THE INDISPENSABLE BOOK
FOR ALL PLANT LOVERS—

The Beginners—those who need the basic
directions for growing house plants to beautify
their homes and offices . . .

The Learners—those who cherish a philodendron,
African violet or hedera helix, and, understanding the
rich rewards of growing house plants, wish to
enhance their abilities and successes . . .

And Those Advanced House Plants Growers who are
almost professionals, who have managed alocasias,
bromeliads, the numerous tribe of begonias and
are seeking a challenge to their skill from new, tender,
unusual, glamorous plants . . .

HEALTHY, SUCCESSFUL, DECORATIVE
HOUSE PLANTS ARE YOURS EASILY AND
SIMPLY WITH THE HELP OF THIS DEFINITIVE
ENCYCLOPEDIA BY DOROTHY H. JENKINS, FORMER
GARDEN EDITOR OF THE NEW YORK TIMES.

Also by Dorothy H. Jenkins

❧ THE COMPLETE BOOK OF ROSES

❧ Published by Bantam Books

THE ENCYCLOPEDIA
OF HOUSE PLANTS

BY DOROTHY H. JENKINS

BANTAM BOOKS
TORONTO · NEW YORK · LONDON

THE ENCYCLOPEDIA OF HOUSE PLANTS

A Bantam Book / published January 1962
2nd printing ... September 1962
Bantam Gardening Guide edition published November 1967
4th printing .... November 1968

Illustrations by Alex Tsao

Published simultaneously in the United States and Canada

Bantam Books are published by Bantam Books, Inc., a subsidiary
of Grosset & Dunlap, Inc. Its trade-mark, consisting of the words
"Bantam Books" and the portrayal of a bantam, is registered in the
United States Patent Office and in other countries. Marca Registrada.
Bantam Books, Inc., 271 Madison Avenue, New York, N.Y. 10016.

PRINTED IN THE UNITED STATES OF AMERICA

TABLE OF CONTENTS

CONTENTS

THE ENCYCLOPEDIA OF HOUSE PLANTS

CHAPTER 1

HOUSE PLANTS FOR EVERYDAY LIVING

The azalea, flowers gone but leaves still green, was a hostess gift. The two wax begonias in clay pots were brought home by the youngsters from Sunday School. The pottery burro that still has cacti planted in the pottery baskets on either side of its back also was a gift to the children. The marica and rather limp philodendron that the next-door neighbors left behind when they moved seemed too good to leave for just anyone.

Such hit-or-miss accumulation was common twenty years ago and often led to an incongruous assortment of house plants. As certain as September came around, the lady of the house decided that some good plants might be cheerful to have in the house during winter. So, on the next shopping trip, two pots of handsome ivy were purchased. Or, possibly, some long stems of ivy were cut from a friend's garden and brought home to place in a bowl of water. But, by mid-December, the ivy was no longer really green and, in fact, looked

1

rather sad, so it was a good thing it was time to start putting up Christmas decorations.

The wish for both foliage and flowering plants is easy to gratify today (ivy still isn't the easiest with which to begin). Forget about bringing indoors in September the geraniums that are blooming luxuriantly (they'll be green sticks with a few small leaves in a couple of months). Forget about the palm that was traditional in a Victorian parlor, the wicker stands filled with ferns that graced sun porches, and the snake plants that dressed up apartment house and hotel lobbies in the first decades of the twentieth century.

New and more likable versions of these once-fashionable plants can be found today, if desired. They're almost lost, however, among the dozens of other dependable foliage and flowering plants for houses, apartments and offices.

Nowadays it is possible to live with plants from fall until spring or all year around. The majority that can be purchased "down street" or at the shopping center hold their leaves and produce flowers without special coddling. This is fortunate, since architects' plans for so many new houses include built-in places intended for plants and nothing else. Planter boxes and bins, room dividers, glass walls and picture windows leave homeowners no choice but to live with plants.

The picture window of a contemporary house that faces a street needn't keep the family living in a goldfish bowl if an indoor garden is planted at floor level or several large plants are grouped near it indoors. The plants won't cut off light, either.

The sunny bay window of any house built in any decade always has seemed the natural place for glass shelves and hanging baskets of geraniums, begonias, oxalis and other flowering plants. Many of the so-called contemporary architectural devices to display plants in a home are as adaptable to old as to new houses.

Architectural provision wouldn't be so simple to maintain had not one small member of a large and diverse tropical plant family been brought to market in the early 1930's. Philodendron cordatum is the name of this plant with heart-shaped, dull green leaves. It proved it could live in cool rooms and hot ones, that it would stay green in sunless apartments, that its leaves withered only slightly if its owner forgot to water it for a few days. Usually it is purchased as a bushy pot plant but, as months pass, it stretches out into a vine.

More Philodendron cordatum, or St. Louis ivy as it is sometimes called, is probably being grown indoors today than any other house plant. Other philodendrons have become almost as popular, with the result that few stores display less than four or five varieties, and all can obtain any one of fifteen to twenty varieties without delay.

The immediate success of the philodendron family spurred a search for other equally sturdy foliage plants. A legion of handsome ones is now available. A good many of them have names much more difficult to pronounce and remember than philodendron. Since they haven't been around long enough to acquire common names like snake plant and Chinese evergreen, shopping often is conducted on the basis of leaf descriptions rather than plant names.

Foliage plants outnumber flowering plants ten to one, according to wholesale growers' count. That's natural, since most foliage plants live and grow without sunlight. However, some kind of flowering pot plant can be purchased every month of the year, and the homeowner who is sufficiently interested can plan basic groupings of plants so that one or more always is colorful with flowers or fruits.

The azalea wins the popular vote as the most satisfactory flowering plant for its range of color, lasting

quality and ease of bringing into bloom indoors in succeeding winters. Certain begonias, the bromeliads,
amaryllis, veltheimia, and even African violets can be
equally flowery winter after winter. Then there is a
small, select group headed by anthuriums with brilliant
patent-leather blooms and spathiphyllum with white
blossoms like small callas that appear for two to three
months but are valued for their foliage the rest of the
year. Best of all, these plants that are as important for
foliage as for flowers don't have to have sun day after
day.

The realization that so many modern plants live for
years without direct sun has encouraged people to try
different and more effective display indoors. Exposure
has been as influential as architecture in making plants
an integral part of homes and everyday living. Architecture has provided built-in places. The adaptability
of the plants has led to the use of large ones singly or
in groups and of small plants such as ornamental peppers lined up against a glass wall or space divider
purely for massed color.

The specimen plant may be so big that it requires
a pot or container 20 inches in diameter and takes up
as much floor space as almost any piece of furniture.
The specimen chosen for its silhouette or distinctive
foliage as well as the considered grouping of smaller
plants can be an important contribution to the decor of
a room. What's more, plants are less static than draperies, paintings and other elements of decoration.

One handsome bromeliad, perhaps a billbergia or a
vriesia in flower, is just one more plant when it stands
with other foliage plants in a room divider. Standing
by itself, the pot on its own saucer, the bromeliad can
be a picture, particularly in a modern room. So can a
handsome three-foot Ficus decora or a four-foot Ficus
pandurata, better known as rubber plants. The bromeliad or the ficus takes on glamour, as do most specimen

plants, by being lighted at night. A concealed spotlight or an ordinary 40-watt light bulb may do the trick.

Artificial illumination, either for after-dark importance or daytime stimulation of growth, is only one thing that has made it fun to own house plants nowadays. As more and more people have made house plants part of their homes, tools and accessories for their upkeep have been made more convenient and attractive.

Soil, for example, isn't a problem for the apartment dweller at any time of year or for the northerner who must, for one reason or another, repot a plant in freezing midwinter. Small packages of excellent planter mixes can be purchased readily. Fertilizers aren't as messy as they once were, because they come either as pellets or as liquid in a small bottle.

The legendary green thumb is no longer essential to growing plants successfully indoors. It has been outmoded because plants can be found to live in any exposure and under any temperature range.

Because so often sun does not shine on the places indoors where a person wants to have house plants, a healthy plant with interesting foliage has come to be preferred to those that should flower but often don't. Outlines of leaves and habit of growth are so diverse that no one can complain of the "same old plant." The assortment displayed in florist shops as well as other stores are sturdy kinds that stay healthy in homes.

Choose house plants to enjoy, to make rooms more livable, to provide green indoors when it's bleak outdoors, or simply to break the monotony of one dull day after another. A new leaf, the appearance of a bud, the unfurling of a flower, the little plant that suddenly starts to grow at the base of the larger one can go unnoticed when people are busy, but they are major events to a shut-in. All are proof that house plants live and change from week to week, if not from day to day.

CHAPTER II

PLANTS FOR OFFICES

The trend toward living with house plants doesn't end at home. It goes so far as to include carrying on one's work among house plants. Their prevalence in offices and lobbies of office buildings can be attributed to insistence rather than to mere acceptance by the occupants. As a result, in some sections of the country there are almost as many arrangements of polyethylene begonias, philodendrons, geraniums and other foliage replicas as there are of living house plants.

Contemporary architecture is as much responsible for the planter boxes and other groupings of honest-to-goodness plants in offices today as the spacious windows of butcher and barber shops have been, traditionally, display places for magnificent specimens of begonias, coleus, geraniums, lemon trees and other old-fashioned house plants. The lemon tree and one or two kinds of begonias undoubtedly would live in a modern office. The list of other plants is considerably more brief for an office than it is for a house or an apartment.

Whether it is in the lobby of a building, the reception room of a business firm or the offices of its executives and staff, someone has to give plants a little attention occasionally. Finding someone to assume this responsibility is the first hazard of maintaining office plants in good condition. Plants that are seen every business day by all sorts of people must be as fresh-looking as the paint on the walls.

The determination of an architect or executive to have plants as part of the office decor is all too often regarded unsympathetically and uncooperatively by the staff. Even if there are only two pottery vases with Chinese evergreens on a bookcase, water must be replenished as necessary and a leaf that turns yellow should be removed.

Office workers can be relieved of 90 per cent of the upkeep if plants or plantings are installed and maintained by a florist shop or greenhouse grower of indoor plants. A few plant shops or professional growers in every city specialize in this sort of work. Someone in the office may have to water between visits by the professional, but even this may not be necessary if the budget permits his services often enough.

The professional caretaker will replace the plant that isn't doing well with one that he thinks will be more satisfactory. He knows also that when new leaves are progressively smaller on philodendron, or a succulent such as kalanchoe starts to shrivel, or any other plant hasn't opened a bud or leaf in months, it's time to replace it with a more rugged sort.

Plants on display in an office must look as though they are thriving in spite of all the factors against it. First, lack of light restricts the selection. Yet in the center of a big office building, a circular reception room is decorated with curving planter boxes filled with real plants. The plants have looked fine every time I've waited there.

7

Second, temperature and lack of humidity can be drawbacks. Air conditioning doesn't seem to counteract the prevailing unfavorable temperature and humidity. Drafts are another hazard for many plants.

Above all, plants in an office must be able to withstand one obstacle to which plants in a home are not subjected. That is, most offices are closed every week from Friday evening to Monday morning.

Unpainted clay pots are the worst possible containers for house plants that are to live in offices, for these pots are porous and heat and dry air draw moisture from the soil. Clay pots that have been painted white or a neutral color are more satisfactory. Potted plants arranged in some sort of container with damp peat moss between the pots and on top of the soil are best equipped to stay healthy and handsome in spite of the adverse climate of an office.

Planter boxes of some sort are the standard method of incorporating house plants into office decor in New York City. Often the boxes are built to fit a wide window sill or an area of wall space. In San Francisco, groupings of indoor plants in tubs or other appropriate containers have been popular. But, in both New York and San Francisco as well as in cities and suburbs between the two, all sorts of variations may be seen.

Some people still like dish gardens of cacti, although little gardens now are likely to be more imaginative and display different kinds of plants. Glass containers range from a brandy snifter planted with mosses and small green plants to a round glass table with a planting on its base to be viewed through the top surface or the glass sides. Water gardens, a recent innovation, need less upkeep and look well for a longer time.

The aspidistra, a plant that now is seen in the best of circles, was nicknamed the saloon plant years ago in Brooklyn. It was a common adornment of saloon windows and reputedly was watered with beer, yet never seemed to die. Such haphazard care is not recommended even for philodendron today. Briefly, this is what house plants need, not to grow noticeably fast, but to stay green and alive in an office:

TEMPERATURE .. 70–72 degrees maximum; 55 degrees minimum.

WATER .... Cacti and succulents twice weekly; other kinds daily, but never so much that soil is constantly wet or muddy. Maintain water level in container with Chinese evergreens, ivy or other plants.

FOOD .... No fertilizer for at least 3 months, or better yet for 6 months; then 1 tablet of plant food inserted in the soil and watered.

GROOMING ..... Wash smooth or shiny leaves with water once a week; dust off fuzzy or plushy leaves such as those of geraniums. Or reduce frequency of washing by coating smooth leaves with one of the liquid products formulated to keep them shining.

Some of the foliage plants suggested as being rugged ones will look fresh and natural for months in offices that are closed every weekend. It is possible, if an executive insists, to have some flowers most of the year.

Rugged Foliage Plants

Aglaonema (Chinese evergreen)

Araucaria (Norfolk Island pine)
Aspidistra
Bromeliads
Cacti and Succulents (most cacti, many succulents)
Cissus antarctica (kangaroo vine)
Cissus rhombifolia (grape ivy vine)
Dieffenbachia (dumbcane)
Dracaena
Fatshedera
Ficus decora (rubber plant)
Nephthytis
Palms—Kentia, Phoenix, Chamaedorea, Rhapis (bamboo)
Pandanus veitchi (screw pine)
Peperomia, especially P. obtusifolia, P. sandersi
Philodendron, especially P. cordatum, P. hastatum, P. monstera, etc.
Pilea, especially P. cadierei
Pittosporum
Podocarpus
Pothos aureus (vine)
Rhoeo discolor
Sansevieria
Schefflera
Schismatoglossis
Spathiphyllum
Syngonium
Tradescantia
Zebrina

Flowering Plants in Season

SPRING .... Azalea
Clivia

SUMMER .... Chrysanthemums

FALL .... Chrysanthemums
Wax begonias

WINTER .... Anthurium
Ardisia (red berries)
Azalea
Bulbs such as amaryllis,
lily of the valley,
veltheimia
Chrysanthemums
Otaheite orange (fruits)
Primroses
Spathiphyllum

ALL YEAR .... Bromeliads

CHAPTER III

MODERN FOLIAGE PLANTS

The mainstay for decorating at home and in offices is foliage plants. Many of them do flower, but this may happen only occasionally. As a general rule, blossoms are inconspicuous and cannot compete with foliage in interest.

House plants, selected and grown primarily for their leaves, aren't look-alikes. Arrow-shaped is the right description for leaves of Philodendron hastatum, nephthytis and syngonium, but even those who don't know one house plant from another could tell that these three aren't all the same plant. If someone suggests a palm, don't think of those lining the avenues of Los Angeles or Palm Beach. The ones grown as house plants are only a tiny fraction of their size, and range from the lacy miniature date palm from India to the feathery cocos from Brazil and the coarser-leaved fishtail palms.

Foliage plants have leaves of every conceivable shape and size. Some are only ⅛ inch long, and even the philodendron family includes kinds with leaves from two inches to two feet or more. There are shiny ones and plushy ones, leaves that look pleated and others that grow like shingles on a house.

Plants are as diverse as their foliage. Creepers, trailers, vines that climb or hang down, little shrubs and bold treelike plants, soft green mounds or graceful fountains certainly should include some plants that are to everybody's liking. If not, there are the man-made forms such as the totem pole (a cylinder of sphagnum moss anchored in a pot and completely covered with Philodendron cordatum) or the cones that look like outdoor topiary (cones of wire mesh concealed by an English ivy or grape ivy).

The increase in the number and diversity of leafy plants has been brought about by necessity. Many people who haven't a sunny window like to have plants around. Most foliage plants do not need to be in sun in order to live and grow. As a matter of fact, most of them do better in full light but not sunlight, many of them get along in indirect light and a few don't die if they're kept in a dim corner.

The demand has risen for plants that will grow well indoors where it isn't sunny, as well as for plants that don't need special care such as a shower in the bathtub at least once a week. Few of the plants that graced the domed glasshouse or conservatory of fifty years ago fit the homeowner's definition of an indoor plant that is long-lasting in return for minimum attention. Air conditioning, central heating, low humidity and minimum light are conditions which people survive and expect their plants to do more than survive.

So, long-known house plants have been evaluated in the light of present-day living conditions. In many cases, hybridists have developed improved varieties. Growers have tried new kinds of foliage plants from near and far—from Puerto Rico, Mexico, the countries of South and Central America, Africa and Asia, and the

Philippines. That's why so many of the foliage plants bear completely unfamiliar names. We haven't been growing them long enough to substitute for most of them as descriptive a common name as "hen and chickens" for echeveria.

The search and the testing have brought to light plants that can be chosen for coloring, texture, size and shape. Some are distinctive enough to be used alone; others contribute to a fascinating group of house plants. The various colors and textures of plants make possible a harmonious selection for different rooms and their furnishings.

Of course, when a philodendron produces several leaves that are much smaller than they should be, it's time to move it to a location where there is more light and try another plant in the vacated spot. When ferns dry up and turn brown, temperatures are too high, atmosphere too dry, and a tougher plant such as a bromeliad would be a better choice.

There are tough foliage plants and delicate ones. Some few thrive only in temperatures of more than 70 degrees in daytime and not less than 60 degrees at night, which most homes do not maintain. Whatever the requirements for steady growth, all foliage plants need much the same care.

Generally, a new foliage plant shouldn't need to be fertilized for six months or repotted for a year. If the pot breaks accidentally, replant in the same size pot unless roots were practically bursting out of the old one. In that case, find a pot only one size larger.

Whenever you replant, make certain that drainage will be good. Drainage depends on two things: (1) an inch of gravel, pebbles or rough stuff left after sifting soil in the bottom of the pot; and (2) the soil mixture. For the majority of foliage plants, the following is good: one-third good garden soil or loam, one-third leafmold, humus or peat moss, and one-third sharp sand (builder's, not beach sand), tossed and turned until it's one color, and then sifted.

Loosen the soil about once a week with a fork, apple corer or other small pronged tool. This cultivating will break up any crust that is forming and make soil porous to air and water.

The frequency and amount of watering depends not only on the kind of plant but also on the temperature, humidity and light in which it lives. Again in general, foliage plants need watering less frequently than the more rapid-growing and soft-leaved flowering plants. Watch new foliage plants closely until you find out whether they need watering daily or less often.

Humidity in the air is as essential for many of the foliage plants, especially those of tropical origin, as is watering the soil. Rooms where temperatures are almost constantly 70 degrees or higher in winter, must be humidified in some manner (see page 275).

Circulation of air is essential to the welfare of the most tropical-looking foliage plants. Drafts can be harmful, but fresh air never is. Open a window every day, even if only for ten minutes. To prevent drafts, it may be necessary to lower a window from the top.

Keep foliage clean (see page 279). Pick off yellowed leaves. Never hesitate to pinch back an upright plant that is growing tall and straggly or a vine that is getting stringy.

No plant grows at a steady pace twelve months of the year. House plants must have a dormant or rest period, too, just as roses and perennials are dormant outdoors during winter. Few house plants are as obvious in this as are deciduous trees, roses and perennials in the outdoor garden. Instead of dropping their leaves, house plants rest by not growing. For some the dormant period is in summer; for others, such as ferns, it is in fall and early winter.

Less favorable conditions for growth and only minimum care can be given to prospective house plants in florist shops and other stores. It stands to reason, then, that their stock is going to consist of the tough plants that can look well, at least for a time, under the most trying conditions. Few plants grown primarily for their leaves can be rated as fragile, but those that are newest or unusual, or need specific conditions to continue growth will have to be hunted down in greenhouses or special shops.

ACANTHUS MONTANUS: A thistlelike shrubby plant from West Africa with long, cleft, spiny leaves, similar to those of the classic acanthus leaf in decoration. Both A. montanus and A. mollis with even bigger leaves show off well as specimen plants in tubs. A montanus does well under average home conditions but is seen most frequently in the Southwest.

ACORUS GRAMINEUS ALBO-VARIEGATUS, as you might suspect from its name, has grasslike leaves. Variegated green and white ones grow in a tuft. Since it needs strong direct light and temperature of 65 or so degrees in daytime and 50 to 55 degrees at night, a window sill is a fine place. So is a terrarium. Water this bog plant from Japan daily and generously, but do not allow it to stand continuously in water.

AGLAONEMA: Chinese evergreens do come originally from China, and also from Borneo. Best known is the one with plain, dull green leaves that grows equally well in soil or water. Quite different in shape and coloring is the variegated Chinese evergreen (A. commutatum) with olive-green leaves marked with silver. Other forms are blue-green with silvery patches, A. pictum; and the light green and creamy A. Treubii.

All of the Chinese evergreens are slow-growing and tolerate dry, hot rooms. They stay green even in dark corners and dim light. They'll look livelier if foliage is kept free of dust and soil is watered frequently or

water is kept sweet with charcoal, but even neglect
cannot kill.

AMOMUM CARDAMON: Ginger plant also is a good
choice for sunless places. The green leaves of this bushy
plant have a spicy fragrance. Warmth, humidity and
ample watering keep it healthy.

ANTHERICUM or CHLOROPHYTUM is an old-fashioned
house plant usually called spider plant. Its narrow
green leaves striped with white grow in tufts. Similar
but smaller tufts form at the tips of branches that hang

ARALIA

over the side of the pot and can be taken off and potted
to make additional plants. Undistinguished white flowers
are lost against the mass of foliage.

Chlorophytum mandianum has broader leaves banded
with white. C. picturatum has a golden center stripe.

ARALIA is the simplest of the several botanical names
by which botanists and some growers classify this handsome treelike plant. Best known probably is the broad-
leaved spreading Aralia japonica or sieboldi, also known
as Fatsia japonica. If you remember the castor-bean
plant in late summer gardens, this will give you an
idea of the aralia's leaves. But Aralia elegantissima is

almost as tall a plant but not nearly as broad, and its palmlike leaves are so thinly divided as to look lacy. Sawtooth and Filigree are equally distinctive. Parsley is a dwarf-growing sort. Victoriae is white and green, Chartreuse variegated, and Marginata has round leaves edged with white. The taller or broader aralias are splendid tub plants for an important location.

In any case, aralias are not window plants. Light (not sunlight) is sufficient. They need ample watering plus humidity, and leaves must be kept clean.

ARAUCARIA EXCELSA has long been known as Norfolk Island pine and hails from the island of that name near Australia. It is recognized by its concentric circles of spiny star-shaped branches. In its native island, Norfolk Island pine grows to 200 feet, but as a house plant in temperate climate, I have never seen one more than two or three feet tall. It is slow-growing indoors and can be kept for years. The green one is most common; but obtainable—at a higher price—is the silvery blue-green A. excelsa glauca.

Norfolk Island pine grows in light or dark but not sunny places, and in either cool or warm rooms. This is one house plant that can be transformed into an honest-to-goodness living Christmas tree by decorating it at holiday time.

ASPARAGUS contributes not only a popular vegetable but two house plants, usually called asparagus fern. One (A. plumosus) is an upright plant with flat, lacy leaves that look like very fine fern fronds. The other one (A. sprengeri), sometimes called emerald feather, has trailing or hanging stems with needlelike leaves. Sprengeri is perhaps more popular as a house plant because it fits a hanging container.

Both of these asparagus ferns can be grown from seed, and they are outdoor perennials where winter is mild. Indoors, they can stand warm rooms, but need only light, not sunlight.

ASPIDISTRA LURIDA, which earned the name of saloon plant in Brooklyn, is more politely known as cast-iron or barber-shop plant or parlor palm. It's almost all leaf, for each of the long, broad tapering ones sprouts from the base of the plant. They're so dark green as to be almost black. A variegated sort has white stripes.

This is a plant to stay green under the worst possible indoor conditions. At best, it needs only light and regular watering.

AUCUBA JAPONICA, an outdoor shrub in the southern states, is a handsome glossy-leaved plant indoors where winters are cold. Japonica has green leaves, Variegata is sometimes called Gold Dust plant because its green is flecked with gold. Gold Leaf has completely golden centers edged with green. Any of the aucubas look well in planter boxes, room dividers or tubs.

Aucubas, particularly those with gold, need to stand where light is good, or possibly in filtered sunlight during midwinter. Cooler temperatures than average (65–70 degrees daytime; 50–55 degrees night) are preferable. Don't neglect ventilation, but don't overwater.

AVOCADO isn't a plant that you can buy. Instead, it's a plant you can take a gamble on by starting a seed from a ripe avocado bought for the table (see page 298).

BAMBOO, a husky member of the grass family, is graceful and a pleasure to look at. Many of these tropical plants grow as tall as trees and look like huge branched blades of grass. Although they don't grow as tall in this country, some are hardy here. Dwarf bamboos (Sasa kumasaca, S. tessellata and others) are distinctive additions to indoor gardens. The fernleaf bamboo (Bambusa multiplex), which will grow eight to ten feet tall outdoors, will not reach that height in the house and makes an excellent background plant. Clumps and height increase slowly.

Unlikely as it sounds, bamboos won't thrive in warm rooms. Cool sun porches or rooms where temperatures average 65 degrees during the day are favorable places. Light, including indirect light, and abundant moisture are other essentials. Deep containers with rich soil are necessary. When it's time to prune off old canes, don't leave stubs, for they will decay.

CISSUS consists of a group of trailing plants, far sturdier than the ever-popular ivy. Best known and easiest to obtain are the kangaroo vine from Australia (Cissus antarctica), grape ivy (C. rhombifolia), Begonia cissus (C. discolor) and, daintiest of all, C. striata. Kangaroo vine has large, leathery green leaves with notched edges, on rather stiff green stems. Grape ivy has glossy green leaves in groups of three, on red-tinged stems; tendrils and the silvery pink look of new leaves account for the grape part of the nickname. Begonia cissus has leaves variegated purple and silver, while striata has the smallest leaves of all. So thrifty are these four well-established vines that others of the group with different-shaped and different-colored leaves also may become better known. All four of these common vines may grow as trailers or be trained upward on bark or other supports. The little striata makes an excellent ground cover for an indoor garden or terrarium.

These leafy vines stay healthy in light, cool places. They can grow in high temperatures, but then such pests as mites or red spiders are more likely to appear.

COFFEE trees that never outgrow a flower pot are a fascinating possibility. You aren't likely to gather any coffee beans from these small plants, although in the conservatory at the Brooklyn Botanic Garden I have seen clusters of the red berries on a plant tall enough to be a real tree. You can grow your own coffee tree from seed, but not from the dried brown beans that are ground to make the beverage. Sometimes, small trees to grow as house plants are available as premiums for a brand of coffee.

Coffee plants grow slowly, always a recommendation for a house plant (seeds are slow to germinate, too). Eventually, the stem becomes woody and is topped by handsome green leaves. Light only or shade against sun is most favorable. Moderate temperatures and water as needed keep it growing.

CYPERUS is the umbrella plant or palm or Nile grass that is often seen in a pot standing in a corner of an aquarium. It can be placed among other house plants so long as it is watered freely and often. The leaves that top long stems look somewhat like palm leaves. Cyperus alternifolius is best known. Recently a more compact form that grows no more than ten inches tall and has broader leaves (C. diffusus) has been introduced. This newer one is said to get along with less moisture.

Either of these umbrella plants is not only attractive but tough. Moderate temperatures are best, and shade or light, not sunlight.

DIEFFENBACHIA, whatever the variety, is a spectacular house plant. Many species have been sent here from Central and South America, but the one that is responsible for the name Dumbcane doesn't make a satisfactory house plant. Folklore has it that those who chew a leaf of D. seguine lose the power of speech for about twenty-four hours. Striking as are the large leaves, variously mottled, spotted, streaked or patterned with white, cream, yellow or chartreuse against dark green, they aren't likely to leave the person who first sees them speechless. D. picta with rich green leaves blotched a green-tinged white is most common; D. amoena with leathery foliage and white variegations along the veins the toughest. Variety Rudolph Roehrs isn't as delicate as its yellow-green leaves blotched with ivory and edged with dark green look. Bausei

21

chartreuse with yellow and white spots; Leopoldii, dark green with white midrib and crinkled; Splendens, velvety green with small white dots; and the dwarf Hoffmanni with white blotches—these are only a few of the twenty-odd dieffenbachias obtainable.

In spite of their spectacular appearance, all of the dieffenbachias in commerce are tolerant of poor growing conditions, especially of high temperatures. Light

DIEFFENBACHIA

(not sun) or shade is essential. Excess moisture is not to their liking, and a thorough soaking of soil in the pot once a week is recommended instead of a little water daily.

DRACAENA is one of the most varied groups of foliage plants. Leaves—broad, narrow, solidly dark red or green, or spotted, striped or otherwise marked with color—are as different as the plants—tall and slender, wide and broad, fountains of foliage. D. sanderiana is rightly one of the most popular, a slender plant with gray-green leaves banded in white. Godseffiana, equally well known, has glossy leaves dotted with yellow, on wiry stems. These two and D. fragrans are three of the oldest house plants. New varieties include Florida Beauty, heavily marked with creamy white, and General Pershing, whose new leaves are creamy pink.

Dracaenas will live forever—or so it seems—in high temperatures, with good drainage and lots of water. As is not the case with dieffenbachias, the soil around dracaenas should never dry out. Light, not sun, is best.

EUONYMUS in its luxuriantly growing outdoor varieties is often called wintercreeper. This, however, is hardly appropriate for the miniature varieties of Japanese euonymus that are adaptable house plants. Silver Queen and Golden Queen have tiny dark green leaves with borders the color of their names. Two other varieties have green and white leaves. All are bushy, compact plants that grow slowly and are ideal for dish gardens. Fresh air, moderate temperatures (not over 70 degrees), direct light but shaded from sun, and frequent watering are their requirements.

FATSHEDERA is a modern house plant, originated by crossing Aralia (or Fatsia) japonica and Hedera helix (ivy). The resulting upright, shrubby plant resembles both parents. Leaves are small editions of the aralias, yet at first glance will remind you of ivy. A newer variety has white margins around the large green leaves. Both are sometimes called "botanical wonder" or tree ivy. Whatever you call it, this is a stunning plant in a tub, and will grow to as much as eight feet.

Sunlight is taboo. Cool locations (65 degrees maximum) are essential, for if fatshedera stands where it is too warm, young plants' growth will be stunted. Ample moisture is needed at all times.

FERNS aren't completely unfashionable, even though the Boston fern is no longer permitted to usurp a corner of any room. The Boston fern as well as the smaller, lacy table ferns (Pteris) were the pride of many a housewife circa 1920. The green fronds are quite likely to dry up and turn brown when exposed to heat and dry air. Nowadays people want ferns that will live for months and stay green constantly without a lot of fuss and bother. Don't bring home the lovely maidenhair, the feathery Boston ferns or the irresistible little pteris ferns and expect them to survive.

Safe choices that can tolerate some forgetfulness are Davallia (rabbit's foot or hare's foot), with lacy fronds almost as dainty as the maidenhair and fuzzy rhizomes that creep over the surface of the soil and edge of the pot; holly fern (a cultivated Polystichum), with long fronds composed of glossy segments that do call to mind a holly leaf; bird's nest (Asplenium nidus), in a whorl, with uncut fronds; and the European hart's tongue (Scolopendrium cristatum) also with straplike leaves or fronds. Something must go really wrong with weather, the furnace or liquid poured on the soil to prevent any one of these four true ferns from staying green and healthy from October to June in any living room. Ask for Polypodium mandaianum by its full name, although it is usually called polypody. Its blue-green leaves are crested along the edge. This one looks exotic but doesn't behave that way.

These ferns produce fronds of thicker texture than the short-lived pteris, maidenhair and temperamental Boston fern. Heavy texture is also characteristic of Blechnum gibbum, sometimes called a dwarf tree fern because it develops a trunk as it grows older. Glossy green fronds are two feet long or more.

The exotic-looking tree fern (Cibotium) and odd staghorn ferns (Platycerium) aren't as difficult to grow as you might think. Either sort might be chosen if you have a room where it would be appropriate decoration.

The tree fern—and it does look like a tree—must grow in a tub. It's a large, commanding plant. Soak soil thoroughly once or twice weekly rather than watering it often. Staghorn ferns usually are fastened to a piece of cypress wood to be attached to a wall, or placed in a hanging basket. They're far from temperamental, but plants should be soaked in water at room temperature once a week or so to prevent their drying out. They tolerate warm temperatures by day and below 60 degrees at night.

No fern needs sun. The tough ones recommended above still need a soil made porous with plenty of leafmold and peat moss and good drainage. A smaller pot encourages growth. Avoid overwatering and high temperatures.

FICUS, literally translated as fig, refers not only to that fruit tree but also to the rubber plant of India and Malaya, and to the banyan and bo tree of India. It's not unusual to see modern forms of rubber plant in a large pot or small tub as an important plant in a present-day living room. The rubber plant (F. elastica), so popular in the early years of this century, has been superseded by the handsome F. decora. Leaves are wider and more oval than in the older sort, and are deep green often tinged with bronze. Added color comes from new leaves, which are distinctly red in sunlight. Ficus decora isn't as likely as the old F. elastica was to resemble a feather duster with a few leaves topping a tall bare stem.

Variegated ficus and the yellow variegated Doescheri are handsome, but they are not common. From a different part of the world comes the durable fiddleleaf rubber or fig plant (F. pandurata), whose glossy, leathery leaves are all of eighteen inches long and a foot wide. The shape of the leaves reminds one of a violin.

The fiddleleaf fig (it won't bear fruit) will drop its leaves if soil dries out around its roots, and the slender oval-leaf rubber plants need frequent watering. All of these large rubber or fig plants tolerate heat but not sunlight or lack of light. Direct light is best.

Two of the smallest-leaved of the ficus creep or climb. Ficus repens, which will creep over and cling to any support, dries up in the average living room, for it needs the humidity of a greenhouse. Ficus pumila with small heart-shaped leaves and F. radicans with variegated green and silver or cream leaves need to be sprayed as well as watered regularly. These last two will trail, creep or climb and can be trained on cones of wire or other forms.

FITTONIA, nerve or mosaic plant, was introduced from Peru almost 100 years ago and is as exasperating as it is handsome. Its beauty lies in its strongly veined leaves —Nile green with every vein outlined in white (F. argyroneura); and darker green leaves with rose red veins (F. verschaffelti). Fittonias display their broad leaves on trailing stems and, if they thrive, form lux- uriant mounds. Actually, I've never had any luck with them in any room, whether it averaged hot or cool. These are tropical plants that need humidity as well as warmth, and such conditions are easier to maintain in a warm greenhouse or a terrarium.

GREVILLEA, the silk oak from Australia, where it is a towering tree, averages two to five feet as a house plant. In warmer parts of the country, it's a less lofty shade tree that also blooms. Some indoor gardeners rate it a satisfactory substitute for ferns, since the silk oak tolerates shade or a certain amount of sun, as well as warm rooms. If you can't purchase one, by all means grow it from seed (see page 294).

HELXINE is one of those cherished plants, passed from neighbor to neighbor, friend to friend, and en- dowed with a dozen names. You may know this little charmer as baby's tears, mother of thousands, Polly- anna, Irish moss, carpet plant, Corsican carpet and good- ness knows by how many other names. It is a creeping plant that forms a dense mat of tiny green leaves. It's often seen growing under benches in a greenhouse. If a bit is planted in each pocket of a strawberry jar, it soon becomes a fountain of green. Or, select pots in three different sizes, fill with soil and stack one on top of the other. Plant helxine in the smallest pot, on top, and then in the soil that circles each pot below it.

Helxine likes warmth, moisture and humidity, but it's next to impossible to kill it. A piece the size of a silver dollar taken from an old plant may simply be pressed into the soil of a small pot. For a few days after transplanting, it looks as though it's going to die. It won't, however, so long as you water it, and it will soon be luxuriantly green and growing.

IVY (Hedera helix) always has been and probably always will be a much-loved vine. It's no exaggeration to say that somewhere in the neighborhood of fifty different varieties can be found to grow indoors. This makes ivy a collector's plant—if the collector can make it grow in his home. Some people are satisfied with cutting short lengths of ivy, usually the larger-leaved and hardy Baltica, from their own or a neighbor's garden about Labor Day and placing them in a bowl of water for some indoor greenery during winter.

For those who aren't satisfied with this, there are climbing, trailing or bushy and almost erect little ivies. Some varieties have glossy foliage, others dull. Leaves range from those of the large Baltica to those no bigger than your thumbnail, and in outline from the conventional ivy to almost star-, heart- or shield-shaped. Besides all these variations, crinkling, pleating, cresting, ruffling or waving may be a distinguishing characteristic.

If you want to ask for ivies by name, Merion Beauty and smaller-leaved Pittsburgh are good standard varieties. Lady Kay is a fine bushy sort, Weber's California ivy has rounded leaves, Maple Queen is small-leaved and self-branching. Curlilocks, Fluffy Ruffles, Manda's Crested and Parsley ivy (H. cristata) are described by their names. Garland has glossy, pleated leaves.

Canariensis, its large green leaves edged with yellow, is said to keep well indoors and grow slowly. Canary Cream is a newer variety. Glacier Ivy and the more

27

dwarf Silver King combine white with gray green in their leaves. Jubilee has tiny oval green and white leaves, while California Gold and Gold Dust are marked with golden yellow.

Ivy is usually grown in pots, as it is purchased. The very dwarf, erect ones are perfect for dish gardens. The climbing and trailing kinds can be trained, espalier fashion, on a trellis anchored in the container, or topiary style against a cone or other form of wire mesh.

Most of the ivies grow equally well in soil or water. Cool rooms, preferably not more than 65 degrees, light, moisture for the soil and fresh air are essential. Only an hour or two of sun daily may be just enough to sicken this vine; it will stay much healthier in a location with light only. Leaves must be kept clean by a shower bath under cool water once a week. And be sure that a strong spray of water hits the underside as well as the upper side of leaves.

Even with strict attention to these details, the healthy-looking ivy plants that you brought home in October may develop a gray or yellow cast to the foliage and feel cobwebby to the touch by January or February. The discoloration and webbiness are caused by red spider, an insect so small as to be almost invisible. It's easier to prevent—by a cold water spray—than to cure.

Many people won't admit that ivy can be other than a thrifty plant, or that they do anything special to keep it growing well. Still, for indoor decoration in general and minimum care, at least three other vines take to the indoors more readily. I still believe that grape ivy, kangaroo vine and pothos are longer-lived and less trouble.

MARANTAS are a distinctive group, with at least one, known variously as prayer plant, rabbit's tracks or husband-and-wife plant, a cherished house plant. Several others are becoming better known, but may be sold

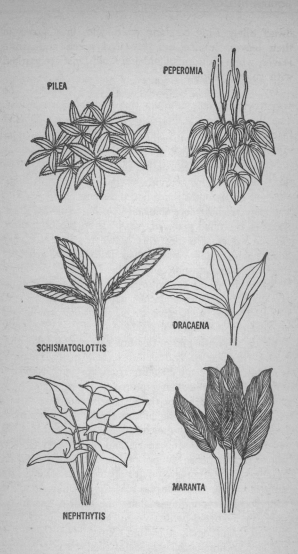

PILEA

PEPEROMIA

SCHISMATOGLOTTIS

DRACAENA

NEPHTHYTIS

MARANTA

either as a maranta or a calathea (the two genera make up the Maranta or Arrowroot family). The arrowroot (M. arundinacea) grows wild in southern Florida; its rhizomes have been a source of tapioca, its roots of medicinal ingredients for two centuries.

M. kerchoveana is aptly named prayer plant because, like a person's hands, its flat, broad, oval leaves fold together vertically at night. It's equally well named rabbit's tracks because of the chocolate markings on the green leaves. Incidentally, the less light, the darker the markings. This maranta is bushy and spreading, and has white, undistinguished blossoms.

Makoyana has more unusual coloring and markings. Blotches are olive green above, pink on the underside. On the upper side, the area between spots is silvery above, with small crosshatched lines, creamy below. Rosea lineata has pink and white stripes at an angle to the midrib, and is purple on the underside. Insignis is a small maranta or calathea with narrow light green leaves, spotted with olive green, and maroon on the underside.

Shade, warmth and water are essential for keeping leaves fresh, crisp and colorful. Soil needs frequent watering and foliage benefits from spraying regularly with water at room temperature.

MIMOSA is another of those plant names that inspire visions of sweet-smelling blossoms and balmy evenings but, alas, it is wrongly bestowed, according to botanists, on the yellow flowering acacia and on albizzia with its silky pink pompons. Mimosa pudica can be grown easily indoors, but is not grown for its flowers. This is the sensitive plant, whose leaves fold up at night, or whenever you run your finger along the midrib during the day. It's a novelty which young and old enjoy having around. Long leaves consisting of many small segments are lacy and make this a graceful small tree.

Sensitive or humble plant is perennial in regions that

are warm in winter as well as summer. In states bordering the Gulf of Mexico, the sensitive plant grows as a sizable shrub or tree and has naturalized itself.

Indoors in a pot, the plant needs ample watering and humidity. It doesn't object to sun. If you can't buy one, grow your own from seed (see page 294).

NEPHTHYTIS has long been known as arrowhead because of its large green leaves. They top slender stems and, since they need some sort of support to keep them upright, usually grow against bark. Lately, plantsmen are listing nephthytis with the syngoniums. The two are interrelated and all have arrow-shaped leaves. If you can't make a person understand what you are looking for when you ask for nephthytis, switch to syngonium, or vice versa.

The old arrowhead nephthytis has rather thin, light green foliage and stems. It can in time grow to a large plant needing a tub rather than a pot. Occasional watering and keeping the foliage clean are its only requirements. Sun is not essential.

Would you like a plant indoors that looks like a miniature holly tree? If so, OSMANTHUS FORTUNEI, or the smaller-leaved O. ilicifolius, will fool anyone. This is commonly called hollyleaf olive or false holly in the South, where it grows outdoors as a shrub. It's an evergreen with dark green, spiny-tipped leaves that seem to be replicas of those of the larger holly. Ilicifolius grows about a foot tall indoors, Fortunei a little taller. If you can provide favorable conditions, tiny white flowers may open in fall. Incidentally, habit of growth and good branching recommend an osmanthus for a specimen plant, small and slow-growing as it is.

Moderate temperature (below 70 degrees), direct light and some sunlight if possible, and regular watering keep an osmanthus in good health.

PALMS in small sizes are the order of the day. Some of the slender, graceful cocos are so small that they fit neatly into a narrow brass planter on the window sill. Other palms belong in a tub as handsome specimen plants for accent. However they are used, palms grow slowly.

Wherever they originated, palms are unmistakable with their crowns of leaves. Foliage of Kentia forsteriana and Neanthe Bella comes closest to the indispensable palm-leaf fan. The lady or bamboo palm (Rhapis excelsa) also has rather coarse leaves. The miniature date palm from India (Phoenix roebeleni) and Cocos weddelliana from Brazil have feathery foliage. Not quite as finely cut but extremely adaptable is Chamaedorea, brought not so many years ago from Mexico. Fishtail palm (Caryota mitis) is fuller, with several branches from the base.

All of these palms are durable, tolerant of high temperatures and insufficient light, and are generally insect- and disease-free. However, do water palms regularly but take care, if their pots are in more decorative containers, that excess water does not collect.

PANDANUS veitchi, the screw pine, is as sturdy a house plant today as it was about 100 years ago when it was brought to England from Polynesia. Its fountain of long swordlike leaves, tipped with spines, forms a plant about as broad as it is tall (from two to three feet). The shiny, leathery leaves are green and white, but neglect will dull the coloring. So will too much sun.

A pot into which roots must be crammed forces strong growth. Soil should not be as rich as for the softer-leaved foliage plants. Water on an average of twice weekly in winter, more often in spring and summer. Fairly high temperatures are tolerated. If offsets looking like small plants appear from the base in spring, these can be broken off and potted individually.

PELLIONIA are creepers rather than climbers, noteworthy for their foliage. P. daveauana has light green leaves edged with bronze, P. pulchra has purple stems and almost purple leaves with dark veining. Both of these unusual creeping plants need warmth and moisture. If you can make them at home, they're a fine ground cover or show off well in a small hanging container.

PEPEROMIAS are delightful small plants, related to the tropical climber that furnishes pepper berries for seasoning. Peperomia, the house plant, is valued for its foliage, which is the most important part of the low, bushy and usually spreading plant. Gone are the days when two peperomias were all the market could offer: Watermelon (P. sandersi) with its oval leaves striped like the skin of this fruit, and P. obtusifolia with shiny green and white leaves. At least two dozen other named varieties aren't hard to locate. White Cloud, for example, is an improved form of P. obtusifolia and has indented leaves as well as much more white. Sweetheart has heart-shaped leaves striped with silver in much the same manner as Watermelon. Emerald Ripple has bright green pleated foliage. Metallica has bronzy leaves with a green stripe along the midrib. And so it goes into endless combinations of greens, gray, silver, maroon, white and brown. Many of the newer varieties such as Royal Gold are trailers.

So long as they aren't overwatered, peperomias are long-lived house plants. When soil is almost dry, soak it thoroughly with water at room temperature. Twice a week should be often enough. They're quite at home in warm rooms, even those with dry air. Light, not sun, is best; but filtered sunlight shouldn't shorten their days.

The true pepper plant from the tropics of the Orient is no stranger in Texas homes. Both black pepper (PIPER NIGRUM) and Celebes pepper (P. ornatum) are climbers with round leaves. They should be trained to totem poles. Humidity and warmth are essential.

PHILODENDRON is a reassuring word, which now refers to more than a hundred plants, without a look-alike among them. This is the green foliage plant that out-does all others. Its name comes from the Greek and means tree-loving, which implies that these plants are vines or climbers. Well, many of them are. Even more useful for decoration are the self-heading philodendrons which do not climb and hence need a support, but produce their growth from a central crown and are independent plants. Both types are diverse as to size and shape of leaves.

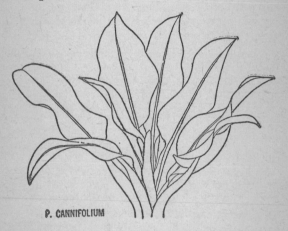

P. CANNIFOLIUM

Some of the outstanding self-heading philodendrons are listed here.

Cannifolium is not too plentiful but is a striking plant with comparatively narrow, glossy leaves on short, plump stems. A slow-growing and beautifully shaped plant.

Crenulatum has enormous leaves, notched almost to the midrib and with every edge wavy.

Eichleri has leaves big enough to be elephant's ears, but with deeply scalloped edges. Both it and P. evansi are excellent. The latter is a hybrid originated in California with some resemblance to Eichleri, which is not one of its parents. New growth on Evansi has a touch of pink on the underside. Evansi is used outdoors in tubs in southern California.

Fosterianum, a Florida hybrid, has heavy webbed leaves on long stems. This makes a large plant.

Selloum has become a popular northern house plant. It is a Brazilian species with deeply cut leaves on long stems that form a graceful plant. A dwarf form of Selloum is also available.

Wendlandii has broad spatulalike leaves that grow on short stems forming a thick flaring crown. This is exceptionally durable, even for a philodendron.

The climbing philodendrons include not only P. cordatum, the first one to become popular, but many other introductions from Central and South America, plus hybrids originated in the United States. Some of the vines can be permitted to trail. The majority are best trained against a support such as tree fern, cork or totem pole of sphagnum moss. Among the many interesting vines are the following.

Andreanum melanochrysum is a better house plant than Andreanum Black Gold. Arrow-shaped leaves are velvety and iridescent green with ivory veins.

Cordatum or oxycardium, often called St. Louis ivy, is the slender vine that will trail or climb and has heart-shaped dull green leaves. When this one begins to look stringy with too much stem between smaller and smaller leaves, never hesitate to pinch back to a leaf of normal size.

Dubium has medium-sized and deeply lobed leaves. As a young plant, it's handsome and looks as though it might be self-heading. However, it is a climber and as it becomes more vinelike, it starts to look straggly.

Florida, with thick, broad, lobed leaves, has creamy areas near the midribs. It's unusual and durable. A variegated form is more difficult to obtain.

Hastatum proved itself long ago. Its glossy dark

green leaves shaped like huge arrowheads is familiar growing against bark.

Imbe is similar to Hastatum but the undersides of the thick leaves are maroon.

Mandaianum, a hybrid developed in New Jersey, has leaves rather similar to those of Hastatum, but more richly colored. Contrasting with the satiny green of older leaves is the red-brown tint of stems and new leaf tips.

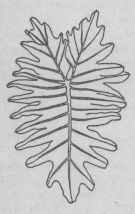

P. EICHLERI

Panduraeforme is the fiddleleaf philodendron, one of the most rugged and unusual. Foliage is dull green, irregularly three-lobed and calls to mind a violin.

Pertusum and Monstera deliciosa, the latter called Swiss cheese plant, are often taken for each other. Some growers believe Monstera is the full-grown stage of Pertusum. Both have large leaves of about the same shape, but those of Monstera are larger as well as perforated. The holes that gave rise to the name Swiss cheese plant were a protective device against the tropical rainstorms. If a Monstera ever develops a fruit, it is edible—prickly before it's fully ripe but at that stage it tastes like a cross between banana and pineapple.

Sodiroi has gained in popularity deservedly. It's a compact climber with small leaves which are slate gray and olive green. Stems are red.

A combination of colors is not unusual with Sodiroi. White, cream or yellow markings are evident on forms of Pertusum, Hastatum and Florida, and there's a green and gold Selloum. Pink tips, stems or undersides of leaves are noticeable on several other philodendrons. Burgundy, a hybrid self-header, has maroon to green leaves on red stems. The propagation of variegated forms is difficult, I understand, but growers will undoubtedly persist until distinctive variegated philodendrons are almost as common as green ones.

Whether it is a vine or a free-standing self-header, care is identical. The smaller kinds grow as satisfactorily in water as in soil. Large- and small-leaved kinds in pots or tubs of soil need regular watering and, should they dry out, thorough soaking. A porous soil containing peat moss is excellent. High temperatures are not a drawback, but they should have full light, not sunlight. Foliage should be wiped clean with a damp cloth once every fortnight. Feeding with liquid fertilizer every six weeks to two months is not amiss.

PILEAS are small plants from the tropical Americas that are as easy to keep looking well indoors as is philodendron. Panamiga or friendship plant (P. involucrata) is an interesting spreading plant with quilted brown-tinged leaves. A group of leaves will be centered with flat clusters of rosy blossoms. Alumnium plant (P. cadieri) has become a greater favorite. It's a neat bushy plant about nine inches tall and is well covered with leaves that are silver-striped and -spotted. It can stand on a coffee table for months without changing its appearance one whit. Aluminum plant contrasts emphatically among green leafy plants.

Pileas need little light, certainly not sunlight.

Warmth, humidity and ample watering keep them growing slowly.

PITTOSPORUM and PODOCARPUS are outdoor shrubs in the Southeast, house plants where winters are cold. In or out, mature pittosporums open tiny fragrant white blossoms in winter. These are a dividend, inasmuch as small pittosporums are grown for their foliage.

Pittosporum tobira looks like a small tree even if it's only a foot tall. A thick woody stem has a crown of branches decked with tufts of dark green leaves. They fall every spring to be replaced by new ones. There's a variegated green and white variety too.

Podocarpus also is grown as an evergreen shrub in the South, where it is planted much as its close relative, yew, is in the North. Podocarpus is covered from top to bottom with narrow linear leaves. In spring slender cones, really flowers, at the tips of the branches drop their pollen dust. One of the best recommendations for podocarpus is that it can be bought in so many sizes, from a four-inch to a four-foot plant. Thus it can be one of several small plants in a container garden or a small tree for accent. At any size, podocarpus is slow-growing.

This is a singularly trouble-free and no-fuss house plant. Moderate temperatures are most favorable, but podocarpus will survive in warm rooms. Don't forget to water, and do spray foliage occasionally.

POTHOS or SCINDAPSUS AUREUS, sometimes called devil's ivy, is an excellent vine for warm rooms. Its heart-shaped leaves are never less than two inches and usually more than three inches long. They're a glossy light green often splashed with cream. Recently, strongly variegated varieties such as Marble Queen and Silver Moon have become available. Porthos doesn't grow rapidly in either soil or water, but it will trail downward gracefully or climb upward against a support.

Pothos definitely needs warmth, and so rooms where

temperatures are 70 degrees or higher in winter suit it well. It can't stand cold air or cold water. If this vine is growing in a pot of soil, keep it on the dry side. Good light, but not sunlight, is desirable to maintain color.

SHINGLE PLANT (Rhaphidophora) is one of the most unusual—and tempting—foliage plants I've ever seen. You might think it some odd philodendron at first. Its rounded oval leaves, not equal on two sides, are displayed alternately on either side of a stem. Of course it needs a wall, bark or a totem pole to grow against, the leaves as tight to the surface and overlapping as shingles on a house.

If you can grow philodendron, you can grow shingle plant. Actually, more warmth and humidity seem to me to be needed by shingle plant.

SAXIFRAGA SARMENTOSA is better known as the strawberry begonia or geranium. It isn't a begonia and it doesn't produce strawberries. The leaves are round but much smaller than most geranium leaves and form a neat basal clump. They are gray green on top, red beneath and rather hairy. Stems also are rosy red.

The charm of strawberry begonia lies in its tendency to produce long rosy runners at whose tips the tiniest of new plants form. When they are sizable enough to handle, they can be snipped from the mother plant and potted individually. Under favorable conditions spikes of delicate white blossoms appear in late winter.

Possibly even more decorative are some of the newer varieties. S. sarmentosa tricolor has leaves variegated with white and a red edge. Magic Carpet has larger leaves than the species splotched with white. Maroon Beauty has not only larger but also darker foliage.

For all its charm, the strawberry begonia is undemanding. It will be more luxuriant in a fairly cool location (not above 65 degrees) and in light or filtered sunlight. It thrives in a humid greenhouse and tolerates the drier air of home interiors. Use water at room temperature and soak soil if it becomes quite dry.

SCHEFFLERA ACTINOPHYLLA, the Australian umbrella tree, is bushy rather than treelike, with large soft green leaves that earn its common name. Leaves are glossy and deeply cut. Both it and SCHISMATOGLOTTIS, called painted tongue, are plants that really stay green and healthy under adverse conditions. For proof, note those in lobbies of office and public buildings where they invariably look as though they'd just been brought in that morning. Don't disdain either one for your apartment or house, particularly if rooms are hot and dry.

Schefflera is the dramatic accent plant with strong enough outlines to stand by itself, and different enough to hold its own in a planter box or bin with an assortment of foliage plants.

Schismatoglottis is closely related to the Chinese evergreen, although it's hard to believe when the leaves are compared. This painted tongue has thicker and more leathery leaves. They are broad, gray green and marked with silver. Often, too, clusters of shiny red berries rather like those on our wild Jack-in-the-pulpit stand erect above the leaves.

Both of these sturdy foliage plants continue to look fine in warm rooms and dry atmosphere. Wipe foliage clean every couple of weeks. If you forget to water, nothing drastic will happen. Schefflera stays green in a room with high temperature where air is dry and soil is allowed to dry out before watering again.

SELAGINELLA is easier to visualize by one of its common names—cushion moss or Scotch moss. It's a little taller and fluffier than real moss, but just as green. What you and I would call leaves are botanically scales. Stems on which they are borne root and thus the plant spreads. Although there are selaginellas native to North American woods, the kinds grown indoors were brought from warmer climates such as the Canary Islands. Most

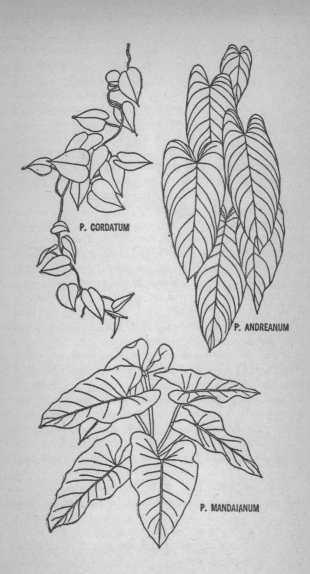

P. CORDATUM

P. ANDREANUM

P. MANDAIANUM

kinds are all green, but there is a variegated form whose "foliage" is tipped with white.

These dainty creeping plants are ideal ground covers in terrariums. They also are good covering for a gravel or stone chip expanse in an indoor garden. Warmth, humidity and moisture are essential. Sun is not.

STROBILANTHES, sometimes referred to as conehead, isn't the easiest plant in the world to grow indoors. It is a prime candidate for shade, but fully as essential are generous heat and moisture. The two latter conditions are difficult to provide steadily and in some places impossible. This is probably more satisfactory to grow as a warm greenhouse plant.

In case you want to try, one strobilanthes is noted for foliage, the other for flowers. S. dyerianus is a shrubby plant that could grow to three feet tall. Its pairs of long pointed leaves are purple and iridescent, with green edges and midribs. If you can grow this one to maturity, it will produce spikes of violet flowers. S. isophyllus is noteworthy for its pink verging into blue or blue and white flowers, which are on shorter stems than are the leaves.

SWEET POTATO vines are as easy to grow as falling off a log. All you need is a plump, firm sweet potato from the kitchen vegetable bin, a tall glass or Mason jar, and three strong toothpicks. Place one end of the sweet potato in the jar so that its tip just touches water. If the glass doesn't have a narrow neck, and too much of the potato would rest in water, support it by means of three toothpicks stuck in its sides (otherwise it may rot).

Place the potato in its jar in the dark for ten days to start root growth, then move into a light place. Top growth should be rapid but you can never tell whether it will be a long vine to train around the window frame or a bushy mass of green stems and leaves. A vine will climb up string or wire.

SYNGONIUMS are a varied group of plants with arrow-shaped leaves, some narrow, others wide, and some cleft as in the widely grown Trileaf Wonder. This was one of the first patented foliage house plants and was originated, if I remember correctly, in or near Cincinnati, Ohio.

Nowadays the syngonium clan includes what was once known as nephthytis. Syngonium for the most part refers to plants that are not as large-leaved or as tall as the longer known arrowhead nephthytis. Foster's syngonium with silvery veining on its dark green leaves is practically a creeper. Emerald Gem is taller with thicker, crinkled leaves, Imperial White has wider leaves that are lighter green with white markings, and Imperial has heavy-textured, bright green and gold leaves. Wendlandii is so small in scale, including its green leaves with silver centers, that it is ideal for dish gardens or water gardens.

Syngoniums are about as tough as the old nephthytis. None of its varieties like fluctuating temperatures. But all of them thrive on constant warmth, moist soil and some humidity, and in light (not sunlight) or in shade from the sun.

TI PLANT, hailed as having been shipped to the mainland from Hawaii, is eminently satisfactory. In reality, it is Cordyline terminalis, often called Dracaena terminalis. A variety of this, Mme. Eugene André, is the Hawaiian ti plant. This is a fine, erect plant with tapering leaves up to 6 inches long, and 2 to 5 inches wide. The most readily available one has dark green leaves with a red margin. New leaves that usually appear around Christmastime are flaming pink. Ti plants come with many variations in coloring, all of them metallic shades based on green, crimson, rose or purple.

Small pieces of ti plant with a couple of leaves can be purchased inexpensively to be grown in water. Plants in pots of soil also are easy to obtain, although these usually are sold as Cordyline terminalis. These potted plants eventually will develop a thick stem with the long drooping leaves clustered at the top. Ample moisture is essential. So is plenty of bright light to encourage red coloring of foliage for Christmas. As winter deepens, unfortunately the bright leaves almost always become spotted and fall off. So perhaps small ti plants are best.

P. PERTUSUM

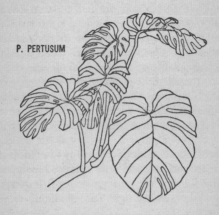

TOLMIEA MENZIESII, better known as piggy-back plant or mother of thousands, is transformed by its habit of producing young plants at the base of its maplelike leaves. If the entire leaf is removed, inserted in a pot of sand and kept moist, roots will grow and a new small plant will soon be ready for potting in soil. The leaves on a full-grown plant are long-stemmed and grow almost horizontal, so that a most luxuriant effect is created.

A piggy-back grows best in a rather cool room where temperature seldom goes higher than 65 degrees in the daytime. An east or a west window furnishes just about the right amount of light in winter (direct sun is not too good). Frequent watering is desirable.

Piggy-back plants created almost as much excitement as the Philodendron cordatum vine, and both were introduced to the public during the 1930's. It's a house plant that is native to the United States and even today can be found growing in forests on the West Coast, notably in Oregon, where it is likely to be called youth-on-age.

TRADESCANTIA keeps alive the name of an English plant hunter, John Tradescant, who sailed to America in 1637 to search for floral wonders. The wealth of small vines still grown indoors should please this venturesome plant lover, and the name tradescantia also honors the perennial spiderwort. The vines have many common names, from inch plant to wandering Jew.

Tradescantia vines grow slowly in water or soil. It's more accurate to call them trailers. It is easy to root new pieces by breaking a piece off at a joint and sticking it in fresh water. Stems are rather brittle and some kinds have almost transparent foliage. There's a small green-leaved one; others have striped leaves in green, silver, purple, yellow, pink or white. T. blossfeldiana has a thick hairy stem and large green leaves that are purple on the underside. It has three-petaled pink blossoms. T. albiflora albo-vittata, Giant White Inch Plant, has large blue-green leaves edged and often striped with white. Its stems branch and trail. Gold Leaf is a pure yellow form of the popular cream and green tradescantia.

Closely related is the stouter trailer, ZEBRINA PENDULA, also called wandering Jew. Zebrina has oval leaves, purple with silver stripes and rather metallic looking. A variety, Quadricolor, according to catalogue description, has leaves with pink, red, white and silver. Daniel's Hybrid has brown-purple leaves with silver stripes.

The tradescantias and zebrinas need strong light to bring out their coloring, which, however, can be faded by direct sunlight. Moderate temperatures and copious watering if planted in soil are recommended. These trailing vines will grow in water and also over a pebbly surface that's kept moist. If new leaves revert to plain green, pinch off the shoot as far back as the more colorful leaves.

TREVESIA SANDERI, also called snowflake plant, is as handsome as any member of the Aralia family to which it belongs. This is not as expansive a plant as schefflera, but is lower-growing and has finer leaves. Its strong stems and leaves that call to mind an oak leaf make trevesia an extremely decorative foliage plant.

XANTHOSOMA variety Magnifica is a truly stunning plant. It's a tropical member of the Arum family, which includes the house plants dieffenbachia, schismatoglossis and Chinese evergreen as well as philodendron and calla lilies. The long leaves are almost arrow-shaped and sharply pointed and grow at an angle so they fall downward. Strong white lines along the midrib and side veins set off the green leaves.

I suspect that Xanthosoma is not as easy to grow as philodendron and dieffenbachia. It needs much warmer temperature (70 to 80 degrees by day, not below 60 degrees at night). It is sensitive to cold, drafts and fluctuating temperatures. Humidity as well as moist soil is necessary.

These, then, are the foliage plants available to anyone who wants to grow such plants indoors. Probably it will be a long time before the list changes as much as it has during the thirty years between 1930 and 1960. Where have all those leafy plants with such odd names come from? A large number have been found in Central America, Africa and other far-off places. The trips of plant hunters are not publicized as are those of many more ordinary mortals. Then hybridists in Florida, other southern states and California and an occasional greenhouse grower-hybridist in other states try their hands at crossing two plants from far-off places to obtain a more durable variety for display in homes in this country. Again, someone with enough imagination experiments with a plant like piggy-back to find out if it need be only a weed in this country, but might possibly lead a more honored life as a house plant. Plantsmen will continue to have bright ideas such as this one, and to produce hybrids about which no one can complain.

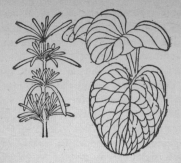

CHAPTER IV

COLORED AND FRAGRANT FOLIAGE

What do you think of when someone says "leaf"? A plant, of course, and isn't it usually one that has a lot of green? Think of all the different kinds of plants—grass, trees, shrubs, bulbs, roses, vegetables, flowers, perhaps even moss—that make such an attractive setting for your house.

Indoors, whether it's a garden or a few strategically placed house plants for interior decoration, again the majority of them have green leaves. Be they large or small, the plants that can produce luxuriant green foliage are the ones on which we depend. Flowering house plants, too, are never handsomer than when their pink, yellow, orange, red or white blossoms open against a background of green leaves.

Let's agree then that green isn't so much a color as a natural part of a plant. No matter how restful green may be to look at, most of us want to break up a mass of it here and there with another color.

Vivid shades and delicate tints can be introduced by

two different groups of plants. The flowering ones are best known. Broadly speaking, it's trickier to manage flowering house plants so that some of them are contributing some color from October to May. The easier route to colors that will contrast with green is by a judicious selection of colored-leaved foliage plants.

Possible indoor plants for houses or apartments, with leaves that are red or a combination of colors other than green, total just about twenty. Then there is a respectable, although smaller, number distinguished for foliage in metallic colorings or in a blend of muted tones often highlighted with iridescence.

This census does not take into consideration the variegated green foliage plants. That is, the plants that have large or small green leaves, perhaps only edged or, in some cases, more generously dappled, splashed, freckled or marked with white, cream or silver. Pandanus, for example, has always had green leaves striped with white, and there's always been a green and white ivy. Aucuba japonica has solid green leaves, A. japonica variegata is splotched with cream, and now there's a variety called Gold Dust with golden yellow leaves edged with green.

Variegated forms are being introduced in more and more house plants that we have long accepted for their green foliage. When variegated philodendron and Chinese evergreen appear—and they are available—it sounds like a revolution.

The rosy red of new leaf buds and growth on Ficus decora, a modern rubber plant, and Philodendron Evansi are only a hint of the rich overall red of such other-than-green foliage plants as alternanthera, coleus and croton.

The more brilliantly colored foliage plants differ from all the green-leaved ones in one important matter. The colored ones need some sun daily, including the winter season, to keep leaves from fading. An east or a west window through which sun shines part of each day is a good location.

In other aspects of care, brilliantly hued leafy house plants are as diverse as all-green ones. Crotons must have high temperatures and frequent fertilizing. Not everyone will be able to provide favorable growing conditions for alocasias and hoffmannias. The plants requiring least care, and therefore the basic group of gay leafy plants are, in my opinion, alternanthera, coleus, fancy-leaved geraniums and iresine.

ALOCASIAS are as exotic as their place of origin—tropical Asia. The big handsome leaves of some kinds are variegated; in others they are precisely patterned along midrib and veins. Strangely enough for a tropical plant, the colorings are cool and metallic, running to gunmetal, aluminum, purple, bronze, copper, pearl and occasionally a touch of red or an off-shade of green such as olive. Leaves of Alocasia cuprea average 18 inches long and 12 inches at the broadest point; of A. zebrina 15 to 30 inches long. Some varieties have distinctly arrow-shaped leaves, others may be heart-shaped.

A. cuprea is one of the most compact. Its thick, wavy leaves are an odd dark green above, maroon-purple beneath. A. chantrieri has dark green leaves with pearl gray veins, which are coppery purple on the underside. A. Lowii grandis with metallic brown-green foliage, silver-leaved Fantasy, and A. sedenii combining olive green, silver and purple are typical of alocasias.

Not everyone will be able to provide the conditions for alocasias. Warmth, humidity and shade are indispensable to growth and, when they do grow, they need room. In the Southeast and Southwest, these exotic leafy plants are often seen, one to a tub or bin, in patios or on sheltered terraces. But they'll also grow indoors if you can provide 70–80-degree temperatures by day and not less than 60 degrees at night. So sensitive are these exotics that southern growers will not ship them during cold weather. They need to be almost constantly moist, and should be fed once a month with liquid fertilizer.

ALTERNANTHERA in comparison is a homely, companionable little plant. My favorite is Alternanthera versicolor. When afternoon sun pours through a west window, the solid red leaves glow like rubies. Joseph's coat is the common name for both A. aurea nana, which is a bushier plant with green and gold leaves, and for A. bettzickiana, with red, pink, green and yellow all in one leaf.

BEGONIAS are usually grown for their blossoms. The Rex begonias, however, have not only large leaves but unusually colorful ones (see page 157).

CALADIUMS, which originated in tropical America, have leaves as large as alocasia but much more softly colored. This plant is grown from tubers planted in spring for summer color (see page 180).

COLEUS plants are indeed a bright rainbow, so bright that no one ever grows them for their modest little spikes of flowers. Dark and bright reds, shades of rose and pink, copper, bronze, yellow from true gold to pale cream, shades of green from chartreuse to olive— two and sometimes three of these colors blend in every leaf. One of my favorites has large maroon leaves with a neat edge like gold beads. The large frilly leaves of another colorful one are predominantly copper, shading into pink and red. Then there's one with a medium-size leaf, scalloped and frilled slightly, in light green, cream and pink.

It's fun to sow a packet of coleus seed, for you can obtain the most surprising variety of plants. It's also possible to buy plants, even named varieties. Firebird has orange-red leaves edged with green; Frilled Fantasy combines red, green, pink, lavender and yellow in deeply cut and frilled leaves. There's a coleus for every preference. Some plants will have leaves three times as large as others. Edges may be scalloped, deeply cut, frilled, waved or small and simple. Plants are usually bushy, but a few trail.

Seed sown in early spring will grow fast enough to be colorful garden plants all summer in a shaded location. In August, cuttings should be taken from the sizable plants and will root within three or four weeks. Rooting cuttings is a better source of indoor plants for

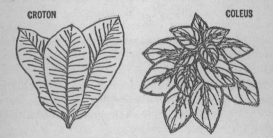

CROTON   COLEUS

the winter months than digging up large ones from the garden.

Although coleus is most colorful in a shaded place outdoors, leaves will be brighter if plants receive some sun during fall and winter. An east or a west window should be a good location.

CORDYLINE TERMINALIS, the Hawaiian ti plant, has bright pinky-red leaves for only a short period each year which, appropriately enough, should be around Christmastime. Other cordylines or dracaenas have green leaves variegated or splotched with color. Many of them combine red, gold or white with green. Baptisti, however, is always red-maroon with bright edges.

CROTONS in their more colorful fashion offer greater variation than the philodendrons, if that is possible. These shrublike plants have oval leaves, some much wider and longer than others. Considerable hybridizing, done in the South, has resulted in dozens of named varieties. New leaves on all crotons, regardless of age, are green and turn color as they age.

If you want to try some of the older and hence less expensive varieties before plunging on this plant, look for Gold Dust, which has green leaves marked with gold; America, which has broad leaves reminiscent of an oak except that they are dark maroon to purple with red veins; Spotlight with narrower leaves that are green and yellow with red; and Columbiana with carmine, purple and green foliage.

Newer—and more expensive—are Jungle Queen blotched with red, pink and maroon and with red veins, Bravo with deep pink to rose semi-oak leaves, and Liberty with red margins and veins and maroon blotches. Harvest Moon is dominantly green with yellow midrib and white veins, and Caribbean Star's heavily veined leaves have orange-red centers in a green to black background.

Croton is the tallest of the colored-leaved plants. They are effective individually in large pots or with others in planter boxes. They can be satisfactory in northern as well as southern homes, if you keep them where temperature is warm (minimum at night 60 degrees), where they're in full light and also receive some sunlight, and if you provide moisture. If temperature drops to 50 degrees or less, or atmosphere lacks humidity, the lower leaves will start to drop.

Soil in pots should be kept moist and soaked thoroughly once a week. If a croton stands in a pot by itself, place at least an inch of sand in the saucer and keep it damp (this will be a sort of humidity factory). In addition, wipe foliage clean with a damp cloth or sponge once every fortnight. Liquid fertilizer every six weeks to two months speeds growth.

DICHORISANDRA isn't quite as difficult to find or grow as its name is to spell or pronounce. And it is handsome. D. mosaica undata (also Geogenanthus undatus) is aptly called seersucker plant, for its leaves are crinkled. They are green and black on top, purple beneath, and have purple stems. It's a nice size for a pot on a coffee table in a room that is warm enough (never less than 70 degrees). D. thrysiflora has silver-green leaves that are red underneath.

Easier to keep, probably, is Reginae, with purple-crimson leaves flecked and striped with silver. This looks somewhat like tradescantia, although Reginae is erect instead of trailing.

GERANIUMS are a clan that offers something to please everyone. One group, often called tri-colored or fancy-leaved, is exactly that. They're worth having just for their often quite gay foliage. An extra dividend is the flowers that start to open before January ends. And this, more often than not, is before the standard green-leaved varieties stage much of a flower display. Another charming addition to an indoor window garden is the scented-leaved geraniums. (See Chapter VIII.)

The name, velvet plant (GYNURA AURANTIACA), is sometimes prefaced by the word purple or royal. The rather fleshy green leaves are covered with short purple hairs, which give it royal coloring and velvety texture. It may grow two feet high, but seldom does as a house plant. It likes warmth (70 degrees is good), some sun and fresh air, but not a draft; also moist soil and air.

The name red ivy is a rather inaccurate but easy way to identify HEMIGRAPHIS COLORATA. Actually, this trailing or creeping plant is more purple than red. Shiny leaves look silvery when sun is not on them. This odd plant will grow quite rapidly and will also produce clusters of white flowers if you can keep it happy. This means quite a warm room, some sun or intense light, fresh air and ample moisture.

HOFFMANNIAS are certain to become a conversation piece if you can grow them. When I was selecting some unusual foliage plants in South Miami to bring home to Connecticut, the couple who operated the nursery warned me that I probably couldn't grow hoffmannia. They were right. My home is too far north and the weather too variable for me to provide enough heat, constantly, for hoffmannias to thrive indoors.

In addition to color, the oblong leaves have such fascinating characteristics as crinkling and silky texture. Quilted taffeta plant (H. refulgens) is both crinkled and silky, with magenta edging the green leaves which are old rose underneath. H. ghiesbreghtii has velvety brown-green leaves that are purple-red on the underside, and a variegated form is enriched with cream and pink as well as brown and green. H. vittata has rosy-bronze leaves with silver veins.

Day temperatures for hoffmannias must be 70 degrees or higher, with some humidity. During the night, temperatures should never go below 60, and preferably not below 65 degrees. Sun isn't essential if light is bright. Moisture is.

HYPOESTES is known by such names as flamingo plant, freckleface, Polka Dot or Pink Dot. Pointed oval green leaves are freely marked with pink. Newer forms such as Splash are much pinker than Polka Dot or Pink Dot. It's a somewhat bushy plant whose stems are inclined to spread sideways before they grow erect.

This is a comparatively fast-growing plant even in moderate temperatures. Filtered sunlight, fresh air and plenty of moisture keep it growing.

IRESINE is as satisfactory as coleus, if not as varied. This bushy little plant is rarely more than four inches tall in the North, but it may be almost as broad. The narrow little pointed leaves may be all red, red splashed with cream or gold, or green and yellow with red stems.

This house plant thrives on being planted outdoors in summer. Small, inconspicuous straw-colored flowers blend with the foliage, and the plant increases in size so that it's possible in August to take innumerable cuttings to be rooted for new plants. Both the small young plants and larger old ones rest in midwinter, but are still colorful.

Peacock plant is an appropriate name for KAEMPFERIA ROSCOEANA, an almost spectacular member of the ginger family. The broad oval leaves are silky and iridescent in patterns of bronze and green. The stemless leaves form a nest for the lavender-pink flowers about the size of a quarter. Blossoms are secondary to the ornamental foliage. This is a plant to enjoy in summer and fall, for it rests in winter. Either tubers or plants can be purchased, the former from January to May.

Moderate to warm temperatures (up to 70 degrees or more) are satisfactory. Filtered sunlight is desirable. Peacock plants also need moisture, and on this score a rather precarious balance should be maintained between not letting soil become soggy and never allowing it to dry out.

Leopard plant is the descriptive name for LIGULARIA KAEMPFERI. The round green leaves are spotted with yellow. There may even be small daisylike flowers. Rare is Argentea, which has blue-green leaves edged with white, plus a pink tinge to new leaves.

The common leopard plant is an old-fashioned and tolerant one for windows. Moderate temperatures in the 60's are best, but it survives greater warmth. Some sunlight or filtered sunlight is desirable, as are fresh air and regular watering.

Colored-leaved plants evidently have been so appealing that people couldn't resist out-of-the-ordinary common names for them. Moses in the cradle, Moses in the bulrushes, Moses on a raft, three men in a boat are typical names for RHOEO DISCOLOR. This plant, which southerners take for granted to edge walks and driveways, is a captivating—and easily grown—house plant wherever winters are cold. Incidentally, it is closely related to tradescantia.

Leaves are a metallic green, purple to red on the underside. They are about eight inches long and fan out from a central stalk, and at their base in a boat-shaped bract appear small white blossoms. Why

RHOEO DISCOLOR

shouldn't such a plant have such original names? R. vittata, also given the same common names, retains purple on the underside of its leaves, but the green on top is striped with pale yellow.

Sun isn't essential for Moses on a raft or Moses in a cradle to be colorful. This places it among the easiest-to-grow house plants which everyone can enjoy. Moderate temperatures (65 to 70 degrees by day, 50 to 55 at night) and regular watering are all you need supply.

All colored-leaved plants have eye appeal. So do flowering plants. We usually think of flowers as being sweet-scented but there is a group of leafy house plants that are notable for their scent or flavor. These flavorful foliage plants are herbs. A few can be grown indoors in order to have a fresh supply conveniently at hand all winter. A few others are grown only because their leaves appeal sweetly to the nose.

The fragrance of flowers is quite likely to fill a room. Fragrant foliage is more subtle, for a leaf must be touched, rubbed or broken in order to sniff its special odor. This is one reason why so many indoor gardeners always have a pot of lemon verbena (LIPPIA CITRIODORA). It isn't a verbena, but the leaves do have a lemony scent. So do the smaller leaves of lemon balm (MELISSA OFFICINALIS), which is hardy outdoors but also can be kept in the house in winter.

One plant each of lemon verbena, lemon balm and rose geranium provides fragrant leaves for floating in finger bowls. Or, on a dreary winter day, you might just want to pick off a leaf, crumple it and smell its clear fragrance. That's why I like to have a pot each of nutmeg, French lace (lemon) and peppermint geraniums indoors all winter.

AMOMUM CARDAMON is commonly called ginger plant or grains of Paradise. Its green leaves are rather spicy but its seeds are not the true cardamon seeds of the spice trade. Common ginger, which grows in tropical countries, is Zingiber officinale. Small specimens can be grown as house plants in warm and humid locations but the tuberous rootstocks, not the leaves, are the aromatic part.

Bay leaves for soups and stews can be plucked from a laurel, or sweet bay (LAURUS NOBILIS). This is not the same tree as the Oregon myrtle or California laurel of the West Coast, or the small magnolia tree of the Southeast. It is the laurel of history, native to the Mediterranean region. It can be grown as a small evergreen shrub or tree in a tub indoors and moved outdoors in summer. Leaves are stiff and dull green.

Equally classic is the myrtle (MYRTUS COMMUNIS), a
shrubby evergreen with scented leaves about two inches
long. Dwarf myrtle (M. communis microphylla) has
smaller leaves. Both myrtles are available in green and
white forms. Myrtle leaves have quite a pungent scent,
rather similar to that of boxwood.

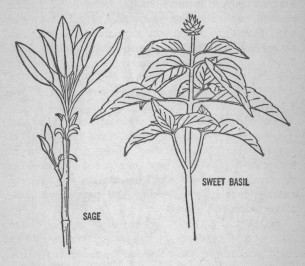

SWEET BASIL

SAGE

Both sweet bay and myrtle will flourish indoors only
if they are in a rather cool room or glassed-in porch.
Moderate temperatures (preferably 65, not over 70 degrees by day, 50 to 55 degrees at night) and strong,
direct light or filtered sunlight are requirements. Fresh
air or ventilation is another need. Remember that these
plants come from the Mediterranean region, and must
not be watered too often. Let soil become moderately
dry and then soak it with water at room temperature.

Not grown for yourself but for the cat of the house-
hold is catnip (NEPETA CATARIA). It's a hardy perennial
outdoors, but you might try a pot or flat of it in the
house during winter.

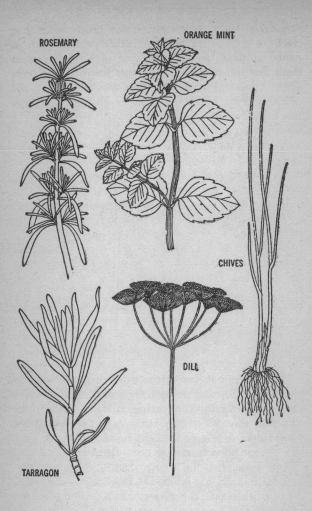

ROSEMARY

ORANGE MINT

CHIVES

TARRAGON

DILL

A dozen herbs for seasoning may prove easier than catnip to grow in the house. Whether yours come from rooted cuttings, seedlings or part of a garden plant that's dug up, plan on 4-inch pots for each one. Pots of herbs are perfect along kitchen window sills. Or the pots might be placed on brackets attached to either side of the window frame or on glass shelves across the windowpane.

A small terra cotta strawberry jar is another attractive way of growing herbs. Plant a different kind in each pocket of the jar. Stands with arms that hold a pot and saucer can also be effective.

If you keep your herbs in pots, have a saucer beneath each one. If you prefer a window box, narrow enough to fit on the sill, give each herb room to spread.

Herbs are plants that are tolerant except of hot rooms with dry air. A sunny window, or an east or a west window that is sunny part of the day, is best for most herbs. Don't overwater, but don't let them dry out. Ventilating for fresh air without a draft is beneficial every day. Turn pots once a week to assure even growth. Spray foliage with water occasionally to wash away dust. Plucking or snipping off leaves should keep them within bounds.

Your nucleus of herbs grown indoors may well be tarragon, rosemary and sweet marjoram. This is especially true if you live anywhere from Philadelphia northward, for these three herbs cannot survive the winter outdoors north of this latitude.

TABLE OF HERBS

HERB	BOTANICAL NAME	SOURCE	EXPOSURE
Balm, Lemon or Sweet	Melissa officinalis	Cuttings from garden plants in Aug.	Light
Basil, Sweet	Ocimum basilicum	Plants dug from garden in Sept.; seed sown in Feb.	East or west window for some sun
Chervil	Anthriscus cerefolium	Seed sown from Jan. onward.	Shade or indirect light
Chives	Allium schoeno-prasum	Clumps dug from garden in Oct.	East or west window for some sun
Dill	Anethum graveolens	Self-sown seedlings from garden in fall.	Sun
Marjoram Pot	Marjorana onites	Plants dug from garden before frost.	Sun
Sweet	Marjorana hortensis		
Mints Orange	Mentha citrata	Cuttings from garden plants in Aug.	East or west window for some sun
Pineapple	Mentha rotundifolia variegata		
Parsley	Petroselinum hortense	Dig and pot small plants in Sept.	Direct light
Rosemary	Rosmarinus officinalis	Move pot or tub plants indoors.	Sun
Sage Garden	Salvia officinalis	Cuttings from garden plants in Aug.	Sun
Pineapple	Salvia rutilans		
Savory, Summer	Satureja hortensis	Cuttings from garden plants in Aug., or self-sown seedlings.	Sun
Tarragon	Artemisia dracunculus	Move pot or tub plants indoors.	Some shade

LEAVES	USE	COMMENT
Bright green, intensely fragrant	Soups, sauces, stews, salads	Pinch back for leaf production.
Green or purple, about 1 inch long	Soups, stews, tomato sauce, garnishing	Pinch back for bushy plants and to prevent flowering.
Bright green and small	Soups, sauces, salads	Slight licorice flavor; seeds sprout quickly.
Slim, spiky (like onions)	Soups, vegetables, eggs, cheese	Leave pots outdoors until after a freeze, for sturdier growth indoors.
Fine, feathery	Sauces, salads, garnishing	Indoor growth dwarfed.
Narrow, fragrant Gray-green, most fragrant	Sauces, salads, garnishing	Sweet marjoram won't survive winters outdoors north of Philadelphia.
Dull green, slight purple edge Green and white	Distinct, strong scents Garnishing, jelly	These two trailing; other mints too robust-growing for indoors.
Curly, dark green	Pungent flavor Salad, stews, garnishing	Cut back to soil level for new tender growth.
Linear, green above, gray below	Sauces, stews, garnishing	Not winter-hardy north of Washington, D.C.
Slender, gray-green Broader, rich green	Poultry dressing Fragrance only	Crimson flower spikes open on pineapple sage for Christmas.
Long, narrow	Poultry dressing, salad, sauces, garnishing	Not winter-hardy north of Philadelphia.
Long, narrow; taste and smell like anise	Salads, sauces, vinegar, garnishing	Not winter-hardy north of Washington, D.C.

CHAPTER V

THE BROMELIADS

Bromeliads are American plants. These natives of the tropical regions of the Americas have only begun within the last decade to be appreciated as house plants. But, just as the English made garden plants of our roadside goldenrod and asters, so bromeliads have been popular house plants in Europe for more than a century. The European interest in this plant family goes far back, and two groups or genera, Tillandsia and Billbergia, were named long ago for Swedish botanists, Vriesia for a Dutch botanist, and Guzmania for a Spanish naturalist.

Recently in the United States, growers, hybridists, plant hunters, florists and you and I have been making up for our tardy recognition. The rewards are great, for bromeliads are unusual plants in appearance and behavior.

Flowers or foliage or both make bromeliads spectacular. They're adaptable to any and all indoor conditions. Thus bromeliads are splendidly equipped for interior decoration in houses, apartments and offices.

Less often grown as a house plant is a member of this plant family familiar to everyone through its fruit—the pineapple. So important is this plant that the whole family is known either as the Bromelia or the Pineapple family.

Leaves of all bromeliads are tough and rather leathery. The texture as well as the manner in which leaves grow are advantages in hot, dry rooms. Not all of the leaves on any one plant are the same length but all come from the base. The result is a cup that holds water.

You should pour water in this cup of leaves. This keeps the plants from drying out and protects them against dry air or low humidity. Soil also should be watered on an average of once a week, but it is the leaf cup that must not be permitted to be empty of water.

The water in the cup of leaves will keep cut flowers fresh too. And this is exactly what many owners of bromeliads are known to do—when guests are expected, cut flowers are placed in the plants that aren't blooming. The group of bromeliads called Aechmea double so well as containers for flowers that they often are listed as the "Living Vase Plant."

A few of the bromeliads are terrestrial, meaning that their roots grow in soil. The majority are epiphytic or air plants. They are found growing on other plants to which the bromeliads attach themselves by their roots. The roots also take moisture from the air. Since no sustenance is taken from the supporting tree or other plant, the epiphytic bromeliads are not parasites.

Because of their air roots, bromeliads require a light, porous soil. You'll need to know how to mix soil for them in order to pot the new little ones that inevitably appear around the full-grown one you buy. Often, bromeliads are potted in osmunda fiber, as orchids are. Or it may be a mixture of leafmold, peat moss and sharp sand, plus about a teaspoon of a fertilizer such as dried cow manure to each pot. Plants may be fed as often as once a month with a liquid fertilizer.

Temperature is no more of a consideration for bromeliads than is humidity. High temperatures during winter and warmth all year are customary. However, many of the bromeliads can stand moderate to cool temperatures, but they won't survive frost or freezing temperatures. In summer, if possible, move bromeliads outdoors to a screened terrace or porch or under trees. You might try hanging them on branches of trees, as they are found in the jungles of Brazil.

If rain fills their cups, that means less watering by you. Incidentally, water in the leaf cups should always be fresh.

Pests are generally unknown. But a neglected or abused bromeliad might develop scale or a healthy one become infected from another plant near it. If any of these tiny insects cling to the foliage, wipe or scrub them off with soapy water. Take care that the water doesn't get into the cups, or, if it does, rinse it out thoroughly.

Light (not sunlight) or shade is natural for these plants, since so many of them come from tropical jungles. If you want to place a bromeliad near a window in order to show it off, bright light or sunlight should be filtered through some kind of curtain or shade. Plants probably would not die in a sunny location, but the coloring of the foliage would not be as strong.

Except for the tillandsias, which are gray, no one color can be used to describe bromeliads' foliage. Usually, leaves are striped, patched, banded, blotched or mottled. Wine red, maroon, pink and other shades of rose or red, purple, bronze, cream and yellow, and all shades of green from gray green to sea green and emerald can be found in various combinations. Many leaves could only be described as multicolored. A frosty finish isn't uncommon. Fortunately, leaf formation gives the plants a strong, sculptured look that can afford all this coloring.

The flowers are as brilliant as they are odd. These are not the sort of flowers with soft petals to which we are accustomed. Instead, the spike is technically known as an inflorescence. Some droop over the foliage; most of them stand erect above it. If the inflorescence is blue, it's often an ultramarine or a purple blue. Or, an inflorescence that is blue at first may gradually turn purple and rose. Lemon yellow, crimson, orange and scarlet are other typical colors.

On one score, you need not worry. The inflorescence won't wilt or fade before you get the plant home from the florist shop. The flower stays bright and lasts for months. On a few species and varieties, colorful berries form.

Each bromeliad plant produces only one inflorescence. That one bloom and sending up new plants are its reason for existence. But, during the months the flower lasts, the plant has been sending up offsets or suckers. Eventually, the original plant will die. But by that time you'll have several new little plants. Unless the big plant dies soon after its inflorescence does, you needn't hurry about potting up the new ones. When you do, fill a 4-inch pot for each one with the soil mixture suggested earlier. New plants flower within one to two years.

Only one of the innumerable members of the bromeliad family is valuable for food. This is none other than one of our favorite fruits—the pineapple. In fact, this whole plant family is called the Pineapple family as often as it is the Bromelia family.

AECHMEA is one of the most popular groups of the Pineapple or Bromelia family. Its species and varieties are the ones most commonly called "living vase plants." Leaves are broad, graceful and recurving.

Aechmea fasciata or urn plant is a common one and easy to obtain. Light green leaves are banded with silver. Its spike of bloom is made up of blue flowers held in feathery pink bracts. The blue later turns to rose and purple. Silver King has frosted leaves.

A. orlandiana has toothed, bright green leaves banded with chocolate. When it flowers, bracts are orange-

AECHMEA

scarlet and blossoms light yellow. This species was brought back from Brazil by Mulford Foster, who makes his home in Orlando, Fla., except when he's off searching for more fascinating and new bromeliads. No one, probably, has done more to make people in this country aware of bromeliads than has Mr. Foster, and his enthusiasm and admiration for his favorite plant are unbounded.

An Aechmea hybrid has been named Foster's Favorite. Glossy wine red leaves are green at the base. Deep blue flowers are followed by equally blue berries.

A. pubescens has leaves green above, brown red on the undersides. The inflorescence appears on a red stem and is first straw colored, then a deep blue. Blue berries form later on and stay colorful for as long a period as the flowers did.

ANANAS, the botanical name for pineapple, was adapted from the aboriginal South American name. To grow as a house plant, ananas was once hard to find. The variegated pineapple plant (A. sativus variegatus) is well worth searching for, since its leaves combine rose, yellow and green and are edged with red. This form is said to produce real pineapples for eating. Southern nurseries and specialists in tropical plants are the places to inquire for pineapple plants.

It's possible to grow your own house plant anytime you buy a pineapple fruit in the market. Carefully cut off the stubby crown of green leaves, taking some of the pulp. This topheavy crown can be anchored in a pot of sharp sand to form roots. When it has, it should be potted in light sandy soil and watered thoroughly.

Cutting off the crown and setting it aside to form a callus before potting it is another recommendation. And I've heard that some people root the top of a fruit in water. As the crown develops roots, its leaves will start to grow. They become longer and narrower and, eventually, you'll have a graceful plant.

California acquaintances have assured me that they or their friends have actually picked edible fruit from a pineapple plant in their patio. I've never heard of anyone in the Northeast plucking a fruit from a pineapple plant grown entirely in the house. However, it takes time—and sunshine—for fruit to form. Like all bromeliads, pineapple plants don't thrive on being chilled. With or without fruit, the pineapple will be decorative.

BILLBERGIAS have less spectacular foliage than other bromeliads. Leaves tend to grow taller and more grasslike. Flowers rival those of other groups.

Billbergia nutans is often the first bromeliad a person buys. Its leaves are narrow, but form a vase. Since its flowers droop, queen's tears is a common name. Green and blue blossoms with yellow anthers are held in a rosy bract.

Fantasia, a recent hybrid, has light green leaves with creamy markings.

B. zebrina has green leaves with silver stripes. From

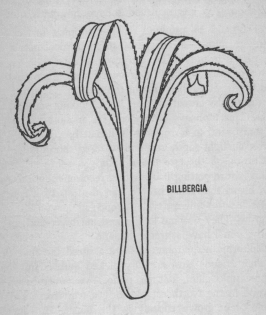

BILLBERGIA

the tall tube of foliage appears a drooping spike of green flowers in salmon bracts.

CRYPTANTHUS are added evidence of the variety offered by bromeliads. Most of them have leaves that grow flat. Earth stars and zebra plant are common names.

Cryptanthus roseus pictus (bivittatus) is distinctly star-shaped, with rosy stripes lengthwise through the leaves.

Many unnamed hybrids are available, all of them showy or striking, or just plain beautiful.

DYCKIAS are rosettes of leaves, small, flat and slow-growing. These are hardy bromeliads.

Dyckia sulphurea has fleshy rather than leathery-looking leaves. They recurve and have sharp spines, making this species difficult to handle. A hybrid, D. fosteriana, also has recurved foliage but with only a

CRYPTANTHUS

toothed edge. The gray-green foliage has white teeth and an almost purple tinge.

GUZMANIA maintains its family's reputation for being different. Leaves are soft and recurve gracefully, usually forming a plant as much as eighteen inches wide. Foliage is basically green.

Guzmania lingulata has smooth green leaves. The inflorescence looks more like a flower than usual; it is star-shaped with many rows of "petals." On this species it is orange and satiny.

A variety Magnifica has red lines from the base to about the middle of the leaves. Its flower is a red star held in clear view above the leaves.

NEOREGELIA SPECTABILIS is the fingernail or painted fingernail plant. It could never be confused with any other because its bronzy leaves banded in silver are tipped with bright red. Flowers are blue but less noticeable than on most bromeliads. This plant also can serve as a natural vase when it isn't flowering.

Hybrids have been developed in this country and Europe. One variety, named Pinkie, has leaves that are predominantly pink. Tricolor has outer leaves of deep green with ivory stripes, around inner leaves of orange red.

NIDULARIUM has large prickly-edged leaves that form a rosette. It produces showy bracts for its inflorescence. Unforunately, this group is not very common.

N. amazonicum has large flat leaves of a dark, metallic purple. N. fulgens has green leaves with darker spots around inner, shorter leaves of red. Flowers are chiefly white and purple.

TILLANDSIA includes Spanish moss, which hangs like enormous gray beards from trees in the South. Small beards even hang from utility wires, since this is an air plant. Larger plants, although still miniature for the Bromeliad family, will grow on bark and can be shown off wherever you please.

Tillandsia ionantha has a rosette of silvery leaves, at the most three inches high. If it's kept in sun, foliage turns rosy red in spring. The small flowers are violet.

T. lindeniana has narrow foliage, green and brown, plus deep blue flowers. T. circinna has powdery gray rosettes of leaves.

VRIESIAS are always described as spectacular. They are as unusual and outstanding as the name, flaming sword, implies. This describes the flower spike.

Vriesia splendens is the true flaming sword. Blue-green leaves are barred with dark mahogany. The tall, flat flower spike is vivid orange-red.

V. hieroglyphica also is well named, for the brown markings look like hieroglyphics on broad, light green leaves. Tall, branched flower spikes are sulphur yellow.

Hybrid Marie of V. carinata is called painted feather. Solid green leaves are topped by a flat feather-shaped flower spike of bright red and yellow. Imperialis has green leaves which look deep red in strong light. Its tall, branching flower spike has yellow flowers in maroon bracts.

Only enough species and varieties have been described to whet your interest in these odd and often bizarre plants. Dozens more are available, and excellent new ones are introduced every year as a result of hybridizing.

VRIESIA

Having brought home one bromeliad, you're almost certain to find room for more. Of course, your original plant will provide you with several more of the same kind within a couple of years. However, you'll probably want others that are colored quite differently. Remember that form and size vary, too, from the star-shaped cryptanthus that is striking on a coffee table to the urn-shaped and important aechmea for the foyer. You might want to group several billbergias or neoregelias in a focal spot, or select vriesias for a planter box in a dark corner.

Remember, bromeliads are plants that can stand neglect. You can shut the door and leave them for a weekend or a week without worry. On your return, they'll be looking as gay as ever, ready to have their cups filled with fresh water.

73

CHAPTER VI

FLOWERING PLANTS

A flower may be large or small but it must have petals for most persons to consider it a blossom. Wax begonias, azaleas, orchids, primroses, jasmine, camellias—these are some of the house plants with honest-to-goodness flowers. White ones can be as enchanting as pink ones or those of any other color. Indoors, fragrance isn't always as desirable a characteristic as it is outdoors. The extra-sweet or heavy scent quickly becomes tiring within the confines of a room. Still, on a house plant a flower is cause for rejoicing.

Most indoor gardeners as well as those who have house plants only because interior decoration demands them struggle to grow some of the flowering plants. Flowers add a certain richness to surroundings, especially during winter. And, after all, what is any garden, outdoors or in the house, without some flowers?

There's no trick to having bromeliads blossom. They do so as readily in an office or apartment as in a house where living conditions are much more favorable. But, dependable, long-lasting, vivid and odd as the brome-liad's flower spike undeniably is, it doesn't have a ring of petals and so it's hard to accept its inflorescence as a real flower.

A good many different kinds of house plants are chosen primarily for their attractive flowers. No one could grow all of them, even if there were room. Some of them, like the leafy alocasias and hoffmannias, require special conditions that few houses, let alone apartments, can supply. Others seem to me too unimportant even in full bloom to bother giving them space and care.

Then there are house plants that flower for some people, but never for others. For every person who manages to find a place where African violets bloom ten out of every twelve months, a dozen other persons never have any luck.

After the demanding and the temperamental flowering plants have been sensibly passed by, there is still a varied group to try in the house. From the more reliable possibilities, at least half a dozen should flower every year indoors sometime between November and May.

In order to flower, all except a handful of house plants need sun. Many require as much as four hours of sunlight daily for bloom. This means that placement in or near a sunny window is essential to stimulate development of flower buds. Not all flowering plants, fortunately, have to be in a south window. Many of them bloom nicely if their location is in or near an east or a west window through which sun shines for only two or three hours daily.

Essential as sun is for bloom, lack of a south or a west window in the house needn't be a total handicap. Nor need a sunless apartment lack flowers growing in pots. If bromeliads and the few plants that bloom in light places don't satisfy the craving for flowers, it's still possible to have real ones by forcing some of the bulbs (see page 164).

Those whose homes have windows on all sides can enjoy all sorts of flowering plants indoors. Modern houses with picture windows or glass walls that let in maximum light or sun are equally satisfactory. With different exposures available and as much light coming indoors as prevailing weather permits, you can pick and choose among flowering plants instead of having to be satisfied with whatever can manage to bloom.

As winter wears on, more and more house plants begin to flower. February, when days are lengthening noticeably, is starting time for many of them. Others that should have blossomed by December or January may have been delayed by weeks of prevailingly cloudy weather—a common occurrence in the Northeast and Midwest.

The flowering year indoors really commences in October, for that is the month when African violets start again. So also will impatiens and wax begonias rooted from cuttings of garden plants, browallia and others brought indoors from the garden. From October to May, therefore, it should be possible to work out a succession of bloom. To achieve this succession, it will take experiment and patience, plus much more care than foliage plants need.

In general, flowering house plants need considerably more attention than foliage ones. But no comparison really can be made between the most durable of the flowering and foliage groups. Flowering plants almost always need more frequent watering, especially when they're in bloom. Those with extremely soft, hairy or plushy leaves must be watered with care too.

Probably, also, more of the flowering plants are susceptible to insects such as white fly and thrips. These pests may be impossible to prevent and difficult to eradicate. A few flowering house plants, of course,

76

are as unlikely as many foliage ones to be ravaged by insects and diseases.

Except for the collectors of African violets or some equally captivating plant, few people limit themselves only to flowering plants. An outdoor garden never consists only of flowers, so why should an indoor garden? The proportion of flowering plants to foliage ones will depend on how much sun and direct light your home provides and, to a lesser extent, on how much time can be allotted to indoor gardening.

A bay window or two or more standard windows flooded with sunlight every day are natural places for shelves to hold all sorts of flowering plants. Elsewhere, flowering house plants are better used as accents. A floor-level garden against a glass wall facing west probably would consist of as many foliage as flowering plants. Here, for example, a bougainvillea vine in the corner next to the glass should blossom. Then wax begonias or impatiens as an edging toward the room side might be sufficient color.

Flowering plants, strategically placed against a background of foliage plants and vines, show up well. By the same token, so does a stunning flowering plant in a box or other container that must be filled mostly with leafy plants because of restricted light or sun. In a planter box in the foyer of a city apartment, one anthurium in a pot contributes a strong and exotic splash of color for weeks.

So long as the anthurium, azalea or other plant is in flower, sun isn't essential. In fact, open flowers last longer if the plants do not stand in sun every day. When blossoms fade, the plant can be removed and replaced by another that has come into bloom.

That's one advantage of using flowering plants for accent. They're easy to shift when flowers are gone or something else comes into bloom. It's also easy to lift out the pot in order to soak the soil or spray foliage clean with water.

Flowering plants for accent may be grown at home or purchased at a shop. Shrubby azaleas in bud or bloom can be bought at least six months of the year, bushy chrysanthemums every month. This has been brought about by professional growers who control light, shade and length of the days in order to make these plants bloom out of season. Chrysanthemums can be saved to plant in the outdoor garden, azaleas to flower indoors another year by mid- or late winter.

Many of the flowering house plants can be practically lifelong companions. My sweet olive, which grows slowly, is so old that it has graduated from a 4-inch flower pot to a 9-inch tub. It's taken at least eighteen years to do so, but it's still shapely and still opens its tiny, fragrant blossoms every winter.

Some of the most successful flowering house plants are shrubs or perennials in outdoor gardens in the South. Hibiscus, plumbago and jasmine are as notable examples as pittosporum, podocarpus and Moses in a cradle are in the foliage plants. Wherever they originate, the flowering group offers a selection of small and large plants, and of plain-jane and spectacular blossoms.

ABUTILON, or flowering maple, grows in the manner of a symmetrical small tree. Its leaves call to mind a maple leaf, its flowers are pendent bells, crinkly like Japanese paper lanterns hanging from every branch. Flowers of Abutilon hybridum, best and longest known, may have yellow, white, apricot, pink, rose or red blossoms. Souvenir de Bonn has rosy yellow bells and green and white leaves. Yellow spotted foliage and apricot flowers deck the taller-growing A. Thompsoni. Then there's a trailing abutilon (A. megapotamicum variegatum) with slender stems of yellow, green leaves and slimmer blossoms of orange and red.

Abutilon has been a standard house plant for 100

years or more. This should be a testimonial for its flowering performance. These are plants that need room; a bay window, a sun porch or an indoor garden is an ideal place. Small plants can be purchased, or a good crop grown from seed. Young plants probably will need pinching back to make them shapely. A sunny window and ample watering are the chief requirements.

Fresh air daily—but without a draft—will help to keep this plant pest-free. If you want to enjoy flowers from late fall through the winter, then don't let the abutilon bloom while it is spending the summer outdoors. Pinch out buds, and pinch back new growth to keep the plant from growing oversize.

ACACIA'S lovely yellow flowers remind us in February that it's spring in other climates. Along the Mediterranean, in Australia and in southern California, the acacias grow and bloom outdoors as shrubs and trees. Wattle is the common name in Australia, mimosa in this country and Europe. The long flower clusters consist either of tiny golden balls or equally colorful "catkins."

Acacia armata pendula is a dwarf shrubby sort that fits a large pot. Sweetly scented yellow flowers start to open in February. Since acacias grow slowly as house plants, some of the taller kinds are indoor possibilities. A. baileyana, often called golden mimosa, opens fluffy, fragrant yellow flowers from February on into spring. The fernlike foliage is more silvery blue than green. A. longifolia has bright yellow flowers, its variety Floribunda creamy yellow ones. Both have green leaves and bloom readily. There are many other species and varieties to investigate, once these beginner's kinds have earned their space.

Acacias are even larger than flowering maples. Room to grow is essential, but a sun porch or glass wall should solve this problem as well as that of temperature. Acacias need a cool location, even for flowering—50 to

55 degrees at night, 65 to 68 degrees by day. Fresh air is beneficial. These are plants that shouldn't be over-watered, as their Mediterranean habitat should imply. Let the soil get quite dry, then soak thoroughly.

ACALYPHA HISPIDA, better known as chenille plant, may be more familiar as a hedge plant in the South. Chenille plant has fluffy red tassels, sometimes ten inches or more long, for flowers. Firedragon plant (A. Wilkesiana) also has showy red tassels but is grown more for its leaves mottled with bright hues of copper, crimson and bronze. It also is a low hedge plant in Florida.

As a house plant where winters are cold, acalyphas want warmth (70 degrees or higher by day), strong light and, if possible, some sun every day. These are thirsty plants, so don't neglect watering.

ALLAMANDA is prized for its large, rich yellow flowers that open from February or March on into summer. Flowers appear on a vinelike shrub with glossy green leaves. Allamanda Hendersonnii is considered most free-flowering. A. Williamsii has smaller yellow flowers with red coloring in the throats.

Allamanda has always been one of the first vines any new greenhouse owner acquires. It also can be grown in the house if there's room to train its long stems. It must have all possible sun in order to bloom, but isn't as particular about temperature. It thrives in the range from 65 degrees to well above 70 degrees by day, but should not be where temperatures may fall below 60 degrees at night. Ample watering is essential but not to the extent that soil is soggy.

ANNUALS from the garden are a distinct possibility. Self-sown seedlings, dug up before frost, will produce smaller blossoms than normal in a sunny window. Try nicotiana, cosmos, marigold, balsam, ageratum and even zinnias. If stocks, for example, haven't flowered outdoors before frost threatens, by all means dig up and plant each one in a pot to bring into the house.

It's worth sowing seed of some garden annuals for indoor color. Black-eyed Susan or clock vine (Thunbergia alata), if sown in September, will open flat round flower disks in shades from yellow to apricot, most of them with a black eye at the center. These blossoms open on graceful, rather short, trailing vines. Another vine, morning glory, will flower within ten weeks if seeds are sown in early February. Colorado Sunshine marigold produces fine, large, yellow flowers almost as freely in winter where it's warm and sunny as it does in summer outdoors.

If you're ambitious and willing to plant these annuals each in its own small pot, they can add a brave splash of color during the fall and early winter months. This is definitely a group with which to experiment. Keep in full sun, water often and watch out for insects.

ANTHURIUMS are striking plants with stunning and brilliantly colored flowers. Flamingo flower, boat sail, tail flower are some of the common names. Large leaves are handsome, and in some varieties veins are a contrasting color, and the glistening flowers last for weeks. They are vivid shades of dark or bright red, salmon, coral, pink or white, and some are spotted.

Anthurium andraeanum, which comes from Colombia, is the common one in cultivation. Many hybrids have been developed. It has plain green foliage. Hybrids also have been developed from A. Scherzerianum, a rather dwarf form discovered in Guatemala.

Species and hybrids have odd flowers whose structure is similar to that of the calla lily. The highly colored, shiny, flat tongue or boat-shaped part is not a petal but a bract. It surrounds the actual flower spike, which is called a spadix.

On Anthurium crystallinum, the bract as well as the flower spike is fairly inconspicuous. This one, however, has magnificent leaves. They are large and heart-shaped, velvety deep green, with veins outlined in sparkling silver. The plant looks well for months in a spot never reached by daylight.

These tropical plants thrive on humidity but tolerate moderate or high temperatures (minimum at night 55 degrees). They need to be potted in a loose soil rich with leafmold or in osmunda fiber or sphagnum moss. Do cover the aerial roots with sphagnum. Always keep the soil mixture damp. Anthuriums rest in summer, flower the rest of the year. They seem to resent transplanting, so don't shift to a larger pot until roots seem about to break the original one.

APHELANDRA SQUARROSA LOUISAE is said to be a stunning plant for both its flowers and foliage. Actually, I have never tried it but, since it also comes from tropical America, it could well make a reliable house plant. Leaves eight to ten inches long are lighter green on the underside and have white veins. Pale yellow flowers open above golden orange bracts.

ASTILBE, more commonly called spirea, is a garden perennial. If you will dig up a clump from the garden in November, pot it and store in a cool place until February, it can then be brought indoors to force open not only leaves but also lacy pink, rose or red plumes. Or, on a mild February day when the ground isn't frozen too hard, dig up a clump, plant it in a pot and bring it into the house. An astilbe will require a large pot, probably at a minimum a 6-inch one.

This perennial should be replanted in the garden in spring, and the soil well fertilized. However, it probably won't flower outdoors for another year or two.

BLEEDING HEART can be forced indoors with the same treatment. It is charming in full bloom, particularly if this can be managed by February. If it's possible to obtain plants of astilbe and bleeding heart from a local

82

nursery in January or February, this certainly is the easiest way to enjoy their flowers indoors.

AZALEAS are wonderful house plants. One that is sent as a gift should earn heartfelt thanks, for it's one flowering plant that anyone can keep for years and bring into bloom every winter. Ten to one, it will have as many blossoms in succeeding years in your home as were forced by the professional grower. At one time azaleas appeared in florist shops in February and were choice gift plants for Easter and Mother's Day. Now, this springlike plant is generally available for Thanksgiving and Christmas.

Indoor azaleas are of two major kinds. One is the Kurume type, which grows into a shrubby little plant covered with masses of dainty blossoms. The pink one, which I believe is variety Coral Bell, is seen everywhere. This is the one most generally forced, but there are many other Kurume varieties in white and shades of pink.

Azalea indica is a treelike plant with a bark-covered stem topped by a crown of green leaves and handsome flowers. The blooms are larger than those of Kurume, double and quite open, and the petals are often waved. Colors are clear tones of red and pink, pure white, or any of these striped or spotted with one of the others.

Those who live north of the latitude of Washington, D.C. and Kansas City, Mo. must treat A. indica as a house plant. It can be moved outdoors for the summer in May after all danger of frost is passed, but must be brought back indoors soon after Labor Day. The Kurume azaleas are quite hardy and may be planted outdoors to grow into a low shrub, or may be kept in a pot and brought indoors again in September to flower along about February. Neither type grows rapidly, but the shrubby little Kurumes will treble their size in perhaps five years.

When an azalea comes from the florist shop, don't

place it in full sun if it is nearing full bloom. Flowers will last longer where they receive full light and buds will open where sunlight touches them for only an hour or so in the morning or afternoon. When flowers fade, an east or a west window is a fine location.

Azaleas are thirsty plants with a ball of roots that soak up water like a sponge. While they are flowering, they may need water twice daily. Set the pot in a large saucer if a matching one didn't come with the plant. If the saucer is filled with water in the morning, all of it has usually disappeared by evening. Out of bloom, azaleas thrive if they are watered once a day, and if the pot is submerged in a sink or a pail of water to soak its fill once a week.

A temperature around 65 degrees by day is ideal to encourage bud formation on old plants. By night, 55 degrees is good, although a drop to 50 or 45 degrees will do no harm.

When an azalea must be shifted to a larger pot, use a package of an acid soil mixture. Fertilize it before it is moved outdoors for the summer, and two or three times thereafter at intervals of about six weeks. Feed again once a fortnight from November until flower buds have formed.

BEGONIAS are one of the most popular plant families for indoors. Not only are they eminently satisfactory, but they are diverse almost beyond comprehension. Most of them are grown for flowers, which are profuse from February on through spring, but a few groups are cherished for their foliage. The person who has no intention of collecting, seldom lacks two to six different kinds among the house plants (see Chapter IX).

BELOPERONE GUTTATA is aptly named shrimp plant. The bracts are larger and brighter than the small white flowers. They overlap and hang from the tip of a slender stem like the segments of a shrimp. Yellow Queen is prettier, with chartreuse to lemon-yellow bracts. This is a native of Mexico which has made itself at home in gardens of southern United States as well as in pots indoors.

Shrimp plant is undemanding and long-lived. Sun and frequent watering are its only requirements. By the time winter is over, shrimp plants will probably be tall and thin-looking, but there'll still be bloom at

BELOPERONE

the end of the stems. When this plant is moved outdoors for the summer, choose a sunny spot, perhaps in the flower border, and cut back the stems to about four inches. This will encourage growth for a bushy plant to be potted up in fall.

BOUGAINVILLEA is never forgotten by anyone who visits Bermuda or the Caribbean. Vivid clusters of bloom tumble luxuriantly over stucco houses and, so tall do the slender stems of this woody shrub grow, that it appears to be a vine that has no trouble reaching the rooftops. As a house plant in a tub or pot, it isn't going to displace the ceiling of any room. It will bloom quite steadily all winter, although clusters will not be as large as in warmer climate. Stems can be trained and tied to bamboo stakes stuck in the pot or tub.

Some people dismiss bougainvillea as gaudy, though indoors it could hardly be called more than gay. Bracts that enclose the inconspicuous flowers are to blame. Their papery texture, which gives it the name paper flower, contributes to harsh coloring. Sanderiana, which will bloom in small pots, has distinctly magenta bracts. It's floriferous, too.

Variety Crimson Lake with bracts as richly red as its name has become the popular variety for planting near houses. It also is good indoors. Barbara Karst is another crimson. Variety Laterita is almost as showy a brick red.

Oddly enough for a tropical plant, bougainvillea isn't particular about temperature indoors. It blooms more if temperatures are 70 degrees by day, but it tolerates as low an average as 60 to 65 degrees. Sun is essential. Don't be too generous with water. Allow soil to become almost dried out before soaking it.

BOUVARDIA as a cut flower has long been a staple of wedding bouquets. Pot plants start flowering in fall and continue steadily well into the winter. Albatross is a good white, with four waxy and fragrant petals. Fire Chief produces quantities of bright red flowers on plants that are semi-trailing rather than shrubby. My favorite is the pink, one variety of which is Giant Pink.

Although bouvardia is grown under glass for florist-shop cut flowers, it's a surprisingly satisfactory house plant. A group of plants in 4-inch pots is most effective. Sun, daily watering, plus syringing of the foliage once a week, and temperature around 65 degrees are satisfactory conditions for flowering plants. When bloom is over, move them to a cooler location and water less for a few weeks. Then cut back the plants, move them to a warmer place and water regularly to induce new growth. Plants can be moved outdoors for the summer.

To stimulate bloom by October, shade them for a week or so after they're brought back indoors.

BROWALLIA SPECIOSA MAJOR is the sapphire flower of outdoors and indoors. It can be grown from seed, or small plants can be purchased. They show off best in hanging baskets or in pots at the edge of a planter box. The sizable violet-blue, starry flowers appear on trailing stems. By sowing seed, it's possible to have Sapphire Viscosa Compacta, a more compact plant with light-eyed blue flowers.

Browallia isn't fussy about temperatures; 65 to 70 degrees by day and not less than 55 degrees at night keep it flowering from fall through spring. Some sun is desirable, at least in fall and winter, when days are short and often cloudy. An east window is ideal. Don't neglect watering or hesitate to feed every six weeks or so.

CAMELLIAS are second only to roses in the popularity poll of garden flowers. Those who can't grow this shrub outdoors because of severe winter climate may be able to compensate by having a shrub or two indoors. There's no point, however, in stopping at a nursery in Florida and buying a couple of camellias in cans to bring home. Some varieties are better suited to indoor culture than others. Don't try any camellia unless there is room for a good-sized shrub in a large tub or pot and unless there is a well-lighted location where the temperature averages 50 degrees and never rises much higher, and humidity can be maintained at close to 50 per cent. A sunroom or enclosed porch should meet these specifications.

If you can provide the room and the conditions, good bloom can be expected from February into April. Debutante, the ever-popular and charming pink, is a dependable variety to try. So are crimson Mathotiana and white Mathotiana Alba, semi-double white-blotched-with pink Elegans, pink-mottled-with-white Lallarook, dark red C. M. Hovey, white Purity, or white Alba Plena.

Camellias outdoors are not grown in full sun, and they must be protected from it indoors. Soil must be kept moist and the foliage sprayed frequently with water to help maintain a damp, cool atmosphere. Start feeding as soon as flower buds show, repeat when bloom is over and again when the shrubs are moved outdoors in summer. With their glossy green foliage, camellias are handsome plants on a shaded terrace or porch during summer.

Prune the plant immediately after bloom, removing weak and droopy stems and trimming outer branches to shape it. Inner branches may be thinned if it seems advisable. Potbound plants flower best, but camellias can outgrow their containers. If they need shifting, do this also immediately after bloom. Soil should be acid, as for azaleas, and porous with plenty of leafmold or peat moss.

CAMPANULA ISOPHYLLA is a delightful plant, usually called star of Bethlehem, but sometimes bell flower or falling stars. The blue or white blossoms on trailing stems are thick as stars on a clear August night. If you don't plant it in a hanging container, do place the pot so that stems and flowers can be seen as they shower down over the edge. This may be a country cousin, for I can't remember ever seeing it in a city.

Bloom all year indoors is said to be possible. However, I've found that it flowers in early fall and then again from spring until June or July. Some sun and some humidity are essential. Be careful not to overwater, so that stems won't rot. Give the container a quarter turn every week so the plant will be covered with blossoms on all sides.

CARISSA GRANDIFLORA, although it's commonly called Natal plum, is grown indoors for flowers rather than fruit. Boxwood Beauty is a dwarf compact plant with glossy evergreen leaves and fragrant waxy white flowers like small stars. The scarlet fruits like small plums are edible.

For flowers, if not fruit, bright light is essential at all times, and sun whenever possible. Warmth from 65 to 70 degrees is desirable, as is regular watering.

Fragrant as jasmine are the CESTRUMS. In fact, they're often called jessamine. Most appealing is the night-blooming jessamine (Cestrum nocturnum), with small creamy blossoms that are delightfully sweet-scented. Blossoms of willow-leaved jessamine (C. parqui) pour out their perfume at night. Leaves are narrow. Day-blooming jessamine (C. diurnum) isn't nearly as tempting.

Plants are shrubby and glossy-leaved. Jessamines react poorly to low temperature and drafts. Keep them in sun, where it's warm, and water regularly for flowers.

CHRYSANTHEMUMS are a reliable source of color. Garden varieties with medium-size decorative flowers can be purchased in bud or bloom every month of the year. Yellow is the great favorite of professional growers, but white and pink also are available a good deal of the time. The forcing has been done on these plants, so all you need to do is to water. Sun isn't necessary, but good light is.

After bloom, the stems should be cut back and watering reduced. Store in a coldframe, cool cellar or porch until it's time to plant them outdoors for future color in the garden.

Paris or Boston daisies (Chrysanthemum frutescens) are good indoor residents. These are the single yellow daisies that appear abundantly on plants with finer foliage than garden 'mums have. A white kind, also single, is generally called marguerite. Boston daisies and marguerites know no season and may bloom the year around. In winter, you may want to cut some of the blossoms.

Sky-blue daisies with yellow centers are produced by Felicia amelloides, the blue marguerite or kingfisher daisy. This also usually is free-blooming.

All of these daisies can grow to be big plants needing a large pot or small tub. Some spring before they are moved outdoors, try dividing a large clump and potting the two or more sections separately. By fall, when they're brought indoors, they should be flowering size. In addition to watering daily, soak the pot in a pail of water at least once a week. Cool situations are best, with temperature around 65 degrees; the closer to 70 degrees, the more watering will be needed. Sun is essential to maintain bloom. Feed occasionally.

CLERODENDRUM THOMSONAE, Glory Bower, is an evergreen shrub with slender twining stems. In other words, its growth is similar to bougainvillea. It's possible, though, to keep Glory Bower as a bushy plant by pinching it back. Large showy clusters of odd white and scarlet flowers appear several times during the year. Winter is the season when shrubby C. ugandense opens its bright blue flowers. The dwarf C. fragrans has double white flowers that are sweetly scented, some say almost like arbutus.

The clerodendrums grow most luxuriantly in a cool greenhouse. They will flower, but not grow too big, in moderate temperatures in a house. An average of 65 degrees by day in as sunny a location as possible would be ideal. They can stand temperatures up to 70 degrees, and not lower than 55 degrees at night. Regular watering and high humidity (this plant's home is West Africa) must be maintained.

CLIVIA, or Kafir lily, has such spectacular bloom and has been displayed so often at big city spring flower shows, that it may seem hard to believe it can flower in anyone's home. Knowing that it's a relative of amaryllis should make this fact more believable. Clivia grows not from true bulbs but from a tuberous-rooted plant. Huge umbels of blossoms in some shade between orange and true red open indoors between February and May. At other times, the wide straplike leaves, which are evergreen, make this a good background plant. Clivias flower outdoors in southern California gardens.

Indoors, clivia flowers best when it becomes potbound. Still, have a 7-inch pot ready for the new plant. A good soil mixture consists of two parts garden loam, one part rotted cow manure, leafmold or peat moss, and

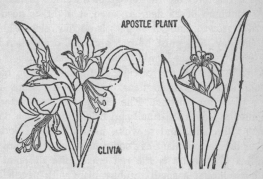

APOSTLE PLANT

CLIVIA

one-half part sand. Mix one tablespoon of bonemeal into each pot. Set the plant so that its crown is about two inches above soil level, then water thoroughly.

Clivias need plenty of direct light and some sun, but if they stand in sun day after day, leaves may burn. The most favorable temperature range is between 60 and 65 degrees. Water frequently.

The cycle of care is important for bloom on clivia. It consists of watering and feeding new annual growth, reduction of watering after bloom, moving to semi-shade outdoors for summer and feeding and watering while it is there to restore vigor, then a waterless (or almost waterless) dormant period during fall and early winter.

CROSSANDRA is an old conservatory plant that was

rediscovered, as it were, during the 1950's. Seeds or small plants can be purchased (seeds should be sown only in spring, and bloom should occur seven to eight months later). I myself have never seen it bloom anywhere except in a greenhouse, and a warm one at that. Anyone who can make crossandra flower has an unusual and attractive house plant. Leaves are glossy green, rather like those of a gardenia. Flowers always remind me of a large candytuft but their color is a soft orange-salmon. Blossoms top the foliage of the small plants.

A minimum of 65 degrees, even at night, is needed for best growth, and 75 degrees is not unwelcome during the day. Soil must be rich and well-drained. Adequate watering and humidity are other essentials.

CUPHEA, cigar flower or cigar plant, is grown in both indoor and outdoor gardens, although the kinds for each place are distinct. The single flowers scattered among the leaves are small and bright red with a dark ring at the end, and a white mouth. Their coloring makes firecracker plant as good a name as cigar flower. Cuphea platycentra is the red one. Quite different is C. hyssopifolia, a small shrubby plant with needlelike foliage and small, starlike lavender-pink blossoms.

Moderate and quite warm temperatures (to 70 degrees or more by day) suit these plants from Mexico. All possible sun encourages bloom. Daily watering is needed to keep them from drying out.

DAPHNE ODORA is a shrub often three feet tall in the South. As a northern house plant it seldom reaches more than a foot tall, and will flower when it's smaller. Its clusters of pinky-lavender flowers are formed like those of the garden Daphne cneorum, but have much more fragrance. This seems to me sharper than the delicate arbutus scent many people claim. Daphne odora marginata has a creamy white margin around its glossy green leaves.

Whichever daphne you obtain, the plant will grow

slowly and be shapely. Another advantage is the fact that it flowers in a place reached by light, but sunlight should be filtered. Fresh air is as essential as acid soil. Although it's a southern shrub, moderate temperatures (65 to 68 degrees) are best indoors.

Daphne will seem to rest a good part of the time. Catalogues usually say it flowers from November to March, but I have never had any bloom before late January or early February. Water frequently from the time buds form until flowers fade; not so much the rest of the year. Also, when buds appear, start liquid feeding every two weeks.

EPISCIAS belong to the African violet family. The homeland of African violets is tropical Africa; of Episcias, tropical America. No two house plants could be more different. Don't, however, try an episcia unless you have been able to make African violets flourish (see page 122).

FUCHSIAS aren't really house plants. Their normal season of bloom is May to December in California and other regions where it is an outdoor plant all the year. In other parts of the country where frosts come any time after late September, plants usually are brought indoors to be saved for another year. This is easiest to do if plants have been sunk in their pots instead of being removed and set right into the garden soil. They will continue to bloom through October and possibly into November after they have been brought indoors. Thereafter they are dormant until new growth starts in spring.

Sunny windows aren't essential, since fuchsias bloom in shade or semi-shade outdoors. Take cuttings for new plants in early spring as soon as new growth is long enough.

Fuchsia triphylla is one that I bring indoors every September (F. magellanica, the hardy one, survives winter even in Connecticut). Triphylla is a distinctive species with downy leaves green above, purple beneath, and long, slender vermilion flowers. Triphylla hybrids flower best outdoors in the heat, humidity and extremes of summer weather in the East and Midwest, and these also are worth bringing indoors every fall.

One Triphylla hybrid, Fanfare, may even bloom in the house later than October (in the vicinity of San Francisco, Fanfare blossoms outdoors twelve months of the year). Fanfare has long turkey-red blossoms. Although the common fuchsia with orange-red blossoms may not flower for as long a period indoors, it's hard to beat. The shape and color give it the nickname honeysuckle, but this Triphylla hybrid actually is Gartenmeister Bonstedt. Wedgwood is a fine, tolerant, double smoky-blue and white.

Trailing fuchsias to plant in hanging baskets are a modern development. Look for and hang onto Cascade, with deep carmine trumpets and white petals flushed with carmine; or Montilla, with exquisite carmine flowers.

Fuchsias need ample moisture when they aren't dormant. They should be fertilized regularly, too, after bloom starts—although not in the fall after plants are moved indoors (except Fanfare, to keep it blooming). Moderate temperatures, never over 70 degrees in daytime, and preferably less, are best.

GARDENIA is a handsome small shrub, in or out of bloom. Stems are well covered with glossy, bright green foliage. The white flowers are strongly perfumed. The size of these cool-looking, fragrant blossoms will vary according to the variety. They are never as large on house plants as those used for corsages. Indoors in greenhouses and homes, as outdoors in Florida gardens, gardenias start to bloom in spring. A potted plant often continues to set buds after it's been moved outdoors for the summer. The general recommendation to pinch off these buds is seldom followed, for owners are too fond—and too proud—of the pretty scented blossoms.

A gardenia is a long-lived house plant. It's almost certain to set buds by April, but it's never as certain that they will bloom. One person after another tells of buds falling off without opening. To prevent this tragedy, the following are the conditions recommended for gardenias:

Temperatures between 60 and 70 degrees in the daytime, never less than 55 degrees at night.

Sun part of the day.

Tepid water, and soaking the soil. Once a week or so, set in a pail of water and leave until the surface of the soil is moist.

Humid atmosphere; so spray foliage.

Ventilation, but never a draft. Keep a gardenia pretty much by itself to assure circulation of air, rather than crowded among other plants.

Acid soil when it is repotted. Feed monthly except in summer.

Moving outdoors in spring when all danger of frost is past to a partly shaded and sheltered location. Don't neglect to water if it's needed.

Pruning for shapeliness if desired, before plant is brought back indoors in fall.

If buds don't fall, the gardenia has a surprisingly long season of bloom. Buds open slowly and are fascinating to watch.

GERANIUMS are the grand old favorite. If for no other reason than that plants in boxes and elsewhere in the garden are blooming their finest in early fall, about the time frost is expected, people try to pot and bring them indoors. Results are bound to disappoint, for geraniums can't bloom all year any more than daffodils and roses can. This diverse family, however, can contribute colored or scented foliage as well as gay flowers to the indoor garden (Chapter VIII).

The GINGER family contributes plants not only with aromatic foliage (page 17) but also with flowers. These are grown outdoors in southern gardens, both east and west, and Hawaii is famous for them. Elsewhere, they are delightful house or terrace plants for bloom in late summer and fall.

Shell Flower or Shell Ginger (Alpina nutans speciosa) has a spike of blossoms that hangs down like a string of shells. Buds, looking like porcelain, are white tipped with pink. One variety opens pure white. Others are white with crimson veining or bright red. These appear above long, shining and rather coarse evergreen leaves.

The Hedychium group are called Ginger Lilies, but H. coronarium is known as Garland Flower or Butterfly Lily. The wide white petals do look like butterfly wings. Four to six large flowers appear in green bracts that turn brown. Their scent resembles that of gardenia. H. flavum is the yellow ginger and Kahili Lily (H. gardnerianum) has smaller, pale yellow flowers with red stamens. Both are fragrant. The Hedychiums and the Alpinas probably grow best in part shade, need rich soil and plenty of moisture.

Gingers need filtered light or sun, but will not flower if they are too shaded. The tuberous or fleshy roots should be potted in rich soil which should never be allowed to dry out while gingers are in active growth.

HELICONIA, wild plantain or lobster claw, is a tender garden plant even in Florida. Leaves are large—2 to 3 feet—on slender stems measuring 8 to 10 feet—as befits a member of the Banana family. It's the bracts that make one find room for this plant. Heliconia bihai has scarlet ones never less than four inches long, arranged geometrically along a stem. These are popular for flower arrangements. Some forms have yellow bracts, and H. aureo-striata has leaves feathered and striped in yellow.

If there's room for a heliconia, it must be a warm

place. Growing in a large tub or pot in a rich loamy soil makes it convenient to move them about. Ample moisture is needed at all times.

HIBISCUS is one of the most satisfactory plants I've ever grown. Beautiful blossoms, little if any smaller than those on the same varieties in southern gardens, open day after day—sunny ones—in winter. Then about June 1, the plants in their pots or tubs are moved to the terrace, where they flower intermittently during

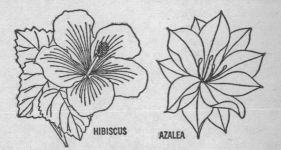

HIBISCUS AZALEA

summer. Flowers of most of the approximately 1,000 varieties of hibiscus now sold by nurserymen, last only a day. Then they roll up neatly and fall off.

For indoor enjoyment, hunt for variety Mrs. James Hendry, whose slightly fragrant flowers last two days, and for Ruth Wilcox, whose single white flowers remain open throughout the evening as well as the day. Kona is double and deep pink, Crown of Bohemia a crested yellow with copper shading, Lamberti a good single red. These are all hybrid varieties of Hibiscus Rosa-sinensis.

H. cooperi may be grown for its leaves, variegated green, white, pink or rose. But since this foliage plant also needs sun to be colorful, who would give it house room when the flowering varieties are so much more rewarding?

If rooted cuttings are obtained—or brought home from Florida—these should be planted in 2½-inch pots filled with a mixture of garden soil, sand and leafmold. A sunny window sill, moderate temperatures by day and never below 55 degrees at night, and daily watering sum up the simple care. Plants flower before they are a year old.

In ten years' time, these plants will have grown to a size that can be fitted only into a 14-inch tub. But they're worth the house room, and are handsome on a

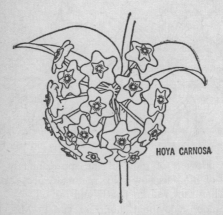

HOYA CARNOSA

terrace in summer. Hibiscus, even in the house, become a branching shrub with stems covered with bark. Don't hesitate to prune stems severely before they're brought back indoors in September.

HOYA CARNOSA, the vine known as wax plant, is becoming increasingly popular. Its leaves are thick and waxy, and it will grow anywhere. H. carnosa with green leaves, and H. carnosa variegata with green and white leaves often tinted pink, produce identical flowers. In spring brown knobs along the stems suddenly produce clusters of blossoms, each one like a pink star and delightfully fragrant. Both of these varieties can grow into long vines that can be trained around a window frame or trellis. H. exotica has leaves the reverse of Variegata, cream centers with green margins.

Hoya bella is a miniature wax plant, bushy with small pointed green leaves and fragrant white blossoms. Similar in habit is H. motoskoi, but its oval leaves are spotted with silver, flowers are creamy pink with a purple eye.

Wax plant vines will not bloom until they have been growing for some time. When they do start, never remove the brown knob from which the flower clusters come. Bloom appears every spring from the same knobs. An east or a west window where the vine receives sun part of the day is ideal. Adequate water and frequent cleaning of leaves are desirable. Since this vine grows slowly, it won't need annual repotting.

IMPATIENS is everyone's house plant. Periwinkle, sultana, patient Lucy, touch-me-not, patience plant, are pet names for this old-fashioned flower that blooms in shaded places in the garden and in light places indoors. It isn't always possible to buy impatiens from the florist, except in spring when seedlings are sold for outdoor planting. If you can't find the color flowers you want, by all means grow your own from seed. They will bloom by late July and be nicely established to bring indoors in September.

A dwarf strain has been developed that won't get so straggly by midwinter. Seed can be had in mixtures or selected colors for flowers of deep rose, scarlet orange, coral rose, cherry red, orange, shrimp pink or pure white. These have all-green leaves. The green-and-white-leaved impatiens has salmon-pink flowers.

Two of this clan are not grown from seed. Impatiens oliveri produces large lavender-pink flowers only in winter. I. platypetela has large orange-yellow blossoms.

Impatiens comes as close to flowering continuously as any house plant could. A location where it receives half a day's sun or direct bright light is best for bloom. These plants make no other demands except for lots of moisture.

Once you have an impatiens, it's possible to grow as many as you want. Soft green cuttings from the tips of the stems root quickly and easily in a small glass of water, a pot of damp sand or in moist earth. Taking cuttings is one way to keep the plant bushy and branching.

IXORA, like clivia, was exclaimed over at March flower shows in northern cities until people learned it could be grown to flower in houses as well as greenhouses. Flame of the Woods is the common name for Ixora coccinea with clusters of orange-red flowers against glossy green foliage. I. chinensis has red flowers, I. lutea deep yellow ones. If it's possible to search among southeastern nurseries, some beautifully colored hybrids in named varieties may be found. A buff one is called Biscuit, Henry Morat is a pink one and Red Velvet describes itself.

The bushy ixoras are slow growing. If they are kept moist and well fed in a sunny window where temperature averages 70 degrees in the daytime, ixoras will bloom for weeks, maybe months. Fertilize at least once a month while they are flowering. When bloom is over, reduce watering for about a month, then fertilize again and increase watering.

JACOBINIA and JUSTICIA belong to the Acanthus family and are mistaken for each other most of the time. The difference is chiefly a botanical difference in the flower structure. Mexican plume plant or king's crown (Jacobinia carnea) has plumes of rosy blossoms on large bushy plants (I understand small specimens are more certain to bloom indoors). A better choice probably is the smaller-growing, shrubby J. pauciflora. This grows only two feet tall in its homeland, Brazil, and has nodding scarlet flowers that have given it the name

Brazilian fuchsia. Justicia extensa has foliage marked with silver, and red or rose flowers.

High temperatures and ample moisture in the soil and the air are necessary for good growth. Therefore, in spite of the fact that only strong light or filtered sunlight is needed, not everyone can grow Jacobinia.

JASMINE and jessamine are two words that are interchangeable. Cape jasmine is a common name for gardenia. Still another plant is crepe jasmine. Star or Confederate jasmine is a fragrant waxy white-flowering shrub. Carolina jessamine is a vine with fragrant yellow flowers—and is the state flower of South Carolina. Then there is the genus Jasminum of the Olive family, called jasmine or jessamine. The jessamine of poetry supposedly is Jasminum officinale, with sweetly scented starry white flowers that are either single or double.

Spanish jasmine (J. grandiflorum) is my favorite for the house. It may grow as a slender-stemmed shrub in southern gardens, but indoors in the North it's a slender-stemmed climber that needs support. Leaves are fine-cut and fernlike, flowers are delicate, white, sweetly scented stars. A plant blossoms while small—heavily in fall, then quite steadily from January into spring. I haven't tried J. Sambac (Grand Duke), with its sweetly scented, creamy, double flowers; J. floridum, with yellow blossoms; or J. polyanthum, with pink-tinted blooms against lacy foliage. J. humile, with lemon-yellow blossoms, is probably a better choice than floridum for the house, although the former is a spreading plant.

Star or Confederate jasmine (Trachelospermum jasminoides) is a hardy evergreen vine in the lower South, and a slow-growing woody plant with gracefully half-drooping stems in the North. Its home was originally Malaya. Waxy white flowers are more fragrant than jasmine itself, and open starting in February every year.

Crepe jasmine (Ervatamia coronaria) was christened

Fleur d'Amour by florists and has had quite a vogue for corsages and wedding bouquets. Petals have a crepey texture and are arrayed pinwheel fashion to form beautiful double white flowers, a little smaller and a little less fragrant than gardenias.

Carolina jessamine (Gelsemium sempervirens) is a vine with evergreen leaves and yellow flowers, rather like those of forsythia, but deliciously perfumed. Orange jessamine seems a bit far-fetched a name for Murraea exotica, which has little bell-shaped white flowers—fragrant, of course.

None of the true jasmines is difficult to grow indoors, nor is the Confederate jasmine. They never reach the height that they do outdoors in the South. A sunny window, moderate temperatures (preferably about 65 degrees) and regular watering are easily met requirements for fragrant blossoms. Feed Confederate jasmine monthly. Don't hesitate to cut back Spanish jasmine in the fall as well as to cut out any dead or old stems. Orange jasmine need not be in full sun.

LANTANA, with yellow to rose, red or orange flowers, that blooms outdoors all summer won't make a particularly satisfactory house plant. After all, it can't bloom all year. I like the trailing perennial L. sellowiana with small clusters of lavender flowers. If planted in a basket or other hanging container, the lavender lantana is a joy all winter. It is extremely free-flowering. Another reason for my preference is that the trailer seems less susceptible to white fly than are the annual lantanas.

Lantana must have sun. Spray foliage occasionally to keep it clean, and soak the soil periodically. The trailing lantana flowers in almost any temperature.

Lion's tail or lion's ear describes LEONOTIS LEONURUS, which has odd tubular flowers of red orange. Plants may be quite large (up to three feet) and branched. If a plant can't stand in full sun, it probably will flower if it receives some sun. So long as it doesn't freeze, and is watered daily, this is an undemanding plant.

LOPEZIA COCCINEA, with its host of small, airy red blossoms, is easier to call mosquito plant. It is interesting and different, and is worth trying also because it blooms during fall. Plants must be kept where it's quite warm and sunny. See to it that soil never dries out completely.

MALPIGHIA COCCIGERA is an evergreen shrub well suited to indoor culture. Although it is native to tropical America, don't visualize the luxuriant growth typical of that area. In its own habitat, Barbados cherry is the common name. In the temperate zone and as a house plant, it's called miniature holly. This is an outdoor shrub in the Gulf States.

The leaves are like tiny holly leaves in outline, with prickly edge and glossy dark green coloring. Completely delightful are the pink-tinted white blossoms that call to mind minute fringed orchids. Tiny red berries occasionally form on house plants. Plants less than a foot tall will bloom, starting in late summer and continuing through early winter.

Fortunately, these charming little flowers open without sunlight. Keep plants where they receive good light; if sun can reach them, filter it somehow. Malpighias flower freely if they are potbound. This condition necessitates frequent watering, even if malpighias weren't naturally plants that could use water every day. Moderate temperatures (65 to 68 degrees by day, 55 at night) are best. If the room which malpighia adorns averages 70 degrees or more during winter, growth can make stems leggy. Don't hesitate to trim or cut back malpighia, which can be trained in the shape of a nice little tree.

Apostle plant, twelve apostles plant, toad lily and house iris are obvious names for MARICA or NEOMARICA. The flower that opens suddenly at the tip of a full-grown leaf does look like a miniature iris. N. coerulea is pale blue, N. gracilis yellow and blue, and N. lutea yellow barred with mahogany brown. N. northiana has somewhat larger lavender and white flowers.

Each blossom lasts only one day, but there should be a good many of them between late January and April. The leaves grow as a fan. Neomarica gracilis has smaller, more slender leaves, so this may be the best choice for a small room or window; N. northiana has large, broad and rather coarse leaves.

Nothing seems to bother house iris. It just grows. As long as it is standing in a sunny window and isn't in too large a pot, winter bloom is certain. Roots, incidentally, take proportionately much less room than top growth. Moderate temperatures and regular watering are desirable, but house iris is a tough plant. When plants grow too large, they can be divided and replanted.

New little plants form where blossoms opened and withered at the tips of the leaves. Let these new plants develop on the parent plant until May, then cut off and insert in sand to form roots, and pot individually in fall. Young plants probably won't bloom before the second winter.

NIEREMBERGIA GRACILIS, cup flower, must be grown from seed. This is a South American perennial, a North American annual. To grow your own, sow seed early indoors and set out seedlings in the rock garden or in hanging baskets in spring. All except variety Purple Robe are creeping plants with white or lavender cup-shaped flowers. Purple Robe is a dwarf plant, about six inches high, and will be covered with one-inch, violet-blue flowers.

Nierembergia will bloom outdoors the first summer. Well before frost, hanging baskets should be moved indoors and rock-garden plants dug up and potted. Cut back the plants somewhat to prepare them for the shock of moving and to stimulate winter bloom. It may be easier to take cuttings in August and root them for strong, new plants. It's easier to grow Nierembergia from cuttings than it is from seed, so do not hesitate to ask someone who owns a plant for a cutting or two in late summer.

Bloom indoors may be spotty until midwinter, but it increases with the approach of spring. Warm temperature (about 70 degrees), plenty of moisture plus spraying of foliage to create humidity, and sun are requirements indoors.

Oleanders (NERIUM) are sizable evergreen shrubs that flower in spring and early summer in the South. From Mid-South northward, oleanders are tub plants that bloom on terraces or porches in summer, but must be moved indoors for fall and winter months. If oleanders in tubs can be kept in a window garden, sun porch or similar protected location, they will start to flower in spring before it is time to move them outdoors again. They need some sun or bright light for bloom.

However, it seems to me that one must decide when and where oleander bloom is desired. If it's to be full bloom on the terrace in summer, then store in a cool, dim place so that plants will be fairly dormant during the winter. Unlike hibiscus, which can bloom on sunny days throughout the winter as well as on the terrace in summer, oleanders have a more fixed period of bloom.

There are many delightful varieties of oleander. Variety Mrs. Roeding has double blossoms of salmon pink; Compte Barthelemy has double red ones; Cardinal, bright red. One variegated variety, whose green leaves are edged with creamy white, has double pink blossoms. Often called yellow oleander is Thevetia nereifolia, a rather dense evergreen with linear leaves similar to true oleander but with double yellow flowers. True oleanders flower in shades of red, rose and pink, as well as white. Whatever the color, oleanders are sweet-scented, and are either musky- or vanilla-perfumed, according to one's interpretation. Against these natural recommendations is the fact that the milky juice from any part of an oleander is poisonous.

Oleanders are, in fact, contradictory plants. They're easy to grow, even from cuttings, which often form roots in water. On the other hand, flowering-size plants are extremely susceptible to mealy bug and scale insects. Spray foliage forcibly with water every week, and with the proper insecticide at the first glimpse of a pest.

ORCHIDS and bromeliads are companion plants from tropical Florida to Brazil. Orchids will flower as successfully as bromeliads for amateur growers of house plants. The two plants require quite different conditions in order to flower indoors, but there's really no reason why anyone who wants to can't grow orchids, including the fragile-looking lavender or white cattleyas that are the familiar corsage flower. This has been done in city apartments as well as in suburban homes.

Cattleyas are only one small part of the orchid story. Orchids are at home in tropical America, but almost as many kinds originate in the tropics of the Eastern hemisphere. Many people include the waxy slipper orchids (Cypripediums) in their collections. Others prefer to grow spray orchids, from the exquisitely colored cymbidiums to small, odd-shaped and odd-colored oncidiums and epidendrums. Miltonias, the pansy orchids, which also open on sprays, are comparatively easy for the would-be orchid grower to bring into flower. Every orchid, large or small, is exotic-looking.

Types as well as varieties are so numerous that it's a good idea to discuss the project of growing them indoors with a professional orchid grower and to seek his advice. After all, the best possible selections should be made if the number of plants is limited by window-sill space. Plants of many varieties will be available for

$5 or less, so the cost need not prevent anyone who buys plants from trying orchids.

In addition to Miltonias, Oncidiums or butterfly orchids are popular with beginners. So are Epidendrums, which also are sometimes called butterfly orchids. Miltonias, Oncidiums and Epidendrums, as well as Cattleyas, laelias (similar to cattleyas) and many varieties of Cypripediums bloom in average, comfortable temperatures for people. Cymbidiums and Odontoglossums require cooler temperature; Phalaenopsis, Dendrobiums and Vandas higher temperature. All except Cymbidium and Cypripedium are epiphytes, or air plants, and are potted in osmunda fiber or a similar recommended medium. Cymbidiums and Cypripediums are terrestrial orchids and grow in a porous soil.

Other terrestrial orchids are Phaius grandifolius, the nun orchid, and Calanthe. These two are easy to grow as house plants. Phaius blooms from February to May, with many two- to three-inch flowers on a spike. Calanthe bears white or pink flowers on long arching sprays, beginning about Thanksgiving and continuing until Christmas.

Try to select orchid plants that flower at different times of year. And when they flower, note their fragrance. Orchids in corsages fresh from the florist's refrigerator have had the fragrance chilled out of them. When the flowers open naturally on plants, many pleasing and interesting odors can be enjoyed and compared.

Cultural directions are included with the plants by all reputable orchid growers. Temperature, humidity, ventilation and light are the basis of successful culture. Temperature range varies with the type of orchid. The amount of light varies, too. In general, all orchids need some sun. The early morning and late afternoon sun is all that most orchids can take without being sunburned and, except in December and January, most of them must be shielded from full sun the rest of the day. Ventilation is desirable, even on cold days.

Watering and humidity are the two greatest problems. How to water must be learned. Until you're sure, it's safer to water too seldom and too little than too often or too much. The question of humidity is comparatively easy to solve. Orchids are certain to need more humidity than is present in the average room. To supply moisture to the air, for each orchid plant fill a clay saucer or foil pan with pebbles or stone chips. Add water to the level of the stones, which will evaporate and provide humidity.

Fertilizing, division of plants and repotting are other points which the orchid grower learns. Catalogues are fascinating reading and any collector or grower is always ready to talk about this, his favorite flowering plant. Many a person who plunges on one orchid plant finds himself buying a glass container, known as a Wardian case, or building a small greenhouse. That first orchid plant can be the beginning of a hobby.

PASSION FLOWER is a handsome vine from every standpoint. Its unusual flowers will open indoors sometime from January onward—at least the four-inch flowers of Passiflora coerulea will. This actually is an annual vine for northern gardens in summer, and can be grown from seed started in spring for transplanting outdoors or from cuttings taken in late summer for the house plants. Leaves are deeply lobed into five parts and appear thickly along green stems.

The fat buds open into large flowers which, according to legend, the Spanish missionaries adapted to interpreting Christianity to the symbolic-minded Indians of South America. The ten creamy white petals flushed with pink stood for the ten apostles present at the Crucifixion, the blue filament above the petals for the crown of thorns and Christ's halo. Partly hidden by the filament are five stamens, emblematic of Christ's five wounds and the nails that made them; the three styles the hammers that drove in the nails. The coiling tendrils of the passion vine stand for the scourges, and the delicate leaves for the hands of Christ's persecutors.

Passiflora coccinea, the Bolivian passion flower, has scarlet blossoms and coarser leaves. P. racemosa has red

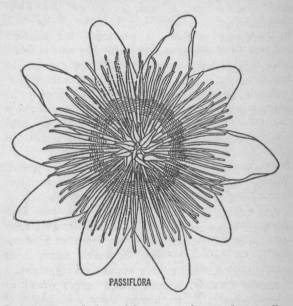

PASSIFLORA

flowers, too, and glossy foliage. P. trifasciata has smaller, creamy yellow blooms and foliage with broad rosy purple bands that turn silver along the midribs.

Short cuttings of passion vine are attractive in a bowl of water. If you want midwinter and spring bloom in the house, the cuttings should be planted in pots after they have rooted. Place the pots at a sunny window and provide string or other support up which they can climb. Sun, ample moisture and warm temperatures are to this vine's liking.

PENTAS LANCEOLATA and PLUMBAGO CAPENSIS are two more southern shrubs that are not only satisfactory house plants but make a delightful combination. Pentas has clusters of small pink blossoms, plumbago clusters of larger pale lavender blue or white flowers. Pentas is much lower-growing than plumbago, for while it is shrubby at the base, its stems are soft and inclined to bend downward. I have only had the pentas with blossoms pink as those of bouvardia, but southern nurseries have several varieties with blossoms in white or various shades from pink to rose and carmine. In full sun, pentas will bloom for a good part of the winter.

Flowers of plumbago or leadwort look like phlox. In addition to the blue and the white ones, there is also a carmine red one (P. indica coccinea). Plumbago blossoms generously in fall until the end of November and starts again in late February or early March.

Plumbago is a shrubby plant that must be pruned severely before it is brought indoors in early September. If it weren't, it would soon outgrow house room.

Like pentas, plumbago likes all possible sun. Both will need daily watering, and will benefit from a weekly spraying of foliage with water. Moderate temperatures (65 to 68 degrees by day, 55 degrees minimum at night) are best. Fertilize once a month during winter.

PETREA VOLUBILIS is aptly called purple wreath or queen's wreath. Showy flowers are a combination of lavender and violet-purple. The blossoms resemble those of verbena, and long after they drop the colorful star-shaped calyces hang on the stems. Oblong leaves, rather thick, rough and wavy, open along the woody stems of this shrubby climber. It is a rather uncommon plant in this country, and is highly distinctive if suitable conditions can be provided.

Warmth, humidity and sun are essential, in addition to an extraordinarily rich soil mixture. It's a better bet, probably, in a small warm greenhouse than in the house.

PRIMROSES never have and probably never will go out of style. From January to March they are a staple of any store that sells plants and flowers. Everyone knows Primula obconica, with its chunky clusters of large rose-colored flowers topping rather hairy green leaves (these leaves cause a rash on the hands of many persons who touch them).

Far more decorative, to my way of thinking, are the fairy (P. malacoides), Chinese (P. sinensis) and star (P. stellata) primroses. Fairy primroses have airy clusters of small blossoms displayed on tall stems. Colors range from pure white through delicate pinks and lavenders to salmon rose, deep rose and rose red. These are easier to buy than Chinese primroses, with flowers almost as large as those of P. obconica but of finer quality and clearer coloring. At one time seeds could be bought by named varieties such as Dazzler (red), Salmon Beauty and Coral Pink, but today colors are as fine in mixed packets.

Primroses supply color from January through March, three months in the North when flowers are likely to be scarce. Light, rather than sun, assures that the primroses' flowers will last as long as possible. Watering must be frequent and generous, probably twice a day. Keep pots in saucers which are filled with water when plants are watered in the morning. Moderate temperature in the 60- to 68-degree range by day is most favorable.

The primroses that bloom in the house are not permanent plants. It's not very difficult to grow your own, but this calls for attention over a nine-month period. Seed of P. obconica should be sown between April and June; of P. malacoides between May and October; and of P. sinensis and P. stellata from April to July. Sow one kind of seed in a pot of vermiculite and keep where it's airy and where the temperature won't go below 45 degrees at night. Keep moist.

When seedlings show their second pair of leaves, transplant to a flat of soil. By late summer or early fall, these seedlings will be large enough to be transplanted into small pots. In another two months, shift again into larger pots with a richer soil mixture. Feed once a month from the time seedlings are planted in pots until buds appear. Again, temperatures that average 65 degrees are most favorable to growth.

MINIATURE ROSES have been riding a wave of popularity, both as house plants and in the garden. It seems almost miraculous to have roses bloom indoors in midwinter, but it can be done. The miniature varieties have flowers no larger than the tip of a person's little finger on bushes that average six to nine inches high. The only one that grows any taller is variety Baby Gold Star (to a possible two feet), and this is one variety to avoid for a house plant. There are many more attractive varieties than Rosa rouletti, with rose-pink double blossoms. Oakington Ruby is a vivid red, Red Imp is crimson, tiny Midget is rose red, Pixie and Cinderella white, Sweet Fairy a fragrant pink. Additional varieties are being introduced almost every year.

There is a trick to having miniature roses flower indoors as house plants. Bushes freshly dug in November or December must be planted in pots filled with a mixture of soil and peat moss enriched with a sprinkling of fertilizer. These are then stored in a coldframe and left there for a dormant period of about two months. Bring into the house in February, place in a sunny window and water regularly. In order for the plants to bloom, temperatures should be not more than 65 degrees by day and the air reasonably humid.

Some nurserymen and plant dealers sell potted miniature roses after January 1 that already have had their dormant period in the cold. If you want to do this on your own, purchase bushes in November and handle as suggested. I like to plant miniature rosebushes permanently in the garden after they have flowered one winter indoors, and to obtain new, field-grown plants for forcing.

RUELLIA has two candidates, one a shrubby little plant about a foot high, the other a trailer. R. amoena is erect and produces red flowers like small bells in abundance. R. makoyana, trailing velvet plant, has decorative foliage of dark green with silver veins and tubular rosy carmine flowers. Both are definitely winter-blooming.

These ruellias are tolerant of temperatures ranging from a cool one in the low 60's to a much warmer one in the 70's. An east or a west window provides enough sun; at a south window, sun should be filtered. Plants should be kept evenly moist.

SANCHEZIA NOBILIS is a jawbreaking name for a rather choice plant. The oblong leaves, from four to twelve inches in length, have veins strongly marked with yellow. When yellow flowers in reddish-yellow bracts open, this plant is quite a sight.

Full sun, real warmth and ample, even moisture are its requirements.

SCHIZOCENTRON ELEGANS, Spanish shawl, starts to open its rosy purple flowers in spring and continues its bloom well into summer. Leaves on this trailing plant from Mexico are not more than a half-inch long. This is an attractive plant, excellent for hanging baskets or ground cover on indoor gardens.

Sun is desirable, at least for flowers, although Spanish shawl will grow without sun, too. It needs warmth, and regular watering.

SPATHIPHYLLUM is a demure relative of anthurium. A smaller spadix is surrounded by a delicate-looking snow-white spathe, the same shape but much smaller in most kinds of spathiphyllums than in the flamboyant anthuriums. S. clevelandi has been a standard house plant for years. S. cannifolium has larger and fragrant white flowers among pale green leaves. S. floribundum is more dwarf, and flowers are small. A new hybrid, Mauna Loa, has flowers as large as anthuriums and delightfully fragrant.

Spathiphyllums flower dependably wherever they're grown. Bloom starts in late February and every flower lasts for weeks. Plants tolerate warm temperatures so

SPATHIPHYLLUM

long as they are well-watered. Full sunlight isn't essential.

When it isn't flowering, spathiphyllum is still decorative. Pointed, slender, oval leaves of a rather dull but clean green are held on slender stems and form a thicket.

STRELITZIA REGINAE, bird of Paradise, is the official flower of the City of Los Angeles. There it is planted in parks and on private property. Elsewhere in the country, bird of Paradise is a popular cut flower as well as a coveted plant for the terrace in summer and for the house in winter. The dazzling flowers are held in rigid bracts at almost right angles to the stems. The bracts are several inches long, and each holds a number of flowers with orange or yellow sepals and dark blue petals.

Other strelitzias produce blue and white flowers or miniature gold and blue ones, but S. reginae is the most desirable. Each "bird" opens on its own stem springing from the base of the plant. Since it's a member of the Banana family, leaves are large (4 to 6 inches wide, 10 to 18 inches long) on long stems. All this adds up to a big plant that needs room.

A flowering-size bird of Paradise will occupy a large tub. Furthermore, plants don't flower until they are seven years old (this isn't a folktale but a fact). If you buy a plant wrapped in damp moss and foil at the supermarket, it's probably only one year old and will have to be nursed for several years. Four- or five-year-old plants for indoor culture are much more expensive. Until it flowers—and afterward—strelitzias are handsome foliage plants. Indoors, strelitzia blooms sometime in the spring.

Sun, warmth (70 degrees by day), watering and fertilizing speed strelitzias to maturity. Water daily and feed at least once a month, except for a couple of months after it is brought back into the house in the fall.

STREPTOSOLEN JAMESONI is often called orange browallia and does belong to the same plant family. Clusters of vivid orange flowers start to open in winter and continue through the spring months. Since streptosolen is a bushier plant than browallia, it can be grown in pots, if they are preferable to a hanging container.

Warmth is essential to bloom on streptosolen. Temperatures 70 degrees or higher by day and not less than 60 degrees at night are best. An east or a west window where sun will shine on plants part of the day is another requirement. Water daily. Unlike browallia, streptosolen can't be grown from seeds, only from cuttings.

SWEET OLIVE (Osmanthus fragrans) is one house plant with which I would never part. It isn't especially showy, but its tiny flowers are very fragrant. Its flowering is dependable, and the plant is one of distinction. Clusters of small creamy flowers start to open in November and continue all winter and spring. Balancing their smallness is the denseness of the clusters on the plant. Oval, dark green and rather leathery leaves cover the slender stems.

Sweet olive grows slowly. My plant, now twenty years old, fills a 9-inch tub. Its spread is about 36 inches, and it is undeniably shapely. Insects never bother it. It is watered daily and the foliage is hosed once a week. It is fertilized occasionally, but not regularly. Temperatures in the high 60's by day and never less than 55 degrees at night have proved satisfactory. It stands in sun part of the day.

TACCA CHANTRIERI is a tropical oddity, as the name bat flower implies. This is one for the collector of exotics who can provide a location as warm as it is humid. The weird flowers appear in summer. The showiest part is the sizable maroon-black bracts with long, drooping whiskers. The large leaves, each on its own stem, are dark green with prominent ribbing.

TALINUM, or fame flower, belongs to the family that includes portulaca, the little annual flower that brightens sunny, dry spots in gardens, and the ubiquitous weed, pigweed or pussley. The fame flower, however, is better behaved. T. patens variegatum has green and white foliage with a succulent quality, and airy, elongated clusters of rosy-red blossoms.

Fame flower is a plant for hot, dry rooms, and it will flower under such conditions. It can stand temperatures into the 70's, and foliage need not be sprayed frequently to compensate for lack of humidity. Fresh air, however, is beneficial. Watering isn't necessary every day; it's better to let soil almost dry out and then soak it thoroughly. Fame flower accommodates itself to bright light or sun.

TIBOUCHINA SEMIDECANDRA is called glory bush or princess tree in the South, where it is planted outdoors. House-plant catalogues seem to prefer the name princess flower. Certainly the large flowers deserve a royal name, for they are velvety and purple, with long golden stamens. In a greenhouse or conservatory, it will bloom for as long as six months. Large pointed leaves are covered with white hairs which turn red before the leaves fall.

As a house plant, tibouchina seems to me questionable. It's said to be easy to grow, but its size alone could create a problem. Outdoors in the South, tibouchina grows to ten feet, but can be pruned to grow as a bush. Then, too, it's deciduous.

Tibouchina isn't very particular about temperature, so long as it's warm. Over 70 degrees by day is desirable, but it shouldn't be exposed to much less than 60 degrees at night. Sun and ample watering are essential. Feeding is recommended during the flowering period.

VERBENA, the perennial rather than the multi-colored garden annual, is gay in hanging containers. This is the only way to display these plants, since stems trail. Peruvian Flame is a variety with bright red clusters of flowers. Chiquita has red or rose and white peppermint-striped flowers.

These verbenas will flower freely if they can hang where full sun shines on them most of the day. Moderate temperatures—65 degrees by day, 50 to 55 degrees at night—are best for healthy growth and bloom. Be careful not to overwater. Soil in which these verbenas grow should be allowed to become almost dried out between waterings. Then soak the whole container in a pail of water at room temperature.

CHAPTER VII

AFRICAN VIOLETS AND THEIR CLAN

African violets have won more friends in less time than any other plant in history. In the early 1930's, African violets were viewed chiefly in conservatories at public gardens such as the Brooklyn Botanic Garden. Yet by 1946, so many housewives, businessmen, shut-ins and other people from all walks of life were growing this charming flowering plant in their homes that the African Violet Society of America was formed in Atlanta, Ga.

Since Baron Walter von Saint Paul discovered it in tropical Africa, the African part of the name is as logical as is the botanical name Saintpaulia. The single purple blossoms of the species S. ionantha do have a slight resemblance to the long-loved garden violets, but the African violets belong not to the Violet family but to the Gesneria family.

All members of the Gesneria family are natives of the tropics, many of them of the tropical Americas. Every plant in this family is sensitive to cold and fluctuations in temperature. Most of them are herbaceous plants and many of them have fleshy, prostrate stems.

Known and grown far longer than African violets is the spring- and summer-flowering gloxinia, one of the Sinningia genus of Gesnerias. This native of Brazil has been grown in Europe and America since the early nineteenth century. Potted plants with large, velvety and richly hued flowers are glamorous additions to florist-shop windows every spring.

GLOXINIAS are, in my experience, the easiest of the Gesneria family to grow, perhaps because they are tuberous. I plant the tubers, one to a 4-inch pot, in February, around Washington's Birthday. A mixture of sandy loam enriched with balanced commercial fertilizer fills each pot and barely covers the bulb. Then they are placed near an east window where they receive sun part of the day and are watered sparsely.

The most important factor in growing gloxinias is constant warmth. They need warmth twenty-four hours a day, and a minimum of 60 degrees at night is an absolute must. Any drop in temperature or a draft, day or night, can slow growth amazingly.

With constant warmth, minimum watering and some sun, there's nothing to do but wait for growth and bloom. Large plushy green leaves appear first, and two to four months after planting small buds appear in the center of the whorl of leaves.

Standard old varieties of gloxinias include Blanche de Meru, raspberry red flowers with white throats; Fire King, flaming red; Emperor Frederick, scarlet with pearly margin; Violacea; Prince Albert, violet with white throat; Princess Elizabeth, hyacinth blue with white throat; Queen Wilhelmina, pink with violet iridescence.

New varieties have been added to the hybrid tubers imported in quantity from Belgium every winter. Most startling, however, are the Buell hybrids, a strain developed in northeastern Connecticut. Albert H. Buell has developed extra-large flowering gloxinias, many of them with waved and ruffled petals and some that look almost double. The amazing range of colors extends from brilliant tones to delicate hues, and in some flowers to blended colors.

Gloxinias vary in shape, too. The large open bell flowers are best known. However, some are slipper-shaped, others have a narrow throat under a salver-shaped blossom.

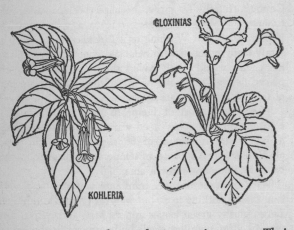

Gloxinias are true house plants, even in summer. Their plushy leaves and velvety flowers need protection from wind, rain and brilliant sun. Plushy leaves can be marred by drops of water, so watering must be done with care. Always water in the saucer under the pot.

When bloom is finished for the summer, reduce watering gradually until foliage shrivels. When nothing is left but the tuber in the pot, store in a frost-free place until the following February.

Hailed as the smallest of all gloxinias is Sinningia pusilla. A plant in bloom fits into a teacup, I'm told. Slipper blossoms are long-tubed in shades of lavender blue with white striping. This miniature gloxinia flowers for weeks under artificial light or in a sunny east window. Little leaves are olive green and puckered. The person who told me about this miniature grew it from seed, which took several weeks to germinate. It also can be purchased as a plant.

ACHIMENES is another gesneria that is grown from tubers for summer flowers. I have always thought that the blossoms, smaller than those of gloxinia, looked a little like ordinary petunias, but common names for them include nut orchid, cupid's bower and kiss-me-over-the-garden-gate. There's an amazing range of colors, which are basically those of gloxinias. Throats may be a contrasting color; yellow eyes and spotting are not uncommon.

If achimenes are planted, five little bulbs in a 5-inch clay pan, when gloxinias are, bloom is likely to continue until September. A rich, porous soil, constant warmth and careful watering are essential. Small leaves on branching, trailing stems can dry out beyond revival if watering is neglected. Tubers in pots are stored over winter as are gloxinias.

The name achimenes comes from the Greek, and means to suffer from cold. This meaning is the keynote for all the gesnerias, including the African violets.

Why has the AFRICAN VIOLET gained a widespread popularity that not even the longer-grown gloxinias can match? Certainly the flowers of African violets have an appealing and special charm. Plants also are long-blooming—from October to May—if favorable conditions exist in a house or apartment. And perhaps the creation of favorable conditions so that African violets will bloom is something of a challenge.

Anyone who grows African violets need never lack friends. In addition to the national society, there are regional and local societies. These groups stage shows which people travel miles to attend—perhaps to exhibit an unusually fine plant, perhaps to see what's new or what other exhibitors are growing, or merely to talk with other African violet fanciers, collectors and hybrid-ists. Many a fine new variety has been crossed, raised from seed, tested and exhibited by an amateur house-plant grower.

New varieties must be grown from seed. Most people increase their stock of plants or share their plants with others by means of leaf cuttings. Nine times out of ten, these leaves are rooted in water (see page 291). Pro-fessional growers who exhibit at flower shows and fairs tell me that many of their plants are almost leafless by the time they get them home, so irresistible is the urge to break off a leaf from a coveted variety and slip it in a pocket.

Leaves, "starter" plants or full-grown plants can be purchased. Suppose that a plant with many buds and a few flowers proves tempting in a florist shop: you buy it and bring it home to a house or apartment. Where do you put it, and what should you do to take care of it?

African violets need plenty of light. A little sunlight, such as that from an east window, is beneficial, espe-cially in winter. Protection is needed against bright summer sun or intense midday sun at any time of year. Many people grow their plants under artificial light (see page 252) which can be controlled to provide an adequate amount.

Give the plant room, too. It shouldn't be crowded among other plants or among other African violets. Let leaves spread out as they will, and remember that they're brittle and break easily. Let the plant have enough space to display its flowers and foliage and to have air circulate around it.

A moderately warm temperature will be satisfactory —70 to 72 degrees should be about right in the day-time, and never less than 60 degrees at night. Fresh air is desirable for healthy growth, but drafts are harmful.

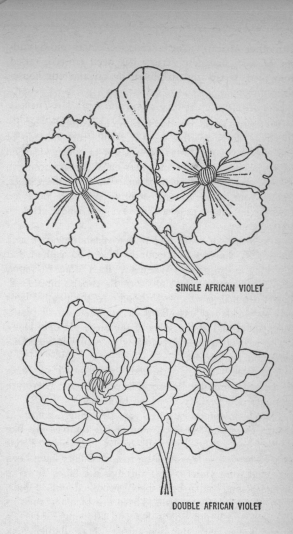

SINGLE AFRICAN VIOLET

DOUBLE AFRICAN VIOLET

123

A dry atmosphere isn't particularly good for these plants of tropical origin. But do not add moisture to the air by spraying the plushy leaves and fleshy stems with a mist of water. Instead, humidify the air by placing containers of water among the African violet plants.

Watering must be done fully as carefully as for gloxinias. It is possible to water soil from the top of the pot, if you're always careful not to spill a drop on leaves or stems. Drops of water cause brown spots on leaves, and start decay of stems. Water in the saucer, unless your hand is very steady. Wick-fed pots are favored by many growers. Always use water at room temperature.

Replanting in fresh soil and a clean new pot isn't necessarily the way to encourage bloom on a plant that has long been green. Whenever it is time to repot, packages of soil in the right formula can be purchased. Select a pot in a size proportionate to the plant. Plants can be divided when offsets or complete small plants form under and at the sides of the large old one. Don't try to save gnarled old plants with flabby leaves. Discard and start fresh.

The disease- and pest-riddled African violet is another to discard promptly before it infects others. There are so many new ones from which to choose.

Double-flowered varieties are becoming almost as numerous as single ones. Some of the doubles are like small roses; others like full, frilled carnations. Petals may be waved, edges may be frilled. Colors have been extended from violet-purple through the blues down to lavender, and pinks have been stretched out to reds, most of these a wine tone. There are bicolors, such as the blue and white Bonne Foi and Glowing Embers, a single flower with the two upper petals lighter pink than the three lower cerise petals. Ringmaster, another single, has red-lavender flowers edged with white, and there are many single and double examples of this style of two-tone blossoms.

Among better-known and time-tested varieties are Blue Flag and soft blue Sailor Girl; Lady Geneva, dark purple edged with white; Alma Wright and White Madonna, both double whites; large-flowered red Fire Dance; double Raspberry Red and burgundy Red King; free-blooming Pink Angel and Lavender Beauty. Experts admit that some varieties are easier to grow and to bring to flower than others. New varieties are

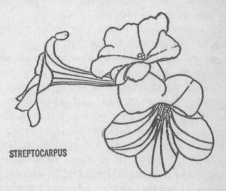

STREPTOCARPUS

introduced at shows and in many catalogues every year.

The popularity of African violets has led to the trial of many other gesnerias. The one most likely to succeed and flower under average indoor conditions—with a lift in humidity—is streptocarpus, familiarly known as cape primrose.

STREPTOCARPUS hybrids were buried in a few seed catalogues and seeds were purchased only by professional gardeners, until the popularity of the African violet was firmly established. Seed sown in early fall in a sterile medium such as vermiculite takes two to three weeks to germinate and will be flowering-size plants by April. Bloom continues into November or December.

Sizable trumpet-shaped flowers open in exquisite shades of pink, blue and lilac, and there will also be some white and perhaps a few reds. They're truly lovely flowers held on stems above the long oval leaves, often in such number as almost to hide the foliage.

Cape primroses flower in moderate temperatures— about 70 degrees by day and never less than 55 degrees at night. Steady warmth is essential to seed germination. Light or filtered sunlight is adequate. Soil must be watered often enough to keep it moist but not soggy. Humidity is of utmost importance and must be provided by one means or another.

Certain streptocarpus plants can be purchased. S. rexii, one of the parents of the hybrids grown from seed, produces tubular lavender-blue flowers on slender stems almost all year. These rise above long, narrow, quilted leaves. S. saxorum is a small, compact plant with succulent leaves. Its lilac and white flowers are produced freely over a long period. S. caulescens has small tubular flowers of dark purple.

EPISCIAS are sometimes called flame violets. Many of them have red flowers; all of them have interesting and often colorful foliage. However, I cannot agree with those who say that anyone who can grow African violets can grow episcias. Nor do I believe that everyone who enjoys African violets will like episcias as well.

The episcias are trailing plants. If they are well grown and in favorable surroundings, episcias show off to advantage in a strawberry jar or some sort of hanging container. If they must be grown in pots with saucers, allow ample space for the trailing stems.

The reason why not everyone can grow episcias, which are at home in Nicaragua, is a matter of warmth. Unless plants are constantly warm, they can look dreadful. Minimum temperature in a house at night is 60 degrees. Daytimes, 70 degrees is minimum, and plants thrive on anything up to 80 degrees. Don't attempt to increase warmth by placing these plants in or near sun. They flower and retain foliage color in reduced light or shade.

Episcias must be potted in an extremely well-drained soil, if only because they require so much moisture. Fertilize monthly. The flowers are usually smaller than those of African violets, mature leaves larger.

Fifteen to twenty species or varieties of episcias are obtainable. No nurseries risk shipping these plants during cold weather.

EPISCIA

If you must try episcias, remember that E. reptans (or fulgida or coccinea) is the one that gave rise to the name flame violet. Blossoms are red. Hairy leaves are brown-tinged with silvery veins. Also possible for beginners is E. cupreata, with bronze or copper leaves and red blossoms. Varieties of E. cupreata include Silver Sheen, with silver leaves and darker margins; Kitty, with bronzy green leaves banded with pink down the center; Chocolate Soldier, with brown leaves and a center vein marked with silver; and Acajou, whose leaves are unusually marked and combine silvery green with mahogany. All these varieties have red flowers.

Episcia lilacina has lilac-blue flowers larger than the more common red ones. Varieties of lilacina have similar flowers but more colorful foliage.

Yellow Topaz has blossoms truly yellow, and is said to flower readily; foliage is green. Tropical Topaz is another name. Dianthiflora and Amazon White have white blossoms against green leaves. Colombia Orange is a fairly new introduction, with bright orange flowers against green foliage. Rose-pink blossoms and metallic bronze foliage indicate the longer-known Pinkiscia.

Other trailing gesnerias include Aeschynanthus (sometimes listed as Trichosporum), Columneas, Codonanthe and Hypocyrta. If you are successful with one of these, you probably can grow all of them. Columneas and Aeschynanthus are somewhat more tolerant of lower temperatures.

The truth is that these four trailing gesnerias are house plants worth looking at only if they can be grown under conditions most favorable to the episcias. They all are more or less sensitive to cold. They grow best in very warm temperatures (over 70 degrees in daytime and up to 90 degrees). Along with warmth, humidity is absolutely essential, and the higher the temperature, the more humidity is needed. They need moist soil, and it's not as easy to water these trailing plants without damage to stems and leaves as it is African violets. Dormant periods are longer than for African violets. Possibly, greater use of artificial lighting makes it easier to grow these trailing gesnerias in an average room of a house instead of in the warm greenhouse or protective Wardian case that has been recommended for so many years. Wherever or however they're grown, they demand time and attention.

AESCHYNANTHUS lobbianus, lipstick plant, has waxy green leaves along its trailing stems, and scarlet flowers that open slowly from purple calyces. Most people consider this more attractive than A. pulcher, which has larger leaves and vermilion flowers with yellow throats. A. grandiflora has larger flowers of orange-yellow.

COLUMNEA'S blossoms have been described as looking like flying fish. Most of these plants are trailers. C. gloriosa opens its tubular red flowers in fall. This little trailer has small opposite leaves, so thickly covered with hairs that they look brown. C. arguta has waxy, pointed bronze leaves and red flowers. C. linearis is bushy rather than trailing, and its shining green leaves are brightened with rose-pink blossoms. C. hirta has three-inch orange-red flowers against shiny green leaves. Other trailing columneas produce flowers in winter from pale yellow through orange to red.

CODONANTHE crassifolia is probably easiest of all the trailing gesnerias to grow. Its stiff waxy dark green leaves have red midribs and red markings on the undersides. Slipper-shaped flowers are waxy, and are creamy white marked with color in the throat. This gesneria is tolerant not only of lower temperatures but also of more light and even of some sun. Humidity is still essential.

HYPOCYRTA nummularia is spring-flowering, sheds its leaves in fall and rests during winter. It's a dainty trailer with bright green leaves on red stems. Tubular flowers are inflated on one side, so that they look like small orange-red balloons or helmets.

ISOLOMA or KOHLERIA HIRSUTA is quite the opposite. This is an upright plant that can grow too large for a window garden. Long, slender green leaves edged with dark red are densely hairy. Orange-red flowers open in the leaf axils.

KOHLERIAS grow only about a foot high. This summer-blooming gesneria includes pink-flowering K. amabilis and white K. lindeniana. Foliage is interesting, being basically green, but usually with markings or edgings in another color, and hairy. Good light but not direct sun brings this one into flower.

NAEGELIA are usually listed now as SMITHIANTHA, and once were called simply gesneria. Some people prize them for their foliage, which is colorful and decorative, but few would be satisfied if the plants did not bloom. Temple bells is the common name for S. cinnabarina, and it does have pendent red bells. Orange

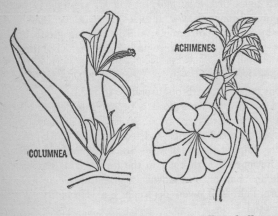

King is a variety with bright orange-yellow bells and velvety leaves of vivid green. S. multiflora has velvety leaves and creamy flowers that resemble foxgloves. Warmth and humidity are so essential that smithianthas still seem to me to be greenhouse plants.

ALLOPLECTUS LYNCHII, now sometimes listed as Nautilocalyx lynchii, and RECHSTEINERIAS are other gesnerias that are probably easier to grow successfully in a greenhouse. Alloplectus is a bushy plant with maroon leaves and creamy flowers that need no sun. It's an evergreen shrub in the tropics. Rechsteinerias have flowers in shades of bright red and closely placed leaves that range from velvety to downy or hairy.

New and different names, often almost unpronounceable, crop up in the Gesneria family as new kinds are produced. Sometimes it's a new plant discovery or propagation and revival of an almost forgotten plant. Again, as with Nautilocalyx, it may be reclassification by botanists. N. bullatus, an upright plant with brown quilted leaves and yellow flowers, was long called Episcia tessellata, although other episcias have trailing stems.

The continued popularity of African violets undoubtedly will warrant a trial to any other gesnerias. But from gloxinias to smithianthas, the majority must have a dormant period once a year during which, in many cases, plants are leafless for weeks or months. African violets may not flower every month in the year, but they do retain their foliage at all times.

CHAPTER VIII

GERANIUMS

If there's one plant about which people are sentimental, it's a geranium. Nothing else explains the reluctance to discard the awkward, straggly plants that occupy space in a sunny window. By midwinter, zonal geraniums lifted from the garden the previous fall usually have only a handful of leaves and an occasional flower about half the size it should be.

Thrift or some inherited instinct may be responsible for the cherishing of geraniums. Our grandmothers who crossed the mountains to Ohio and the plains to the West carried along slips of geraniums and roots of peonies, and probably their mothers and grandmothers brought geranium slips with them from England. Geraniums have been grown in England and North America for more than 250 years. Yet the flower has never lost its fascination, for hybridists are introducing a few new varieties every year.

The majority of new varieties during the last decade have been dwarf and Martha Washington geraniums.

Dwarf geraniums are primarily for the window gardener, Martha Washington varieties for the outdoor gardener on the West Coast. A new variety of zonal geranium appears less frequently.

Color and fragrance in worthwhile amounts are contributed by geraniums to window sills and gardens indoors. Most of this color and fragrance, however, does not come from the best-known type. This is the zonal geranium, a sturdy plant with large round green leaves, often with a darker zone of color, and handsome clusters of single or double flowers. Outdoors in summer, zonal geraniums enhance window and planter boxes and are colorful bedding and pot plants. Zonals are sometimes called fish geraniums because their stems and leaves have a somewhat fishy odor.

Six months of lavish bloom can be expected of zonal geraniums. Whether these six months are to be outdoors in summer or indoors in winter is every grower's decision. Since new young plants are available every spring, it's much simpler to date their finest six months of bloom from May.

No matter how lavishly zonal geraniums are flowering in September, they won't continue to do so after they've been dug up and potted and moved into the house. All cultivated geraniums are tender, except on the West Coast, where they outdo themselves outdoors, and in other southern areas of the country where frost never strikes. The cultivated geraniums all belong to the genus Pelargonium of the Geranium family.

Standard garden varieties of geraniums bloom only by fits and starts indoors in winter. The handsome outdoor bloom soon peters out on the most carefully lifted plants and seldom begins again before February, when it's a mere sliver of its summer glory. This behavior is as typical of large plants that were dug up from the garden and potted, cut back or not, as it is of young plants rooted from cuttings taken in August. Actually, for the greatest amount of winter bloom, cuttings should be taken as early as June. With either method, certain points must be followed for any bloom at all indoors.

Pots that are small in comparison to the top growth are recommended, because geraniums flower best when they are potbound. If rooted cuttings are planted in 3-inch pots, they will not flower until they have grown big enough root systems to crowd the pots. Beautiful leaves but scant and pale-colored flowers can be blamed on a too rich soil. Geraniums flower best in a light soil not too heavily enriched. A mixture of three parts loamy garden soil, one part sand and one part leafmold or compost is adequate. Fertilize as infrequently as every six weeks, starting in early January.

Winter or summer, geraniums need all the sun they can get. At the same time, they need a cool location indoors. Temperatures that do not go higher than 65 degrees by day and never lower than 45 degrees at night are best. Keep plants on the dry side by not watering until soil feels quite dry to touch.

Sunny but cool locations, proper watering—or lack of it—and potbound plants bring out flowers in mid-winter. Geraniums don't have to be sprayed for pests, but you should brush off the leaves once in a while to remove any dust.

Double-flowering varieties of zonal geraniums are readily available in shades of red, salmon and pink, and also in white. Current standard varieties are Olympic Red, Radio Red, Avalon Red, darker Better Times and velvety Pride of Camden. Fiat and Picardy are good salmon varieties, and Fiat Enchantress is a more delicate tint. Mme. Buchner and Snowball are white.

Free-flowering is the orange variety Maxime Kovalevsky. More delicate shades of light pink, lavender, coral, shrimp and the bicolors are hard to find except on the West Coast. Charming, for example, are Halloween, with double apricot-orange flowers with white centers; Alice of Vincennes, a single that, from a large white center, shades from carmine rose to red at the edges; and Apple Blossom, a scarlet single shading to white at the center, and veined and striped in scarlet. These are all standard zonal geraniums that flower best in summer.

For winter bloom, it's worth the search to find certain odd groups of geraniums that closely resemble the true zonal varieties in habit of growth. In Connecticut, the carnation-flowered varieties have flowered best for me. Cactus-flowered, bird's egg and rosebud geraniums are not difficult to bring into bloom.

Carnation-flowered varieties aren't rare, and they do flower consistently if not profusely all winter. Edges of the petals are toothed like those of carnations, but individual flowers are small. Jeanne, sometimes called Sweet William, has small single salmon blossoms. Madame Thibaut has blossoms that open white with rosy veins, and then turn pink. Cerise Carnation is a double cerise to light crimson.

Cactus-flowered geraniums have narrow, rolled and twisted petals. They are sometimes called poinsettia geraniums, not because they look like poinsettias but because of three named varieties that were the foundation of the modern group. Variety Poinsettia has double scarlet flowers with the characteristic petals on compact plants. Specialists usually rate it as more striking than the double light orchid-pink Pink Poinsettia or Double Poinsettia, with double flowers that are deeper red than those of Poinsettia.

Bird's egg geraniums are characterized by small, rose-red spots on the petals. Pink, rose and white varieties are available. Rosebud geraniums have flowers that never open wide, and resemble tiny half-opened roses. The few varieties all have very double blossoms.

MARTHA WASHINGTON

P. echinatum, listed in some catalogues as Sweetheart geranium, is a thorny-stemmed species that rests in summer and flowers most dependably in winter and spring. When it's dormant, it looks like a cactus plant. In late fall, gray-green woolly leaves start to appear, and by Christmas, this geranium is flowering. The blossoms are charming, but if you're expecting a heavy cluster of bloom such as zonals produce, you'll be disappointed. Flowers are single and white, and each petal is marked with red. It's long-blooming.

Dwarf geraniums, which are perfect miniatures of the zonals, bloom from December on through the spring. Each one is in perfect scale, with leaves as small as dimes on some varieties; the size of nickels on others. Blossoms, single or double, are about the size of the little fingertip. A couple of varieties, notably Little Darling (also called Kleiner Liebling or Tom Thumb) reach 12 to 15 inches in height. All others never exceed 6 inches, and some, such as slow-growing Vesuvius and Sprite, stay only 3 inches tall for three years or longer.

Pigmy is the fastest-growing variety, yet it is never more than six inches tall, although it also may be six inches broad. Tiny leaves are light green with a dark zone, small double flowers are cheerful scarlet. In Connecticut, Pigmy shows buds in December. It seldom opens in time for Christmas, but by mid-January it is ablaze with color. By this time other dwarf varieties are starting to bloom.

New varieties are added every year to this delightful group of geraniums. The color range includes salmon and shades of pink, as well as red, white and bicolors. Some, such as Vesuvius, have dark green foliage.

Dwarf geraniums are harder to find than they are to grow. They will flower in any sunny window (seldom does a plant outgrow a 2½-inch pot). Almost exactly the same conditions and care—cool to moderate temperature, no overwatering—bring much more bloom for a longer time than from the large zonal geraniums.

The dwarfs can be moved outdoors for the summer, where they will grow in the same kind of soil as the majority of annuals and perennials. Dappled sunlight or sun part of the day is the preferred exposure. By September, one plant of Pigmy can be split into eight or ten small ones. In fall and early winter, the dwarf geraniums rest.

Fancy-leaved geraniums do flower, starting in February, but the clusters are usually small. The real reason for growing this group is their leaves. Many varieties have at least three quite different colors, as a border, a zone or various markings. Yellow, scarlet, crimson and brown are common.

Silver-Leaved, Gold-Leaved, Bronze-Leaved, Silver Tricolor and Golden Tricolor are standard subdivisions of the Fancy-leaved group. Skies of Italy is one of the gayest and most famous. Mature plants have green leaves that are edged with yellow, zoned with brown and splashed with red. Mrs. Cox's green leaves are edged with bright yellow and widely zoned with scarlet, crimson and brown. This variety also has single salmon blossoms. Happy Thought is another old favorite, with yellow, brown and orange in its green leaves and single, vermilion flowers.

Among Silver Tricolors is Miss Burdett Coutts, whose silvery green leaves have a wide ivory border and a bright zone splashed with rose and brown, and whose small single blossoms are scarlet. Fairyland, a dwarf, also has an ivory border and rose-red zoning on its small gray-green leaves, plus scarlet flowers. Mountain of Snow and Hills of Snow are favorite Silver-Leaved varieties, and Sprite a dwarf in this group. Alpha and Bronze Beauty belong in the Bronze-Leaved group; Cloth of Gold and Dwarf Gold Leaf in the Gold-Leaved group.

Fancy-Leaved geraniums are fairly slow-growing,

and plants must be both well-established and potbound to flaunt their true coloring. Cultural conditions also can affect the coloring. One expert recommends part shade for the Silver-Leaved kinds and says that the Bronze-Leaved, Gold-Leaved and Tricolor varieties are brighter in cool, sunny weather or places. Regular applications of fertilizer will strengthen colors. Pinch back young plants to encourage bushy, compact growth.

Few things could please a geranium fancier more than finding a plant of one of the New Life group, or Distinction, sometimes called One-In-A-Ring. Distinction has small yellow-green leaves that are toothed and ruffled along the edges and have a narrow but distinct dark zone. Small, single flowers are cherry-red. On variety New Life, no two flowers are alike—some are all scarlet, others white with a pink eye, still others red with stripes or flecks with white. Other varieties in the New Life group include Double New Life and Phlox New Life. All are scarce.

Different as can be are the scented-leaved geraniums. Neither color of their foliage nor their bloom is important. The many and varied fragrances don't pour forth into a room as does the perfume of a gardenia or jasmine flower. Instead, a scented geranium leaf must be touched lightly with a finger, or rubbed or crushed to release its definite fragrance.

Rose geranium (P. graveolens) with its finely cut, fernlike dull green leaves and dull rosy no-account flowers is probably best known. At least ten different varieties of rose geraniums can be found. Less subtle is peppermint geranium (P. tomentosum) with broad, plushy, bright green leaves that have a strong mint odor.

Of the spice-scented geraniums, my favorite is the dainty Nutmeg (P. fragrans). Its small silvery-green leaves are no larger than a quarter. By February it has

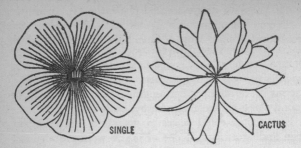

SINGLE

CACTUS

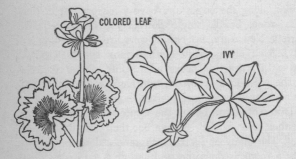

COLORED LEAF

IVY

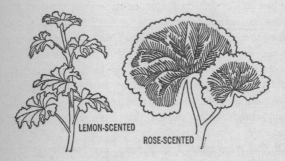

LEMON-SCENTED

ROSE-SCENTED

sprays of delicate white flowers faintly marked with pink. There's a ginger-scented plant, too (P. torento).

Lemon geraniums are almost as traditional as the rose-scented ones. Most of them have tiny leaves, which are curled (P. crispum). Prince Rupert, also called French Lace, has variegated green and cream leaves which are not as lemony in scent. There are lime, orange, apple, apricot, coconut, strawberry and almond scents to be found in leaves of specific geraniums.

Nothing could be easier to grow and enjoy than the scented-leaved geraniums. Although plants are moved outdoors for the summer months, they are most appreciated indoors in fall and winter.

The trailing ivy-leaf geraniums (P. peltatum) are popular everywhere. Their shiny green leaves are ivy-shaped and neither weather nor insects mar their heavy texture. These are the geraniums that make Southern California's "pink lawns," thanks to the pink or mauve flowers that open on the top of the long, trailing stems. They grow like weeds on the West Coast, and are sturdy if not free-blooming plants elsewhere in the country.

It's possible to take ivy-leaf geraniums from the planter box and pot them, or to move the hanging basket with ivy geraniums indoors before frost. As house plants, however, count on them to be green vines. If they ever do flower, it won't be until there are so many kinds blooming outdoors that an indoor one doesn't matter.

Showiest of all geraniums is the Martha Washington or Lady Washington, often called Pelargonium (P. domesticum). These are offered as flowering plants in May, starting about Mother's Day. Except in the West Coast fog belt, Martha Washington geraniums do not flower well anywhere in the country. Outdoors, they don't like spells of day-and-night heat or wet weather.

Husky as the plants are, it's next to impossible to bring them into flower indoors the following spring.

In one way this is unfortunate. Flowers of Martha Washington geraniums are breath-taking, with large, clear colors and beautiful texture. But, after all, other groups of geraniums have a great deal that is distinctive and gay to offer indoor gardeners.

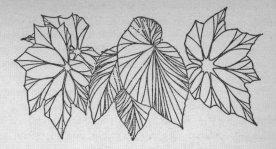

CHAPTER IX

BEGONIAS

Other house plants may come and go, but begonias remain time-honored favorites. Since the first ones were discovered in the West Indies around 1700 and named for Michel Begon, the French governor of Santo Domingo who was interestd in botany, begonias have fascinated plantsmen of all degrees.

A begonia is no more unusual on a New York City apartment window sill than it is in the kitchen of an Iowa farmhouse. In both places, it flowers for part of the year. Early twentieth-century estates noted for their gardens and greenhouses frequently had important collections of begonias.

They are a most diverse group of plants, all of them suitable for pot culture, as it used to be called, indoors or under glass. A few kinds were popular for outdoor bedding in summer. Only one begonia, B. evansiana, is hardy outdoors. This one was brought from China to England in 1804.

Of some 750 species and literally thousands of varieties and hybrids, at least 100 make excellent house plants. Many of the indoor begonias are grown primarily for their foliage. These always are showy plants because of the leaves' size, shape or coloring, or for all three reasons. Most of the begonias have spectacular bloom in white, coral, shades of pink or red, and yellow.

The two most gorgeous of all the begonia displays come in July and December. The July spectacular is furnished by the tuberous-rooted begonias, which have exquisitely colored single or double flowers, some as large as the camellias, carnations and roses which they resemble. Tuberous begonias are not house-plant material, for their normal flowering time is summer, their dormant period winter. They can be grown to bloom outdoors anywhere.

The second peak of magnificent bloom is furnished in December by the so-called Christmas begonias, still popular gift plants. These also are grown from bulbs; and the flowers, although not as large as those of the summer-flowering tuberous-rooted class, are so abundant on a well-grown plant that size doesn't matter. Lorraine and Melior are other names often used in referring to Christmas begonias. They can be grown indoors, but they aren't the easiest of begonias to bring into flower successfully.

Except for the dependable little wax begonia (B. semperflorens), which can bloom almost continuously indoors, the more easily grown house kinds flower from January onward. Each week from midwinter through spring, more and more begonias start to blossom. The blossoms look delicate, but they really aren't. They're borne in clusters, some of them held on tall slender stems high above the foliage. An established plant produces one cluster after another during its flowering season. Not only are flowers long-lasting on the plants, but also they are worth cutting for flower arrangements.

It's impossible to confuse a begonia's flower with

that of any other plant. Under the petals is a three-winged (rarely four-winged) ovary. There, when petals have shriveled and there's been time for ripening, will be found the seeds, which are as tiny as the most infinitesimal specks of dust. The ovary, which is generally called the wings, may be colored as delicately as the white or pale pink petals, or may be more deeply hued.

At the base of the flower or its stem are bracts. These often are so small they can hardly be seen. If these bracts are sizable or colorful, they enhance the beauty of the flowers.

Comparatively few begonias have common names, although varieties obtained by hybridization do. Wax begonias are as often called rose begonias. Christmas is an obvious appellation for the bulbous sort that flowers in early winter, just as Calla Lily is for the group that has ordinary small blossoms, though some of its leaves, usually just under the blossoms, are glistening white and shaped so that anyone who looks at them thinks of a calla instead of a begonia. Sooner or later, someone was bound to use the name Angel Wing for the group with leaves narrow in comparison to their length and prominently lobed at the base. Pond Lily, however, is certainly a more appropriate name than Beefsteak for B. erythrophylla (B. feasti).

The dominant characteristics of begonia plants and the tubers from which some grow are the basis for the six to eight or nine classifications into which they're divided. Of course, a few must always fall into a miscellaneous group. Begonias are grown and increased from bulbs, tubers, seeds and cuttings. Seeds are so impossibly minute that they are not recommended for any but professional or skilled growers.

The tuberous or bulbous begonias make up one distinct group. A handful are classified as semi-tuberous. Fibrous-rooted is an overall term for any begonia that does not form a bulb or tuber. Under fibrous-rooted are several distinct subdivisions, from the handsome Rex begonias, grown primarily for their foliage, to the little, almost constantly flowering wax begonias (B. semperflorens). Rhizomatous, hairy-leaved or hirsute, angel wing or cane-stemmed, are other distinct groups of fibrous-rooted begonias. Some of the tuberous-rooted begonias have pendulous stems of flowers and foliage, a few of the fibrous-rooted sorts trail. By far the majority are sturdy, upright plants.

An important recommendation for begonias is the fact that plants need not be in a fully sunny location in order to flower or display colorful foliage. Filtered sunlight is probably the most favorable exposure for the greatest number, and intense direct light can be reasonably satisfactory. Moderate to warm temperatures are best. Begonias require a richer soil than many other house plants, but they can be overfertilized to a point beyond typical growth. Regular and adequate watering is essential. Take care with any plants having round leaves with cuplike centers, for water does not drain off as readily and some may be held and start rot.

Some of the fibrous-rooted begonias as well as the tuberous-rooted group spend fall and early winter, if not all winter, in their dormant stage. These should be avoided when only a few are selected for enjoyment indoors. Of the 100 or so that make good house plants, here are a few that are among the least demanding and best performing:

1. WAX BEGONIA—single-flowering varieties in white, pink or red.
2. ANGEL WING—one or more varieties such as Corallina de Lucerna with large dark green leaves, spotted with silver; salmon-rose blossoms produced freely.
3. POND LILY (B. erythrophylla or Feasti)—round

leaves, green above, red beneath, and pink flowers. Variety Bessie Buxton is more upright and free-blooming.

4. STAR BEGONIA—Fischer's ricinifolia, a fairly small plant with many pointed leaves, and pink blossoms on tall stems.

5. METALLICA—glossy green leaves with purple veining; large, light pink, bearded flowers.

6. SCHARFFI—leaves olive green above, red beneath. Large clusters of light pink flowers for a long period.

7. GILSONI—stout rhizome supporting sizable green leaves, pointed but not as markedly as the Star type, smooth upper surface, hairy underside and stems. Tall stems with pink blossoms, some of them double. Free-flowering and not too large a plant.

8. ULMIFOLIA—bright green leaves the size and shape of elm leaves, and the plant actually resembles an elm tree (it can grow four feet or taller). Leaves are rough and hairy. Small white flowers in clusters are freely produced in late winter. Requires light only.

9. DREGEI—small, maplelike, bronzy leaves; white flowers produced freely (semi-tuberous).

10. WELTONIENSIS—maplelike leaves larger than those of Dregei; pink or white blossoms (semi-tuberous).

These—and many others—are almost certain to be permanent plants. Many in time grow so large that size alone makes them impressive. Success can lead to trial of others with tempting descriptions in the catalogues.

Tuberous Begonias

B. EVANSIANA can be grown outdoors and will survive

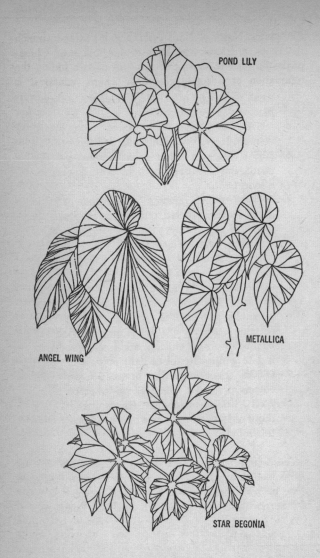

POND LILY

ANGEL WING

METALLICA

STAR BEGONIA

148

the winter. North of New York City, it's safer to mulch the roots. A friend who lives in Virginia near Chesapeake Bay has this plant growing in masses hiding the foundation of a screened porch. There, where it is shaded by pine trees and camellia bushes, it flowers profusely from late spring until fall. Cuttings from her plants were brought to Connecticut and rooted for both indoor and outdoor plants. Indoors, it blooms from early spring through summer. The plant is decorative in a hanging container.

Evansiana has good-sized, soft green leaves and long-stemmed clusters of bright pink flowers, which are worth cutting. A white-flowered variety is available. Stems are quite erect, and fifteen inches or more tall. Bulbils that form in the axils of leaves fall to the ground and send up new plants the following spring.

HOLLYHOCK begonia (B. martiana or B. gracilis) is dormant in winter. Even though it is summer-flowering and does particularly well in a partly shaded location in the garden, this is one you may want because it is so different. The three-to-four-foot stems are lined with rather round glossy green leaves. Single rose-pink flowers open close to the stems, as the larger blossoms of hollyhocks do. Bulbils form in the leaf axils, but this is not a hardy begonia.

B. martiana and B. gracilis are similar. However, some authorities say that flowers of B. gracilis are fringed, those of B. martiana are not; also that leaves differ slightly.

B. HIEMALIS are the Christmas or winter-flowering group. They have been developed from crossing B. socotrana brought from a hot, dry island in the Indian Ocean with Andean tuberous species. Many named varieties are available in beautiful shades of rose, pink and salmon, with a few in red, gold and white. These are not easy plants to grow successfully. Bloom is easier to achieve in a greenhouse than in a house or apartment. These holiday-blooming begonias can be grown from leaf cuttings or bulbs, but require months of careful attention.

At all stages of growth and bloom, these begonias must be watered carefully. Plants should never dry out but, on the other hand, water should not be left standing in the saucer under the pot at any time. Temperatures of not more than 70 degrees by day and under 60 degrees at night are satisfactory if air is humid. A partly sunny window or one with bright light encourages bloom, but turn the plants once a week so they will grow symmetrically. Try to keep a gift plant for several weeks (see page 191), but don't try to grow your own.

B. DREGEI and B. WELTONIENSIS rank among the best of house plants. Both have small leaves and are likely to be called maple-leaf begonias. Both make bushy plants. Dregei perhaps is a more branchy one, Weltoniensis somewhat inclined to droop or trail.

Dregei has small, serrate, green to bronze leaves. The color depends on the amount of light. Small clusters of white blossoms appear in succession. It's easy to grow, and for fifteen years my plant of Dregei has never failed to flower.

Weltoniensis, the pink-flowered one, has given as little trouble for almost as many years. Light green leaves are lobed and serrate and have red stems. There is also a white-flowering kind. Weltoniensis is supposed to have a dormant period when, besides not flowering, it drops its leaves. I have never had my plant lose all its leaves at one time, although growth and bloom do stop for several months.

Fibrous-Rooted

B. SEMPERFLORENS, wax or rose begonia, is probably the most widely planted and best known of all begonias.

The single-flowered varieties are certainly the best introduction anyone, anywhere, could have to the family. A group of plants in 4- or 5-inch pots is a cheerful sight from October to May. They flower almost continuously where they receive plenty of light, or, better yet, in an east or west window where the pale winter sun reaches them for a couple of hours a day.

Wax begonias have glossy leaves, rather oval and two to four inches long. Leaves are green, red or bronze, according to variety.

Small clusters of modest blossoms open all over the plant. In the single ones, golden stamens stand out in the center. The double-flowering wax begonias are charming, and the pink ones look like tiny roses. Petals have a sheen which enriches the color, whether it's white, some shade of pink, salmon, scarlet or red or a bicolor.

There is great variation in the height of wax begonias. Dwarf plants grow only 4 to 6 inches tall. Another group averages 6 to 10 inches, and a few varieties such as Christmas Cheer, with single red blossoms, and Masterpiece, a large-flowered light pink, normally grow taller than 10 inches. But, plants are always mounds of foliage and flowers. In the house, any wax begonia tends to grow leggy. To prevent this and to keep them bushy, pinch out the tips of any stems that are stretching up fast or cut back the taller stems to four inches. This will stimulate branching and additional bloom.

Single varieties flower more abundantly and continuously than do the double ones. The singles offer a wide choice of color in flowers and foliage. Christmas Cheer with vivid rosy-red blossoms, Lucerna with scarlet red, Dwarf Carmen with light pink flowers and bronze foliage, or Frosty with white blossoms against bronze leaves are exceptional. The Cinderella strain is a modern one with such large clusters of stamens that the flowers are described as crested.

None of the double-flowering varieties blooms as constantly or over as long a period as the single ones. Fall and early winter seem to be natural rest periods, for I always have much more bloom in spring and summer. The doubles also seem to need more sun than the singles. Be careful not to overwater. If any drops fall on leaves, rot will start.

Wax begonias which have been started from seed in December can be purchased as flowering-size plants in spring. They are wonderful in a partly shaded place in the garden. In September, plants can be dug up and potted, after which all stems should be cut back to two-inch stubs before the plants are brought indoors. Or, for young plants, stem cuttings are taken in August. They root quickly in sand or water.

Once you have any kind of wax begonia, you'll have it forever. They self-sow readily, and occasionally, even after a severe winter, seedlings will be found in a sheltered spot outdoors. They also may self-sow in pots indoors. By all means, plant these volunteers.

CALLA LILY begonia is a sport of the wax begonia. It is indeed unusual, but it is a puzzling and difficult plant to grow. Only one thing is certain, and that is that the white leaves and stems are more likely to appear above the basal green foliage in summer or in warmth.

The original calla lily begonia has single red blossoms above its green leaves that look like begonia leaves, and white ones that look like calla lilies. Now single and double varieties with rose-red, cherry-red, light pink or pure white blossoms are available. One is as exasperating as another.

Some people report success by using artificial light a few hours every day or evening. Others say calla lily begonias need sun or no sun ever. The standard recommendations include all possible light, care in watering, and never overwatering, no drafts, feeding only when potbound.

Much easier, so I've been told, is a variegated strain of wax begonia called New Hampshire. Their green leaves are spotted with creamy yellow, and flowers are either pink or red.

ANGEL WING or CANE-STEMMED species and varieties are as easy to grow as single wax begonias, and are certain to give an indoor gardener a reputation for a green thumb. They flower generously, gracefully and quite spectacularly. The name angel wing is deserved because of the shape of the leaves; cane-stemmed because the tall growth is somewhat reminiscent of bamboo's habit of growth. In California, some angel wing varieties reach a height of 15 feet outdoors. Indoors, anywhere in the country, 18 inches to 2 or possibly 3 feet is maximum.

This group can be traced to B. coccinea, which is at home in Brazil. It's still possible to buy this one, with its glossy dark green leaves and drooping clusters of scarlet flowers. Many of this group have spotted leaves like those of the Trout Leaf begonia (B. argentea-guttata). The upper sides are green and spotted with silver, the undersides red. Blossoms are white tinged with pink. President Carnot has light green leaves with faint silver spots and clusters of large red flowers.

Corallina de Lucerna, another spotted-leaved variety, is hard to beat. It almost always has some pendent clusters of large salmon-red flowers. Swisher's Hybrid has large pink flowers and deeply lobed green leaves sprinkled with silver. Helen W. King has bronze leaves, silver-spotted, and pink blossoms. You can try almost any angel wing begonia after you have proved by these time-tested varieties that this group is satisfactory for conditions in your home. They are noteworthy for their readiness to bloom, although some are preferable to others in habit of growth.

HAIRY-LEAVED or HIRSUTE begonias have both leaves and stems covered with soft hairs—white or red, or sometimes just deepening the color of green leaves. Flowers are bearded, which adds distinction. This group as a whole is sturdy.

Metallica varieties and hybrids are especially interesting—and they are tough. There is considerable variation in height. B. metallica's leaves are shining green, with a metallic luster on top and red on the underside. Flowers are soft pink. Fewer stems of bloom will appear on a plant that does not stand in direct sun, but leaves will be more metallic-looking. Scharffi has rounded bronzy leaves that are softly hairy, and white flowers bearded with pink. Scharffi is often called Haageana, or vice versa. Whatever the name, plants reach a height of about two feet. Alleryi, with hairy green foliage, displays its showy white flowers bearded with pink in the fall.

Some of the dependable fibrous-rooted begonias can't be classified except as miscellaneous. Worth looking for under this heading are B. sceptrum (or B. aconitifolia) a tall-growing sort even in the house, and the unusual B. ulmifolia. While you're looking for these, you also might like to find Dancing Girl and Red Kimball. The latter is like the hardy B. evansiana, but its leaves are red.

B. sceptrum's growth may be slowed by somewhat unfavorable conditions in a house, but it will manage to live, look well and to flower. Leaves, which are deeply lobed, are green, streaked and splotched with silver. The undersides have a rosy tinge. Blossoms are comparatively large, white tinged with pink.

B. ulmifolia (*ulmus* means elm) may look more like a small elm tree than like a begonia, but its growth is

the soft growth of a perennial. The stems are quite succulent and green beneath their scurfy or scalelike
brown covering. The green leaves are exactly the shape
and size of an elm leaf and are rough to the touch,
as elm leaves are. Terminal clusters of small white
flowers begin to open in late winter. Ulmifolia doesn't
need sun to flower. In fact, it grows best in light only.
It's an erect plant that can grow to six feet tall, but the
soft green stems cannot always hold the burden of

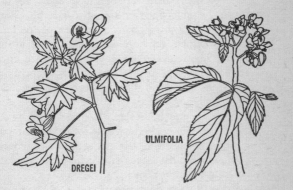

ULMIFOLIA

DREGEI

foliage and flowers upright. This is why large plants
may resemble elm trees with their drooping branches.

Dancing Girl has no two leaves alike in shape or
size. All, however, are basically green, streaked and
splotched with silver and pink. Even though flowers
are red, they are outdone by foliage. Plants are inclined
to be bushy but good size.

The RHIZOMATOUS group is characterized by a thick
rootstock that grows near the surface of the soil. These
rhizomes, which support leaves and flowers, enable the
plant to withstand the warm, dry atmosphere of a
house better than do many other begonias. Rhizomatous
begonias flourish if the atmosphere can be kept fresh
and moist. Through February, a sunny window is a

good location. From March onward, some protection from sun is advisable so foliage won't be burned.

Star, lettuce leaf and pond lily are terms that describe the leaves of some of the rhizomatous begonias. Star varieties, such as Ricinifolia, Sunderbrucki and many others have deeply lobed and pointed leaves. They are richly colored and have a velvety sheen. Maphil or Cleopatra has velvety light green and brown leaves. This is so bushy as to be almost dwarf. The large leaves of many Star varieties have short stems. Flowers, usually pink, open in spring. All in all, Star begonias seem to me to be one of the nicest of the lot.

Bunchi, the lettuce leaf begonia, is interesting in or out of bloom. The round green leaves have frilled and curled edges. Pink flowers open in spring. Bunchi is descended from the pond lily or beefsteak begonia (B. erythrophylla or Feasti). Its large round green leaves are red on the underside. Tall sprays of pink blossoms open in winter. Variety Bessie Buxton, named for an enthusiastic collector of begonias who also writes about them, has bronzy leaves and light pink flowers. Both of these are sturdy plants.

Some of the Rhizomatous begonias can grow much too large to be placed among other house plants or even among other begonias. Verschaffelti, admittedly a handsome plant, is one that can outgrow its welcome and look gross if grouped with other house plants. The rhizomes are thick, the leaves glossy and a good green. Clear pink blossoms hang gracefully from tall stems and open from February through spring.

Gilsoni seems to me a better choice, if not exactly comparable. This one has stout stems holding erect glossy, dark green leaves that are pointed and toothed. It's a floriferous variety that starts to open pale pink flowers in midwinter. Some of the blossoms are double.

B. manicata and its variations are considered easy to grow. The green leaves of Manicata have a red edge finished off with white hairs. However, many people prefer B. manicata aureo-maculata, called the leopard begonia, because leaves are blotched with yellow. B. manicata crispa has leaves with curled and ruffled edges. Tall stems of soft pink flowers are notable on B. manicata.

Rex begonias are probably the most important and certainly the most numerous Rhizomatous group. Rex begonias have a fascination quite out of proportion to their contribution to the indoor garden. Winter is the dormant season, and foliage, the chief lure of the Rex varieties, is more showy in spring and summer. May to August are the months when they are most colorful. However, I've seen variety Merry Christmas living up to its name in a house in January.

Hundreds of varieties have been named and introduced since B. rex was brought from Assam, India, to England in the 1850's. Large leaves are variously colored and marked. Although these plants do flower, the leaves are any Rex begonia's glory.

Merry Christmas is one of the newer varieties that has become famous. Its large leaves are satiny red outlined in bright green, with a velvety red center and edge. Helen Lewis has dark red leaves with silver zones flushed with purple. Cardoza Gardens is dark purple, almost black in the center, with a lighter edge; it is sprinkled and zoned with silver.

Queen of Hanover is better at holding its leaves during winter than are many other varieties. The leaves are green, banded with lighter green and covered with pink hairs. Fireflush has the same habit. Its dark green leaves are edged with black and have an allover covering of red hairs. The white flowers are quite fragrant.

Although many varieties of Rex begonias have huge leaves, plants aren't necessarily too large for general use. There is a group of Rex begonias with short rhizomes supporting plants that are less than ten inches tall and not much wider.

A Rex variety was one of the parents of Abel Carrière, which is unanimously voted a handsome begonia and remains a size to be appreciated (maximum height about eighteen inches). Branching erect stems display small, smooth leaves that are green and silver. On the undersides, veins are outlined in red. Older leaves become flushed with rose. Rose-red blossoms are handsome above silvery leaves.

The markings and variations as well as the colorings of Rex begonias are endless. Sizes of both leaves and plants differ. Some specialists differentiate according to color (those predominantly silver form a large group). Then there is the spiral-leaved type, on which the lobe of each leaf is twisted in two or three spirals. Curly Fireflush has added this characteristic to the brilliantly colored standard of the same name. The spiral-leaved or curly varieties are as handsomely marked as are other Rex begonias.

The Grape Leaf begonia (B. speculata) is another rhizomatous type, and closely resembles the Rex varieties. However, Grape Leaf isn't so spectacular. Its leaves are dull green, puckered with lighter green, and coarsely hairy. Flowers are a creamy or pinky white. Pearli and Illustrata are similar, but have smaller leaves and are more attractive plants. Pearli's leaves are light green, overlaid with pearl, and pebbled. Illustrata has round gray-green leaves, rather mottled, and pinky-white flowers in winter.

The SMALL-LEAVED group is a charming one. B. foliosa probably has the smallest leaves of any of the begonias. They are about half an inch long and grow quite flat on either side of the stem. White flowers open at the tips of the drooping stems. This probably should be grown in a hanging basket.

B. floribunda (or multiflora rosea) and B. digswelliana are fairly easy to grow. Floribunda is tall and decorative, with leaves about an inch long and half an inch wide, and produces small pink flowers in the axils of the leaves. It's graceful, though droopy. As nearly as I can figure out, Floribunda is a variety of B. fuchsioides. Digswelliana is mistakenly called the bleeding-heart begonia. Small, bushy plants have glossy light green leaves, sharply toothed, and long-stemmed, drooping scarlet flowers.

What with the descriptive terms bleeding heart, grape leaf, maple leaf and others being used with the name begonia, this reads like a family of mimics. Certainly leaves and occasionally flowers of a number of begonias have a superficial resemblance to some other well-known outdoor plant. Attaching that name is one way of setting apart at least a few members of a highly diverse and confusing family.

It's a rewarding family. Find two or three specimens that do well in your home, and soon there will be cuttings available to pass on to neighbors and friends. Begonias are friendly plants, and cuttings, fresh or rooted, are frequently exchanged. (Both leaf and stem cuttings can be made, and rhizomes divided.) It's one of the best ways to increase a collection.

They're a friendly plant, too, in that there is a national begonia society as well as regional and local groups. Bulletins and correspondence are mediums for advice as well as for news.

For begonias still are news. New varieties are introduced almost every year. Seed hybridists work to improve wax begonias and find new variations of this simple, sturdy plant. Specialists who've lost their hearts to begonias achieve new varieties, even of the Rex group. Not so much because of the new introductions, but just because so many plants are different, it's hard not to become a collector of begonias.

CHAPTER X

FLOWERS FROM BULBS

Every week from October to May can be highlighted by special flowers some place indoors. This succession of bloom results from forcing bulbs, many of which normally flower outdoors in spring. Good contributions also are made by South African bulbs of the rainy-dry seasons.

Colorful, varied and often fragrant flowers are produced by the bulbs and tubers that can be grown indoors. This is especially appreciated during fall and early winter when short days and meager sunshine prevent many of the house plants from blooming profusely.

Bulb planting starts in late September or early October with autumn crocus, and ends in December with amaryllis. Many people continue to plant until February, to maintain the succession of bloom. Whether or not certain bulbs are planted every two or three weeks from October through January depends on how essential their flowers are to indoor pleasure. In February, a few quite different kinds of bulbs and tubers are planted for bloom during spring and summer, both indoors and outside on the terrace.

The length of time to flowering can be counted in days for two or three bulbs. Others planted by mid-October won't bloom until sometime in February. A continuous succession of bloom from Thanksgiving to spring is as easy to manage in an apartment where daylight is at a minimum as in a house with sunny windows.

Good, healthy bulbs of flowering size should be purchased for forcing. It is important to specify top grade and flowering size of outdoor spring-flowering bulbs. Order bulbs as early in fall as possible. If succession plantings are to be made of narcissus and lily of the valley, order the full supply for the season, and if there's no place to store bulbs safely for succession plantings ask to have deliveries staggered.

Other supplies include soil, which can be purchased ready-mixed in bags, and, for those that grow in water, pebbles, stone chips or vermiculite, peat moss or bulb fiber should be provided. Labels are good to have on hand for keeping track of date and variety.

Decorative containers can be used for bulbs that grow and flower in water and for some of the smaller-flowering ones that must be planted in soil. Any container of the right depth (three to five inches) when bulbs have grown roots will be satisfactory. Choose pottery, china, brass or other metal, appropriate to the place where you want to have the bulbs when they are blooming. For some bulbs, the traditional clay pots or shallower pans, often called bulb pans, are more practical.

The flowers can cost as much—or as little—time and trouble as you're willing to spend. It depends on which bulbs are planted and how they're planted. The ones that are the least demanding might be the ones that give the greatest pleasure.

Most bulbs need a few days or a few weeks in a cool dark place to form roots. Usually by the time they're brought back into the light, leaf growth and, in the case of some bulbs, flower buds are showing. A closet or cupboard has the required darkness, but it's likely to be stuffy. It's a rare closet that has any circulation of air. Find a place where temperatures range between 40 and 60 degrees and where there's some ventilation—even if it means putting the containers in a covered carton out on a porch or a fire escape.

Easiest, of course, are the bulbs that do not need special temperatures or a dark place in which to start growth. This is true of at least six candidates for winter flowers.

Everyone goes into bulb planting, indoors or out in the garden, with one assurance. The bulbs are certain to flower. Long before they were dug from the fields in which they grew, a flower bud had formed deep in the center, where it is protected by layer after layer of plant tissues.

Simplest of all are the bulbs or their kin that grow in water. Four of them can provide a succession of bloom from October into March. These are equally successful in house or apartments.

Water Culture

AUTUMN CROCUS (Crocus sativus) is planted in late summer for September-October bloom in the garden. They have true crocus flowers and, because they open without leaves, were called "naked ladies" by the Victorians. Some bulbs are usually still available after Labor Day. Buy a half-dozen whenever you think of it. Then choose a decorative saucer or small, shallow dish, or even a large seashell such as an abalone. Place about an inch of pebbles or stone chips in the container and anchor three to six bulbs in the pebbles. Then add water just to the base of the bulbs. Leave in the room where they are to flower.

Autumn crocus bloom so quickly that there's no waiting for root growth. Light is good, but sun isn't

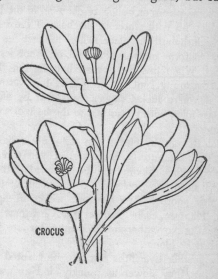

CROCUS

necessary. After bloom, plant the bulbs in the garden, to flower thereafter every fall if the season isn't preceded by too much rain.

The HYACINTH is one of the most delightful flowers for forcing indoors. Some people try the water method for Dutch hyacinths, with their big fat spikes of fragrant bells. Less troublesome, and flowering in less time, are the French-Roman hyacinths with their more slender stems of equally fragrant white, soft blue or pink blossoms.

Dutch hyacinths develop quite slowly in water. Purchase forcing-size bulbs, which are slightly more expensive than the grade bought for garden planting. Special glass jars topped with a cup into which a hyacinth bulb just fits are necessary. These hyacinth jars were made in clear and colored glass during the nineteenth century, so this is far from a new idea. They are still produced in small quantity.

Place some pieces or pellets of charcoal in the bottom of the glass, fill with water to the base of the cup and set a hyacinth bulb in place. Then it must be put in the dark to form roots, which will take not less than six weeks. When this has occurred, bring out the jars to a partly sunny spot where it isn't too warm. In a month, if you're lucky, flower buds will be showing. Keep glass filled with water just to the base of the bulb at all times.

French-Roman hyacinths are not only reliable for forcing, but are utterly charming. If you can obtain pre-cooled bulbs, bloom will be speeded. Otherwise, bulbs will need five weeks in a cool dark place to grow roots, plus another three to four weeks in light for flowers. Plant in early October for Christmas bloom, then again in November and December for late January and February bloom.

These smaller hyacinths can also be planted in pots of soil, but they flower as quickly and as well in a decorative container of pebbles or bulb fiber and water. Place bulbs fairly close together and embed them in the growing medium. Then fill container with water to the base of the pebbles (or other growing medium) and add as needed to keep water at this level constantly, even during the period in the dark. Bloom progresses more satisfactorily if temperatures average about 65 degrees after the containers are moved into a light place.

LILY OF THE VALLEY is perhaps the most delightful flower of the whole winter. Forced ones aren't quite as fragrant as those from the garden, but they're dainty, white and sweet. Don't try to dig up pips (the thickened rootstalks from which leaves and flower stems sprout) from the garden to force indoors. Pips require a special cold-storage treatment and must be plump and extra strong to force readily. Pips grown and treated especially for forcing can usually be purchased about December 1 each year.

They flower in twenty-eight days if planted before January 1; in twenty-one days thereafter. Bulb fiber, vermiculite and peat moss are splendid mediums in which to plant forcing pips. The pips will have long beards of dry roots. Cut them with a sharp knife to the more convenient length of about three inches. This will not only make them more manageable but will permit a wider selection of containers. They're charming in a small strawberry jar, two pips in each pocket. In other containers, set pips an inch apart and pack pebbles, fiber, peat moss or vermiculite around them. Moisten the packing with water and keep it constantly moist but not soggy.

Lily of the valley needs no period in the dark to spur flowering. Plant, water and place wherever you want them to bloom. For continuous bloom, make a new planting every two or three weeks.

PAPERWHITE NARCISSUS is the bulb everyone forces. If you've grown a little weary of the sweet-scented small white flowers in clusters on tall stems, try golden yellow variety Soleil d'Or for a change. It grows in the same way, thrusting up slender green buds among the typical daffodil foliage. February Gold, the early and small-flowering garden daffodil, and Fortune, larger but also early, may flower in water and pebbles. However, these last two will take many more weeks to form roots and, hence, to flower than does Paperwhite or Soleil d'Or.

Failure to bloom or buds that blast is a fairly common complaint about narcissus. Firm, plump bulbs of good quality should certainly flower. If they don't, it's probably because they've been kept where it's too warm. The dark place in which they've been put for the roots to grow should have a temperature not higher than 60 degrees. When bowls are moved into the light, 60 to 65 degrees is high enough. Keep them out of bright sun until buds show, at which stage sun will hasten bloom. When flowers are breaking open, move back to light spot so they can be enjoyed as long as possible. To make the flowers last longer, some people move them into a cooler room every night.

Narcissus forms quite a mass of roots, and therefore needs a fairly deep container. Set bulbs about two inches apart and embed them firmly in the growing medium. Add water until it touches the base of the bulbs and replenish to this level as needed.

When planted during the fall, narcissus needs three weeks or so in the dark to form roots, then at least two weeks in the light for flowers to develop. Count on six to seven weeks from planting to flowering before January 1, and about four weeks after that date. For bloom at Thanksgiving, therefore, start Paperwhite or Soleil d'Or bulbs the first week in October; for the Christmas holidays, November 10 is probably the last planting date. For continuous bloom all winter, plant either of these two varieties every two weeks.

Soil and No Trouble

It doesn't make sense to plant lily of the valley, Paperwhite or Soleil d'Or narcissus or autumn crocus in soil, since they'll flower with their roots in water. Nor do I believe that French-Roman hyacinths are any finer if they're grown in soil instead of water.

Ten other bulbs that are as dependable as these four should be planted in soil. This doesn't mean that they are any more trouble than those that bloom in water.

Four of the most satisfactory ones—lachenalia and veltheimia from South Africa, oxalis and nerine—need no period in the dark to establish a root system. The others have no specific demands that are hard to meet. This is the group that produces the most unusual flowers—some spectacular, all colorful.

AMARYLLIS bulbs produce the most magnificent flowers of the winter. A top-quality bulb will bloom without fail the first winter it is planted. Whether it does in succeeding years depends on how it is handled after the flowers fade.

Fresh bulbs are available by December. Pick out a good, firm one. It needn't be the most expensive amaryllis in the store or the catalogue, but if it's too cheap, it's likely not to be flowering size. Price differs with variety. Old, ordinary varieties, possibly marked only according to flower color, can be purchased for as little as fifty cents, but it's possible to pay ten dollars or more for some of the recent hybrids.

Considerable hybridizing has been done during the last fifty years in Europe, as well as in Florida and California. Among the more famous hybrids on the market—and readily available—are the Royal Dutch hybrids and the Ludwig strains from Holland, the Howard and Smith hybrids developed in California, the Mead, Cammack and Hayward strains from Florida.

Some hybrids and strains have many named varieties; others are sold by colors. Imported bulbs are more expensive, since the American ones are field-grown.

It's possible to find garish colors in amaryllis, but red ones need no longer be the rather hard orange-scarlet. There are both darker and brighter shades, to say nothing of pinks and salmons. Some flowers are a solid color, others are bicolored and striped. Flowers are single, except for the McCann doubles, which are available in mixed colors, or by a few named varieties.

Among the many splendid varieties in the Royal

Dutch hybrids is the all-white Joan of Arc. After seven winters of bloom, a single bulb still produced two spikes last year, each one with not less than four enormous white flowers. Bordeaux, with broadly flaring petals, is a rich wine-red.

Ludwig amaryllis, also from the Netherlands, is noted for unusual colors. Pink Favorite, camellia rose Margaret Truman, watermelon Pink Perfection are some of the noted varieties. Fantasy combines blush rose with white.

Cammack's Star, developed in Florida, has dark red and white flowers, Margaret Rose is rose and white, Wings of Snow salmon-orange with white.

Small-flowered amaryllis on dwarf plants have been another goal of hybridists. Christmas Joy, with its red blossoms, doesn't flower for the holidays, but it is early blooming. Perfect in its smaller scale, it's even more usable than the long-stemmed, big-flowering hybrids. Ludwig Mignon hybrid is an excellent dwarf, miniature-flowered strain.

Modern hybrids are noted for vigor (stems are strong), disease resistance and long-lasting flowers. The large white flowers of Joan of Arc have enough substance to last a full three weeks. They usually are open by March first. March, April and May are the peak months for bloom, although some may open in February.

Two planting rules must be followed. Choose a pot that is an inch wider all around than the amaryllis bulb. Plant the bulb so that two-thirds of it is exposed above soil level, which should be about an inch below the rim of the pot.

An inch of pebbles or broken crock (pieces of flower pot) in the bottom of the pot takes care of drainage. Fill with a sifted mixture of soil, compost or humus, and sand in about equal parts. Mix in a teaspoon of bonemeal for each pot. Water well.

The potted bulb should be set aside, not necessarily in the dark but in a dim place, neither too hot nor too cool. Here it should stay to grow roots and until a green tip pushes out of the bulb. Water occasionally as the soil becomes really dry.

It may take only three or four weeks, or as long as three months, before there is any sign of green. If the first green tips are thin and grow from the center of the bulb, they'll be leaves. Alas, if leaves appear first, it's likely that the amaryllis bulb won't bloom. The flower bud is thicker than a leaf tip, but just as green, and appears from the side of the bulb.

When green does show, move amaryllis to a warm, sunny place (about 70 degrees) and water regularly. As flower buds develop, move the amaryllis to a place in light, but not sunlight. Every bulb should have one stem with not less than three flowers. Many bulbs produce two or more flower stalks every winter, with five or six flowers topping each stem.

When flowers fade, cut off the stem. The care given for the next six months determines whether or not the amaryllis bulb will flower the following winter. Continue watering to keep foliage growing. Fertilize once a fortnight so the bulb can store food and form its flower buds.

When warm weather comes in spring, the amaryllis in its pot can be moved outdoors. Sometime during summer, foliage will start to turn yellow. When foliage has fully matured, the leaves can be pulled easily from the bulb.

After this, the bulb is in its dormant stage. Keep bulb and the soil in which it's planted dry until November. Then the cycle of new growth and bloom starts again.

Several relatives of the amaryllis are neither difficult to find nor to bring into flower. Handsome as are the many stems of scarlet flowers on Vallota or Scarborough lily, the darker red flower of Sprekelia or Jacobean lily, the blood lily or Haemanthus and the curious white blooms of Peruvian daffodil (Hymenocallis), these bulbs do not seem to me true indoor material. Their flowering season is late spring or summer.

Difficulty in providing conditions for bloom is the reason for mentioning but not recommending Eucharis grandiflora, the Amazon lily, and Peruvian lilies (Alstroemeria). Furthermore, both are spring-blooming, although earlier than Scarborough lily and Peruvian daffodil.

Certain of the CRINUMS, however, are well worth planting for indoor flowers. Crinum moorei has bell-shaped pink flowers about four inches across in the fall. Variety Cecil Houdyshel produces deep rose-pink flowers almost constantly from spring to fall. Check season of bloom before investing in a crinum, for not all are good house plants. A crinum needs a large pot or tub, for it becomes an unusually large plant. Its cycle follows that of amaryllis, with a dry, dormant season after bloom.

CALLA, usually but incorrectly called calla lily, belongs to the same family as Chinese evergreen and philodendron. Its relatives certainly are a good reference for the more showy flowering plant. A calla's flower is the clublike spadix, which is encircled with a spathe or bract of white, clear yellow, soft pink or black.

The stately white calla of formal weddings grows two to three feet tall. So does the Golden Calla, Elliottiana. Godfrey, a free-blooming white variety, doesn't grow quite as tall and has smaller flowers in greater numbers.

Prizes for the house, in my opinion, are the dwarf-growing, small-flowered callas in white, pink or black. They reach only 12 to 15 or possibly 18 inches. The miniature or baby white calla produces many more

flowers during winter than does its taller, larger counterpart. So does the miniature yellow calla and the
dusty-rose or soft pink Rehmanni. The black calla, also
small, has black-green spathes that look almost maroon
inside.

Callas aren't true bulbous plants, but grow from a
fleshy rhizome. They can be purchased in spring to

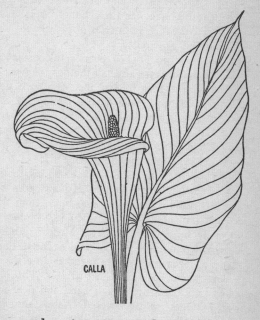

CALLA

flower outdoors in moist ground, or in fall to pot for
winter flowers. Each rhizome or tuber should be
planted separately, six-inch pots for the tall large ones,
four-inch pots for the miniatures.

Plants will be both thirsty and greedy, so keep the
soil level low enough for generous watering. A rich soil
consists of two-thirds garden loam, one-third humus,
compost or leafmold, plus one tablespoon of bonemeal

for each pot. Water thoroughly and set in a cool place (55 to 60 degrees) to grow roots. It need not be dark, but only minimum light is needed at this stage.

When leaf tips appear, move the pots to a light place where temperatures average about 60 degrees. Whenever flower buds are noticed, it's time for sun or artificial light.

The large-flowered callas may not flower before late March. Miniatures take less time, but even so it will be close to four months. Both sizes of flowers are long-lasting if watered generously.

Callas can be saved in their pots for bloom another winter. Continue to water after all the dead flowers are cut off. The glossy green foliage, incidentally, is decorative. Until it matures, feed once a month. By early summer leaves will turn yellow and be ready to pull off. Since callas should be potted in fresh, enriched soil every November, take the tubers from the pots, dry, clean and store in a cool, airy, dark place.

GRAPE HYACINTHS (muscari) are a charming forecast of spring when they flower indoors in January or early February. Set aside a dozen or more bulbs from those that are being planted in the garden in October. To buy especially for forcing, look for Muscari armeniacum, early-flowering, or M. botryoides coeruleum. I plant about a dozen bulbs, close together, in a shallow pottery bowl about six inches in diameter. The bulbs are pressed into a mixture of soil, sand and peat moss so that all but the tips are covered. Water thoroughly and then place in a dark, cool cellar or on a porch where temperatures will never go below freezing and not much higher than 45 degrees. Forget them for four weeks or so and then move into a sunny window. From planting to flowering requires eight weeks at the most, and, since flower spikes open slowly, they are most worthwhile. Continue watering until foliage matures.

IRIS RETICULATA is early-flowering outdoors. Forcing

will bring out its flowers six weeks or more earlier indoors. Diminutive plants produce small but showy iris in a rich shade of violet. They are as fragrant as true violets.

I suppose it might be possible to plant the little bulbs of Iris reticulata for bloom during the Christmas holidays. They're so springlike that they will be more appreciated in January or February. November planting should bring flowers in mid-February. Place half a dozen bulbs in a 5-inch pot and cover with an inch of soil.

LACHENALIA is a small bulb from South Africa, called Cape cowslip. Flower stalks closely hung with orange-yellow or scarlet blossoms open as successfully and gaily in an apartment as in a house. The flowers remain fresh for six weeks.

Plant three bulbs in a 4-inch pot in October; water and place on a sunny window sill. Flowers will open in December.

LILIES are more than a possibility, but need considerably more attention than lachenalia, iris or lily of the valley. Easter lilies, now almost always the Croft strain, require more time than skill to grow for your own pleasure. The Georgia lily, which passes muster for the glistening white Easter lily, flowers in January if planted in late September.

These large lily bulbs must be planted one each to a five-inch flower pot. Mix equal parts of soil and leaf-mold, compost or humus; set the bulb on about two inches of it and cover until only the tip shows. Like all lilies, these are "stemmy," and low planting permits soil to be filled in around part of the stem as it shoots upward. Follow the same routine as for callas. Heat, however, is important after the flower buds show.

Some of the garden lilies force almost as easily as the Easter lily. Try L. rubrum, the red-spotted pink lily that flowers outdoors in late summer, or its white counterpart, the early-flowering small coral lily (L. tenuifolium), or the tiger lily. I haven't tried any of the modern hybrids from the Northwest, but I think chances are reasonably good for forcing them too. And, since the flower stems are much leafier, the Mid-Century and other new hybrids should be handsome plants. Follow the procedure for Easter lily.

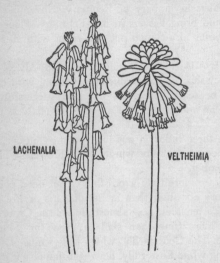

LACHENALIA   VELTHEIMIA

NERINE, Guernsey lily, flowers in November and December. The only reason why more people don't grow it is because the bulbs are hard to find. Nothing, except lily of the valley, could be easier to grow. N. sarniensis and its varieties are the true Guernsey lily. The flower stem is topped with many individual blossoms about the size of, and looking somewhat like, those of wild azalea. The petals, however, have greater substance. They are vivid shades of pink, salmon, rose, scarlet or crimson, overlaid with a sparkling iridescence. They're as airy as brilliant butterflies.

Plant six bulbs in a 6-inch clay flower pan which has

been filled with a good loamy soil. The bulbs should be half in, half out of soil, like amaryllis. Water and set in a light place. September or early October planting brings flowers in November. When the shimmering blossoms fade and leaves appear, move pots into a sunny, cool place (50 degrees is adequate), water regularly and fertilize once a month. Stop watering when leaves turn yellow and store bulbs in their pots bonedry. No more water should be given until flower buds show again in fall. (Repot the bulbs in fresh soil once every three or four years.)

The following September bring pots out again, topdress with enriched soil and start watering. Flowers appear again in November.

OXALIS, to most people, means the old-fashioned plant with masses of shamrocklike leaves on stems long enough to trail and small blossoms of yellow, lavender, pink or white on every sunny winter day. This is Oxalis cernua, Bermuda buttercup, whose little bulbs used to be planted in pots and placed in brackets at sunny kitchen window frames. There's a double yellow Bermuda buttercup too.

Six to ten other and quite different oxalis also grow from bulbs. O. variabilis, or Grand Duchess, has large bright pink flowers; O. bowieana is known as a giant pink and also has large leaves; O. hirta, unlike the others, has long trailing stems covered with feathery foliage, and its flowers, larger than those of Bermuda buttercup, are bright rose. This has a short season of bloom in fall, as does O. melanosticta, with yellow blossoms against gray-green leaves. Brasiliensis has rosy blossoms in winter and spring, Flava large yellow flowers and curled five-parted leaves in winter. Incarnata, or Irish shamrock, has lavender flowers in winter.

Plant oxalis bulbs, water, and place them in the sun. In return for daily watering and occasional removal of yellowed leaves, the majority will be green and flowering for months.

Of the several that do not grow from bulbs, the tree oxalis (O. ortgiesi) is one of the sturdiest plants imaginable. It's an upright and branching plant with three-parted leaves bronze-green above, maroon beneath. Small yellow flowers open at all seasons of the year. It's easy to obtain more tree oxalis from cuttings. O. regnellii opens its white flowers on compact plants at all seasons; and O. rubra, with trailing stems and pink flowers, is just as free-blooming.

VELTHEIMIA from South Africa is a handsome foliage plant before and after bloom. A whorl of glossy bright green leaves starts unfolding in November. The flower stalk pushes up from the center of this green rosette sometime in January and grows about a foot before buds start opening at the tip, not at the bottom. Flowers are dusty rose, arranged closely, and stay fresh for six weeks.

No sun is needed. Plant one bulb to a pot, as you do amaryllis, with about two-thirds of the bulb above the soil level. Water, place in sun or good light and watch for leaves. Continue to water after the flower spike is cut off. When the glossy foliage finally shrivels, store the bulb in its pot until next fall.

Soil and Cold

Daffodils, tulips and Dutch hyacinths are the important spring-flowering bulbs in the garden. Florist shops stock them in winter as cut flowers and potted plants. Their requirements are fairly strict, and indoor gardeners are fortunate that other bulbs can be forced with less trouble and time.

The chief drawback to forcing these spring-flowering bulbs is that their period in the dark must be in a cold place. They really need freezing temperatures before they can bloom. A coldframe will be most convenient. Lacking this, you will have to have a trench dug somewhere in the garden and the pots of bulbs covered with ashes, salt hay or burlap. It's going to be cold and uncomfortable digging them out to bring indoors some January day. A cellar or porch where temperatures never rise higher than 40 degrees probably will do, but remember that the bulbs also must be in the dark.

Not every variety of tulip and narcissus will force well. Catalogues usually mark the best ones in some manner. Early-flowering varieties of tulips possibly are more successful than later ones. Single and Double Early varieties, and varieties of such species as Kaufmanniana, also Cesar Franck and Olaf if you can find them, are good but need just as long a period in the cold and dark as do taller, late varieties. However, flowers open faster when pots are brought indoors. Most of the Dutch hyacinths can be forced, but some are better than others.

An assortment of flower pots should be on hand for planting in October or November. One hyacinth bulb in a five-inch pot or three to a six-inch pan is good. Four to six tulips or three daffodils also fit in a six-inch pan.

A sandy soil mixture is preferable. Two parts of garden soil, one of leafmold or compost, and two of sharp sand is satisfactory. Fill the pots half full, or a little more, and set bulbs in place so that, in the case of tulips and hyacinths, when they are covered the tips barely show; in the case of narcissus, the bulbs should be covered. Water, and move into the cold outdoor location.

In order to grow roots, hyacinths will need ten to twelve weeks, daffodils twelve to thirteen weeks, tulips fourteen to fifteen weeks. Some sign of green leaves is usually evident when roots have made enough growth for the move back indoors.

A light and cool place is the first stop when pots are brought into the house. After a few days, sun and more heat can be given. Temperatures of 65 degrees by day, not less than 55 degrees at night, are favorable. On sunny days higher temperatures are all right. Daily watering will be necessary.

Crocus, scilla and other small bulbs, with the exception of the grape hyacinths, are too uncertain to be worth trying to force them indoors. The taller Scilla hispanica, wood hyacinths that bloom outdoors in May, can be forced but are likely to be slow-starting and not even to be flowering by late March. However, Dutch iris that have been given the pre-cooling treatment aren't particularly difficult to bring into bloom. Two or three weeks where it's dark and cool (but not as cold as for tulips) start their growth. Some varieties such as the familiar Wedgwood are more tractable than others.

After any of these bulbs have flowered, continue to water until the foliage turns yellow. A slight tug then will pull it out easily. Tulips, daffodils, narcissus, outdoor lilies and iris cannot be forced into bloom again, but they can be planted in the garden in the fall. They won't amount to much the first spring outdoors but should flower regularly in succeeding years.

Most of the more easily forced bulbs have a future outdoors if not indoors. Paperwhite narcissus is not reliably hardy in gardens north of South Carolina, French-Roman hyacinths north of Washington, D.C. Elsewhere, discard after bloom. Iris, autumn crocus and lily of the valley may be saved to be planted permanently in gardens anywhere after having been forced.

The bulbs that flower on a wet-dry cycle rather than on a cold-warm one can be saved to flower again in the house. Amaryllis, callas, lachenalia, nerine, oxalis and veltheimia will flower dependably winter after winter, with a dry dormant period and fertilizing.

Out of the Ordinary

Freesias and ornithogalum are enchanting cut flowers. Certainly this should be their "own excuse for being" since they aren't notably attractive as pot plants. Bulbs of either one should be planted in August for flowers in February or later. Ornithogalums bloom in day temperatures of 55 to 65 degrees (not always possible in a house or apartment), while freesias require warm days, cool nights and some shade.

Little bulbs with such names as babiana and ixia may be tempting. Again the results seem to me not only less dependable but hardly worthwhile.

An oddity is sea onion (Urginea maritima). The bulb is so large and full of food that it can be placed, as is, on a shelf or window sill and will send up a flower stalk. Bloom is most likely in autumn. False sea onion (Ornithogalum caudatum) has green-white flowers, as does the true sea onion.

Fascinating to many people in a most unattractive way is hamburger plant, devil's tongue, snake palm, lily of India or amorphophallus (Hydrosme rivieri). Call it what you will, the giant flower has a distinctly foul odor. It's not even pleasant to look at, for the bulbous rootstock produces a huge dark maroon-red spathe like an enormous calla. Leaves that follow are large and palmlike. There's no trick to having a mature rootstock flower in its season of active growth.

Spring Bloom

While the procession of bloom from bulbs and tubers started in the fall is at its height, it's time to pause in admiration—and to begin over again. A mere handful of types can be planted in February for bloom from spring into summer.

ACHIMENES and GLOXINIA (see page 119) are planted in February. Neither one is any more difficult to grow than is amaryllis, and certainly gloxinia has flowers fully as magnificent as those of amaryllis. Bloom on both gloxinia and achimenes should be opening by mid-spring and should continue well into the summer.

CALADIUMS, tropical relatives of callas, provide masses of color red as the brightest rose, pink as crabapple trees in bloom, white as waterlilies and green as ferns. All of this color comes not from flowers, but from foliage. No caladium has a plain, one-color leaf. All varieties—there are dozens of named ones—are variegated, splotched, streaked or veined, or combine in some fashion at least two colors.

Size also is an attention-getter. Twelve inches from tip to tip is ordinary, and many caladiums have leaves fifteen to eighteen inches long. Many are arrow-shaped but some are almost heart-shaped, and there is a group of strap- and lance-leaf varieties. An old name for caladiums is elephant's ears. Each large leaf balances on a slender stem.

The rather thin leaves scorch and the bushy plants dry up if they are exposed to hot sun for any length of time. Dappled or filtered light is the best exposure. Outdoors in gardens, caladiums are colorful in shade. Indoors or on terraces and balconies, pot plants are cool-looking as their leaves bend gracefully in the slightest breeze.

Late March or early April is the time to plant tubers, one each to a 5-inch pot. Soil mixed with humus, compost or leafmold is good, and a tablespoon of bonemeal or 5–10–5 fertilizer should be incorporated for each pot. Cover tubers with about two inches of the soil. Water, and keep soil moist. A light place and warm temperature

(70 degrees) start growth. Fertilize once every three weeks. Caladiums thrive on warmth and humidity.

FAIRY LILIES (Zephyranthes) are delightful small-flowering plants for late spring and early summer. They really aren't lilies at all, but are related to amaryllis. Their timetable is the reverse of that of amaryllis and veltheimia, their care the same. The white Z. atamasco and rosy-lavender Z. robusta are spring-flowering; pink

FAIRY LILIES

or rose Z. carinata begins in late spring; and there are both white- and pink-flowering fall varieties, if they can be found. These also are tender bulbs for outdoor planting.

The small bulbs of fairy lilies are planted close together in a pot of average good well-drained soil. Since the blossoms are a modest size, a dozen or more bulbs in a six- or seven-inch pot make a good display. Soak with water, move into a sunny, or partly sunny, location and watch for flowers. They resemble small lilies, each on its own stem. Later the foliage will appear, but flowers continue to open for two or three months if soil is allowed to dry out and then is drenched thoroughly with water.

CHAPTER XI

HOLIDAY GIFT PLANTS

Easter lilies, shamrocks, geraniums and poinsettias each belong to one special day every year. Easter and Christmas bring out more pot plants, beautifully grown to full flower or fruit, than do any of the other days of the year.

Gift plants, appropriate to the holiday or season, are a pleasant custom. Many kinds are seldom, if ever, seen except just before the special day to which they are linked. If you've wanted to add a pair of orange trees or ardisias, for example, to the indoor house-plant groupings, December is certainly the one month to do so. Although the gift plant's color may be fleeting, many of them turn out to be splendid house plants.

The Christmas gift plants, most of which display flowers in some shade of red or pink, make the richest display. They seem like a small miracle in regions where people do their Christmas shopping bundled in overcoats and furs. Easter and Mother's Day have almost as large an assortment, Thanksgiving and St. Valentine's Day a few special plants. Little pots of shamrocks fill florist-shop windows before St. Patrick's Day. So far, Father's Day is more likely to be remembered with gifts for cook-outs rather than with plants.

A week or so before any of the special occasions, appropriate plants are delivered at florist shops and other stores in every city and town. Whether it's December or May, these plants are the acme of the professional grower's skill. To bring them to this point, all of his tested knowledge of light and shade, warmth, and moisture in the air and for the soil is practiced. As a result, flowering plants are smothered with blossoms and buds, fruit plants have reached a high degree of color.

The development of holiday plants is timed so that they reach a peak a few days before the special one. Although conditions in a store are a shocking change from those in a greenhouse, and there are two trips by truck, it's rare when a holiday gift plant doesn't reach its final destination in good condition.

A gift plant often arrives bearing a tag in plain sight, telling how often to water, and what temperature and how much sun it needs. Follow any such instructions carefully.

In general, gift plants will need to be watered generously. If a saucer in which to stand the pot isn't included, find an odd one large enough. If any pebbles are left from bulb forcing, place a half-inch to an inch in the saucer. Filling the saucer with water to the level of the pebbles after the soil receives its morning allotment should keep the plant from wilting before you get around to it again in late afternoon. Water standing in the saucer increases humidity in the air too. Plants with a spongy ball of roots like those of an azalea, or large soft leaves like those of hydrangeas and poinsettias, will need more than one watering a day.

Strong sun is rarely good. Flowers will last longer and the buds on the plant will open in strong light. Avoid drafts and, if possible, temperatures above 70 degrees. A temperature range in the 60's is better for most plants, even at Christmastime.

The majority of gift plants are for years pleasant reminders of the holiday on which they were received. You may never be able to bring them quite to the peak of bloom they first displayed or to have them flower again right on time for Easter or Christmas. However, those that are permanent house plants will grow enough to require eventual shifting into a larger pot. There's no reason, either, why they shouldn't flower or fruit. The disappointment when you discovered that the flowers on an orchid plant were in small glass tubes and wired in place will be allayed in a year or two when you succeed in having the plant itself flower (see page 106).

A certain number of plants available at each of the three main holidays end up as garden plants, and, for a few of these, a future is practical in either house or garden.

Philodendron, in some one of the handsome large-leaved varieties, has become a year-round choice of gift plant from one business firm to another. These are always available. For personal gifts, African violets can be found every week, except during the summer months. Then gloxinias are available. Potted chrysanthemums, usually halfway to full bloom, are another all-year possibility.

By late January every year, primrose plants herald the upsurge of flowers. First come the large rosy ones, and by St. Valentine's Day the dainty fairy primroses are plentiful (see page 111). Some florists make an effort to have bleeding heart forced into bloom for Valentine's Day. By this time, too, professional growers are supplying tulips and other spring bulbs forced in pots. Cinerarias return before February ends.

Bulbs and bleeding heart hold their flowers only a short time indoors. If they are watered until their leaves turn yellow, they may be planted in the outdoor garden in spring.

Primroses supply about a month of color. There's no point in saving primroses and cinerarias either for bloom next winter or for the garden in summer. About two weeks is as much as cinerarias can be expected to stay colorful even in a light place with circulation of air,

CINERARIA

plenty of water and temperature between 60 and 65 degrees. Cinerarias are annuals, even in southern California gardens where they bloom in early March.

Easter pot plants are flowering ones and are the essence of spring. When Easter falls in March or early April, the selection of plants will be quite different from that for Mother's Day in May. It may seem odd, but the same kinds of plants are available in all regions of the country.

It cannot be said too often that gift plants need frequent and generous watering. The hydrangea with drooping flower clusters and wilted leaves isn't dead; it just needs water. If leaves on a rosebush turn yellow

PLANTS FOR EASTER

PLANT	FLOWER	TYPE	DESTINATION
African violet	Various colors	House plant	Indoors
Astilbe (Spiraa)	Pink to red	Perennial	Garden
Azaleas			
Indica	Various colors	Shrub	House plant; summer outdoors
Kurume	Pink	Shrub	House plant or garden
Calceolaria	Yellow, rose, red, and spotted pouches	Annual	Discard
Calla	White, yellow, pink	Perennial	Garden, or hold for indoor bloom next spring
Camellia	Pink or rose	Shrub	House plant or garden
Cineraria	Various, vivid-colored daisies	Annual	Discard
Daphne odora	Fragrant pink	Shrub	House plant, except in Southeast
Easter lily	White	Bulb	Garden
Genista	Yellow pealike	Shrub	House plant
Geranium	Various colors	Annual	Garden or house plant
Hydrangea	Blue, pink, white	Perennial shrub	Garden
Lily of the valley	White	Perennial	Garden
Marguerite	White or yellow daisies	Perennial	Garden in mild climate; house plant
Rose	Miniature, polyantha, hybrid tea	Shrub	Garden
Spring bulbs	Tulips, hyacinths, daffodils	Bulbs	Garden

PLANTS FOR MOTHER'S DAY

PLANT	FLOWER	TYPE	DESTINATION
African violet	Various colors	House plant	Indoors
Astilbe	Pink to red	Perennial shrub	Garden
Azaleas		Shrub	
Indica	Various colors		House plant; summer outdoors
Kurume	Pink		Indoors or garden
Garden varieties	Pink, red, white		Garden
Caladium	Vari-colored foliage	Bulb	Colorful all summer, indoors or out
Daphne cneorum	Fragrant, small, pink	Shrub	Garden
Fuchsia	Various colors	Shrub	House plant; summer outdoors
Gardenia	White	Shrub	House plant, except in Southeast
Geraniums			
Zonal	Various colors	Annual	Garden, or house plant
Martha Washington	Various and showy	Perennial	Garden
Gloxinia	Various colors	Bulb	House plant
Hydrangea	Pink, blue, white	Shrub	Garden
Lily of the valley	White	Perennial	Garden
Rose	Hybrid teas	Shrub	Garden
Begonias			
Tuberous	Various colors	Bulb	Outdoors in shelter and shade
Wax	White, shades of pink, red	Perennial	Garden for summer; house plant

and drop and small buds fail to open, don't worry too much, and don't throw it away. If it is planted outdoors as soon as possible, new leaves will appear.

It's important to keep watering the pots of bulbs until their leaves mature, if you plan to plant them in the garden. By all means, transplant the Easter lily from its pot directly into the outdoor garden. If possible, choose a location where shallow-rooted annuals or other plants grow over its root run and shade it. The Easter lily, more often than not, provides a pleasant surprise by flowering again outdoors in August or September.

Small camellia bushes in bud or flower are often sold north of Washington, D.C. In the area of severe winters, they are house plants. But they are fine on shaded terraces or porches in summer. Camellias grow slowly.

Whether Easter and Mother's Day plants are destined for permanent contributions to the garden or, as house plants, will only spend the summer there, wait until all danger of frost is past before moving them outdoors. And for the house plants, start the fall trip back indoors soon after Labor Day so they won't be nipped by an early autumn frost.

Genista, without which it wouldn't seem like Easter, is seen no other time of year. This shrubby plant is one of the brooms, and has many hardy relatives for gardens everywhere, including the North. The florists' genista, Cytisus canariensis or C. racemosus, comes from the Canary Islands and is a Mediterranean type of plant, accustomed to alternating dry and wet seasons. Gray-green leaves are enhanced with delicately scented, pea-like yellow blossoms.

Genista is quite sizable even grown in a pot. If it becomes too large, cut it back after flowering or before it's moved to the garden for the summer. It needs plenty of water during its flowering season. As a pot plant, it does best in a sandy, rather poor and acid soil. Indoors, from fall through spring, the location must be sunny, airy and cool (55 to 60 degrees is best, if it is to flower again).

It wouldn't be Thanksgiving without chrysanthemums, in pots or as cut flowers. 'Mums probably will always be associated with fall and Thanksgiving, although they can be purchased now every month of the year.

In a reasonably cool and light place, and with plenty of water, potted chrysanthemums last well. After flower-

CALADIUM

ing, cut back the stems. These plants won't bloom again indoors without special treatment, so if there's no garden in which to transplant them eventually, discard them. If there is a garden, store plants in a coldframe or in a cool, but not freezing, dim place until spring.

By Thanksgiving, it should be possible to obtain pre-cooled lily of the valley pips to start for Christmas bloom. Paperwhite narcissus and French-Roman hya-cinths planted in pebbles and water early in November will be almost ready for the move from dark to light in order to bloom for the holidays.

Old favorites and some new ones appear every De-cember in appropriate colors for the end-of-the-year holidays. Most of the flowering plants have white or red blossoms, although the clear shades of rose and pink,

PLANTS FOR CHRISTMAS

PLANT	FLOWER	TYPE	DESTINATION
Ardisia	Red berries	House plant	Indoors, except in warm climate
Azaleas		Shrub	
Indica	Various colors		Indoors
Kurume	Pink		Indoors or garden
Christmas begonia	Various colors	Bulb	Discard
Christmas cactus	Cerise, red	Succulent	House plant
Chrysanthemum	Various colors	Perennial	Garden
Citrus			
Orange	Small oranges	Shrub	House plant
Lemon	Large lemons	Shrub	House plant
Cyclamen	White, shades of red, pink	Bulb	Discard
Heather	White	Shrub	Discard
Holly		Shrub	Garden
Jerusalem cherry	Red fruit	Shrub	House plant
Kalanchoe	Scarlet	Succulent	House plant
Lily of the valley	White	Perennial	Garden
Orchid	Various colors	Perennial	House plant
Pepper	Red, green, yellow fruits	Annual	House plant
Poinsettia	Red, pink, white	Shrub	House plant, except in Southeast, Southwest
Pyracantha	Scarlet fruit	Shrub	House plant or garden

and even some yellow or gold ones aren't ostracized. December is the month for plants with decorative fruits, which are among the easiest of permanent house plants to grow.

To the list can be added amaryllis bulbs, potted and perhaps with flower bud showing, and lily of the valley pips planted for forcing. Both can be set in any light place to flower.

In December and January, plants will need plenty of moisture to look their best as long as possible. Too much heat can shorten their lives drastically. A draft coupled with a cool location is equally disastrous. How long holiday gift plants remain colorful depends on conditions and care.

The little holly trees, sold in 3- to 5-inch pots for Christmas gifts, had better go into a coldframe as soon as possible. Otherwise, find a light location with temperature between 40 and 45 degrees until they can be transplanted outdoors. All holly trees lose their leaves in early spring and these small ones may do so ahead of schedule.

As for the flowering plants, most people manage to keep poinsettias bright until some time in January, although a few leaves probably yellowed and fell right away. I've heard of poinsettias flowering until early March, but this is exceptional. Three months of bloom is possible for cyclamen; several weeks for Christmas begonias, azaleas and kalanchoes. Heather with its tiny leaves and little white blossoms may last two weeks or longer. Everyone wants as many of the buds as possible to open on any gift plant.

For this to occur on Christmas begonias involves a problem of humidity. The air around this type of begonia must average 50 per cent humidity at a minimum. A mist spray of water is a less desirable means to this end than a saucer filled with pebbles and water under the pot, and additional containers, from which water

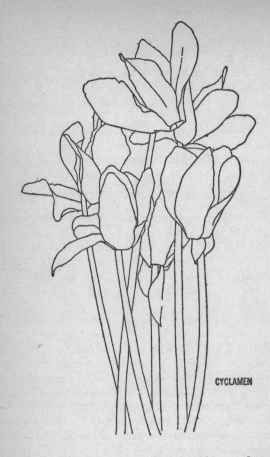

CYCLAMEN

will evaporate, in the vicinity. Soil should never dry out. Keep it wet, but short of being soggy. Maximum daytime temperature is 70 degrees, nighttime 50 degrees. Every day, a little sun and fresh air without a draft will help.

Cyclamen are grown and brought into flower in a

cool greenhouse. Undoubtedly, many more small pointed buds could push up above the leaves to open. Buds will be encouraged by the light or winter sun from an east or north window. A cool, even temperature, little higher than 60 degrees, is essential. Plenty of water will be absorbed, but don't keep the saucer constantly full, for this leads to soggy soil. Whenever a flower withers, or a leaf turns yellow, tug at the stem to pull it out from the base of the plant. Stems are soft and limp and can start rot.

Cool temperature for cyclamen, high humidity for Christmas begonias are the keys to bloom after the holidays. House-plant addicts have been known to hold over the plants and bring them into bloom another winter. This takes a lot of fussing, and results are so uncertain that it seems to me more sensible to discard and add fresh plants to next year's Christmas list.

The poinsettia is quite another story. Florists start a new crop of plants every spring. At home, the Christmas gift poinsettia can be carried from one year to the next and brought into bloom every winter, if not always by December 25th. The red, pink or white "flowers" on poinsettias are bracts. The true flowers are inconspicuous, for they are the clusters of little knobs, surrounded by the bracts.

Each cluster of bracts and flowers is carefully wrapped in tissue paper and the whole plant is bundled up for protection against cold during delivery. However, the professional grower brought the poinsettia to peak display in daytime temperatures of about 60 degrees, nighttime 55 degrees. If the gift poinsettia can be kept where temperatures average 65 degrees, that's fine. Moderate light will suffice, but sun becomes necessary if temperatures go as high as 70 degrees. With inadequate light, poinsettias drop their leaves and bracts promptly. The same thing happens immediately after a sudden temperature change or a draft. Ample watering is essential.

As leaves and bracts wither in January or February, reduce watering. When nothing but bare stems remain, move it to a cool dark place to rest until spring. In May, when it's safe to move a poinsettia outdoors, cut back the stem to three or four inches and repot the plant in a rich soil mixture. Water, of course.

The best location outdoors all summer is one in light shade. Sink the pot in the ground up to its rim and never let it suffer from lack of water during this new growing period. By late August, the plant will look quite luxuriant with all its new growth. This is the time to prune. Reduce each stem by at least one-third of its length. This pruning is indispensable to winter bloom.

Indoors again, even warmth maintains steady growth (65 to 70 degrees daytime, 60 degrees minimum at night). Some sun, some humidity and regular watering of the soil are essential. By November 1, start to fertilize and repeat once every two weeks until bracts are noticeable.

No plant is more Christmasy than poinsettia. In its native Mexico and Central America as well as along the Gulf Coast, from Florida to Charleston, S.C., and in southern California and the Southwest, poinsettias are outdoor shrubs ten feet or more tall. Flower of the Incas and Mexican fire plant are common names in tropical America. In Mexico, *flor de pascuas*, flower of Christmas, pinpoints it more exactly. Poinsettia is a name coined in the United States to honor Joel R. Poinsett of Charleston, S.C., who was so taken with the plant while he was on a diplomatic mission to Mexico in the nineteenth century that he introduced it to this country.

CHAPTER XII

COLOR FROM FRUIT

Every once in a while, a Chinese evergreen or a sansevieria sends out a comparatively unimportant blossom, or a flowering plant such as malpighia forms a tiny fruit. A spike tipped with round, berrylike seedpods is striking on a schismatoglottis, which is grown as a foliage plant and has such inconspicuous bloom that it probably wasn't noticed. The unexpected flower or fruit is not the reason why these particular plants were chosen for the house.

Colorful, decorative fruits ranging in size from currants to small oranges and large lemons are the reason for selecting a few plants. Most of the fruits aren't for eating. All of them do make a wonderfully long and cheerful display from late fall through winter.

Sometimes I've wondered if the red berries of ardisia, which is a staple of the Christmas season, would fall off before tiny white blossoms opened in June. By April, or certainly by May, most people want to move otaheite orange to a less important place, because they have become tired of its glowing balls.

Fruit plants are the perfect means of adding color to a planter box or a grouping of foliage plants. Once they have flowered and set fruits, and the fruits have taken on color, these plants get along beautifully in direct light. Intense light is no more essential for the plants with conspicuous decorative fruits than it is for the leafy green ones. Furthermore, the fruiting plants require little care except watering during this gay season.

Watering soil from the top of the pot will be needed every day. In addition, soak the soil thoroughly once a week. This will not be as easy to do with plants in tubs as with those in pots, which can be set in a large container of water until moisture shows on the surface of the soil.

Every one of the fruiting plants is capable of being an important accent. Several pots of Jerusalem cherries or ornamental peppers are often massed to make a stronger impact of color. The treelike ones such as ardisia and the small citrus fruits are distinctly specimens and should be placed to display their symmetry.

On the whole, the decorative fruit plants are slow-growing. But those that are as long-lived as many human beings are will eventually require either a big, deep pot or a tub.

This is never the case with bromeliads, and some of them have spikes or clusters of fruit that are as colorful and long-lasting as their odd flowers. Most notable in this respect are some of the aechmeas. The long-stemmed arching spray of white berries that turn blue on Aechmea angustifolia is surely one of the handsomest. By early spring, blue berries have replaced the inflorescence of A. filicaulis, and orange-brown berries that of A. maginali. Other aechmeas have equally gay stalks of fruit.

ARDISIA CRISPA or CRENULATA is aptly nicknamed coral berry. The fruits, a coral red, are about the size of currants and cluster thickly just under the crown of narrow dark green leaves. The crown of leaves is quite round and tops a slender, bark-covered stem. It's customary before Christmas to sell an ardisia with a perky bow of scarlet ribbon stuck in the foliage to repeat the color of the berries.

Some of the berries will still be clinging under the foliage in June, when tiny flowers open. New leaf and stem growth also should be apparent. The flowers are a signal to start feeding. Once a month should be often enough until the new crop of berries has reddened.

Ardisia and all other woody-stemmed fruiting plants can be moved outdoors to terrace, porch or garden in summer. A partly shaded location is preferable. Before an ardisia is brought back indoors, some trimming of the top may be desirable. Other fruiting plants may need some trimming or shaping. Indoors or outdoors, watch out for scale insects and eradicate with spray at once.

BANANAS are a distinct possibility if there's room for the broad tall leaves. These, and its lush growth, are sure clues to its tropical origin. The dwarf banana (Musa Cavendishii) is less susceptible to cool spells and is grown in gardens along the Gulf Coast, in the warm Southwest and in Bermuda. Indoors, in a large pot or tub, the plant will grow four to six feet tall. Leaves are one to two feet broad. In summer, the banana plant can be moved outdoors, but only to a place where it will not be exposed to wind, which can rip leaves to tatters.

Banana plants grow in a manner that always makes me think of corn. The leaf stems sheath the trunk, and sucker growth springs from the base. The terminal flower spike appears from the leafy sheaths.

The dwarf one (M. Cavendishii) produces the lady-finger bananas, each one about four inches long. Preceding the fruit is a short, drooping flower spike, the blossoms hidden by showy red-brown bracts. If you're in the market for a banana plant, insist on this species, or Musa velutina with pink bracts and fruit, and do not get the small-fruited forms of the tall, common banana.

The red banana (M. coccinea) is grown as much for the flowers as for the fruit. The inflorescence is not less than a foot long, with yellow-tipped red bracts encasing yellow flowers. This variety is said to mature, or bloom, when it is about five feet tall.

Bananas need the largest-size pots or tubs, not only because they are such big leafy plants but also because they must grow in deep, rich soil. About half-and-half garden loam and leafmold or humus is good. Soil should be loose and porous for good drainage. Plenty of moisture is needed at all times.

Sun is desirable indoors, but should be filtered or dappled outdoors. A warm location where temperatures are never less than 70 degrees is best. Humidity in the air is beneficial. Before a banana plant is moved back into the house in September, cut off any torn leaves at the base.

CARISSA GRANDIFLORA TUTTLEI is better known as Natal plum. Both this one and the variety Boxwood Beauty are evergreen, low-growing (a foot tall, or a little more) and branching. The first named is more spreading and its stems have spines.

White, star-shaped flowers are good size and stand out against the glossy dark green leaves. Flowers are fragrant, and the scarlet fruits, an inch or so long, not only look like plums but are edible. They can be used for jelly, if you can bear to pick them from a house plant.

Moderate temperature (65–70 degrees), some sun and good light the rest of the time, fresh air and regular watering are routine for placement and care. By all means move a Natal plum outdoors for summer. In the South it's often planted for a low hedge.

CITRUS trees—if a plant eighteen inches to three or perhaps four feet tall can be called a tree—produce as fragrant flowers when they are pot- or tub-size as they do in orange groves of the Southeast or Southwest. Huge lemons as well as normal-size ones, kumquats and calamondins are as tasty as those grown outdoors in warm climate. The dwarf or otaheite orange (C. taitensis) has insipid pulp and tart juice inside its small golden fruits. All are ornamental, slow-growing and long-lived, broad-leaved evergreens.

Otaheite oranges decked with a bow in addition to a few fruits are offered as Christmas gift plants in the Northeast. These fruits hang on for months. Waxy white

DWARF ORANGE   DWARF LEMON

blossoms tinged with pink open in late spring or early summer, and by early winter new oranges are turning color.

Meyer's lemon is a dwarf tree that produces medium-sized fruits. It is practically everbearing. White to lavender blossoms are fragrant. The Ponderosa lemon is always a conversation piece because of its enormous yellow fruits, so heavy that they pull down the branches. They are juicy and edible.

Lemon trees, however small, are spiny, much more so than the otaheite orange or the calamondin (C. mitis). Calamondins are bushier plants than the orange or either of the lemons. Fragrant flowers are followed by small bright orange fruits flattened at the end. If you decide to sample a calamondin fruit, you will find it has thin, loose skin which is easy to pull off. The calamondin's segments are quite acid, but the juice is frequently used.

Kumquats, which grow as evergreen shrubs in the South, are closely related to the citrus fruits. The botanical name Fortunella honors Robert Fortune, English plant hunter who introduced this fruit and plant from China in 1846. The tiny white flowers are sweet-smelling. They open in summer, and the small, bright orange-colored, aromatic fruits ripen in early winter. Catalogues describe kumquats as "dwarf, bushy plants," and mine has never grown more than twelve to fifteen inches high.

The small citrus trees will be the healthier if grown in cool temperatures. Daytime temperatures of 50 to 65 degrees are ideal, and nighttime temperatures should be about the same. Sun part of the day, or filtered sun if plants are near south windows, is needed from spring on into fall. Spring is the flowering season. After the fruit colors, light—not sunlight—will be satisfactory. Don't overwater these little citrus trees. Soak the soil thoroughly each time, but let it get almost dry between waterings.

When plants become potbound and must be shifted into a container one size larger, a mixture of good garden soil to which some humus, leafmold or compost has been added is a safe formula. Citrus trees, unfortunately, are not strangers to scale insects and white fly. This is all the more reason for a weekly hosing of the foliage. Control or eradicate insects by means of chemicals. A thorough spraying of foliage with water once a week is good for all fruit plants.

JERUSALEM CHERRY and ORNAMENTAL PEPPERS, or Christmas cherry and Christmas peppers, aren't good to eat, although they are closely related to the potato. They are the most common, least expensive and most heavily loaded fruit plants in December. The Christmas

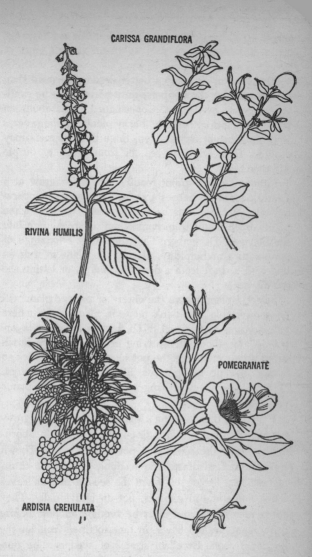

CARISSA GRANDIFLORA

RIVINA HUMILIS

POMEGRANATE

ARDISIA CRENULATA

rry is a dwarf, compact, bushy plant with scarlet fruits of edible-cherry size, so plentiful as almost to cover the dull, dark green leaves.

"Ornamental" is really a better descriptive word than "Christmas" for the peppers, since plants may be available as early as August. Cone-shaped fruits about an inch long stand up from the bushy plants. In the process of turning bright or dark red, these little peppers may progress from white to red, or from green to purple and then red.

Although seeds sprout readily and plants grow at a steady pace, the cherries and peppers can be temperamental. That is, fruits have a tendency to drop when plants are brought from florist shop or greenhouse into the house in December. The cause may be change of temperature or humidity, placing the plant so it is on line with a draft from a door or window, or letting the soil dry out.

Select a place where the cherry or pepper plant will be comfortable and don't move it. Cool rooms where temperatures average 60 to 65 degrees are most favorable. Daily, thorough watering of the soil is essential. In addition, submerge the pot in water once a week so it can soak up all it needs. Strong light is sufficient. With luck, fruits will hang on the bushy little plants until February.

Far easier than keeping a plant looking well, is growing one from seed. Take a ripe-looking cherry in February and sow the seeds in a pot of sandy soil. They'll sprout amazingly fast. The seedlings should be transplanted in a flat of soil when the second pair of leaves show. Sometime in summer, pot up individually. They are tender plants and must be brought indoors before frost. Plants should flower in time to ripen fruit for the holiday season. Excellent strains of seed can be purchased from many seed houses. Ornamental peppers need not be sown until between April and June for gay plants in December.

POMEGRANATE is a splendid house plant. Hunt for the dwarf forms of the tall shrubs that are at home in southern gardens, east and west. Punica granatum nana is the dwarf pomegranate. Leaves are shining green and rather fine. Since the shrub is a semi-evergreen, all the leaves won't fall at one time unless exposed to cold winter temperature. Small, single, scarlet flowers open in summer and are less important than the fruit, which ripens in fall and early winter. Burnt orange to red suffuses these round fruits.

Chico is a new variety said to have flowers resembling small bright red carnations. I haven't tried this yet, and since my information makes no mention of fruit, I presume it must flower later than the dwarf pomegranate. Chico grows little more than six inches tall, the dwarf pomegranate about a foot. Both are bushy.

Prune pomegranates in late winter or early spring while they are dormant. Flowers are formed on new wood. Pomegranates aren't fussy about soil, exposure or humidity. I would compromise on part sun.

PYRACANTHA, the firethorn of gardens, is fast becoming a popular holiday plant. Dwarf varieties loaded with clusters of red or scarlet berries appear in December. Since the gift plants are dwarf, they probably should be maintained as house plants and spend only the summer in the garden.

Outdoor varieties are evergreen in mild climate, semi-evergreen north of the latitude of Washington, D.C. and Kansas City, above which all old leaves fall off in spring before new ones appear. Clusters of dainty white flowers in May precede the green berries, which turn red in early autumn.

As a house plant a cool location is desirable. So is regular and generous watering, as well as spraying foliage clean once a week. Prune when necessary, but only enough to keep within bounds and shapely.

RIVINA HUMILIS goes by the name rouge plant or blood berry. The bushy plants, with a maximum height of three feet in greenhouses, are both interesting and undemanding in a room of the average house. Leaves are softer and thinner than those of most of the fruiting plants. A long slender cluster of white flowers, sometimes tinged with pink, gives way to soft and richly red berries.

Rivina grows, flowers and fruits in moderate temperatures. Heat up to 70 degrees should be satisfactory by day; not less than 55 degrees at night. It will need daily watering. Bright light is sufficient; sun is not essential.

STRAWBERRIES, the little Alpine kind that can be grown from seed, are something I intend to try indoors some winter. Variety Baron Solemacher produces bushy plants about six inches high and wide from seed sown in spring. Plants are flowering about ten weeks after seed sprouts. The small pointed red berries are edible, if rather dry. I think, however, that I shall dig up established plants of Baron Solemacher from the outdoor border and plant one to each pocket of a small strawberry jar. It seems that these are worth a trial at least, in an east or a west window with moderate temperature and regular watering.

Seeds of orange, grapefruit and dates can be saved from these fruits that are bought for eating during winter, soaked overnight in a cup of water and planted in pots of soil. They sprout and grow with reasonable promptness, to form little green thickets about four inches tall.

Of course, seedlings can be separated and some planted individually in pots. They grow slowly, but the orange and grapefruit ones eventually become specimen plants of good size. Sometimes these specimens do a bit of flowering, but fruit is seldom set. It takes special varieties and grafting to insure edible fruit.

Planting these seeds, then, can be fun for youngsters, if not particularly rewarding for adults. The little plants provide a patch of green, need no special care and probably thrive even if neglected.

CHAPTER XIII

CACTI AND SUCCULENTS

Crown of thorns, which displays pairs of scarlet blossoms against a background of thorns, isn't a cactus. It is a succulent plant. The Christmas cactus with cerise flowers hanging from the tip of every stem doesn't have spines but it is a true cactus.

Cacti and succulents are splendid house plants on many scores. Spines aren't a true indication of one or the other. Because they are xerophytic plants, they do not suffer in rooms where temperature is always 70 degrees or higher and where the air is dry, for xerophytic plants are native to arid regions and, in order to exist for months without rainfall, have developed a structure in which they can store moisture.

The day-to-day and week-to-week care of cacti and succulents is minimal. The chief danger is overwatering. There are no problems such as supplying humidity to the air or finding a cool enough location so flower buds won't blast. They are ideal plants for warm, sunless apartments and also can be used effectively in a house.

Cacti and succulents fascinate many people because of their unusual shapes and forms. Starfish, sand dollar, star, prickly pincushion, fishbone, barrel, stone are fitting descriptions. The stone plants (lithops) do look like small rocks—until they flower. Because an array of small plants is available in these two classifications, never think that they just vegetate on a sunny window sill. They will grow larger, and many kinds will bloom.

Flowers appear in winter and are always exciting. The blossom may be little larger than a pinhead, or it may be the size of an orchid. It may be as delicately tinted as arbutus, or as vivid as a rainbow. Most of them flower by day, but some are night-blooming, the cereus being the most famous of these.

Because so many are small, one window can house a sizable collection. To the collector, acquiring these little plants is like eating peanuts. If there's already a rosary or heart vine (a succulent), then a burro's tail is next on the list. Or, if there's a pincushion cactus, then the larger hedgehog cactus must keep it company.

All cacti are succulents, but not all succulents are cacti. Spines occur on both cacti and succulents, but not on all of them. In fact, the succulent plants come from many families and from many places. Poinsettia is a succulent. So are kalanchoe that blooms scarlet at Christmastime, sansevieria or snake plant, rosary or heart vine, aloe, jade plant, a crassula that looks like a centuries-old tree even in a pot, and bryophyllum that is a weed in southern Florida fields.

Many more kinds of cacti and succulents grow outdoors than indoors. High mountains as well as deserts are their homes. The key to their classification, from a grower's standpoint, is their xerophytic character.

Many of the small succulents are splendid for dish gardens. Echeverias, sedums and kleinias offer exquisite shadings of color even if they never bloom. Small cacti also can be combined so that the dish garden represents a desert scene in miniature.

Cacti and succulents will flower in dish gardens as well as in individual pots. To have poinsettia, kalanchoe, Christmas and Easter cacti, and epiphyllums bloom is only a matter of understanding the plants' cycle of growth. But the blossoming of a small cactus or an unusual succulent is cause for wonderment.

Many true cacti will flower indoors, even in apartments in eastern cities. Before bloom can occur, the plant must have grown to flowering size. Miniature cacti, such as some of the mammillarias (pincushion and fishhook cacti), notocactus, rebutias and gymnocalycium, flower when they are no more than one inch tall. The larger-growing echinopsis (hedgehog cacti), cereus and cleistocactus will reach flowering size in a four-inch pot if they are rootbound.

Once these plants have reached flowering size, they must have a dormant, dry period every winter. During this two to three months, never water them. Sometime in March, syringe the plant to remove dust and soak the pots in water. This should start growth and bloom, and then normal watering is resumed.

Cacti and succulents may be grown in individual pots in preference to dish-garden groupings. Most cacti fit a 2-inch pot, and few succulents grow too large for a 4-inch pot. Select a clay or a glazed pot a little larger than the plant's circumference, including the spines.

For the sake of your fingers, handle plants with tweezers or tongs. Another indispensable tool is a rubber syringe for watering.

Whether these small plants are to grow in pots or dish gardens, good drainage is a must. An inch or more of broken crock, pebbles or stone chips over the bottom will help to drain away excess water. Recommendations on soil differ. One collector will recommend half garden soil and half gravel, plus a tablespoon each of crushed charcoal and hydrated lime or crushed eggshells. Another expert settles for coarse or builder's sand and screened leafmold or humus, half and half, mixed until the mass is all one color. Still another suggests one part garden soil, one part leafmold, one part coarse sand, plus a little charcoal and lime. Almost everyone agrees that the surface of the soil should be covered with gravel or coarse material.

To plant, fill the pot or other container to within an inch of its rim. Then make a cone-shaped depression in which to set the plant, picked up by tweezers, and fill in around it with sand. If cacti are being transplanted, always cut back the roots. Repotting should be needed not oftener than every two or three years, or possibly longer.

After potting, plants should be watered sparingly for ten days to two weeks. For the same length of time, a shaded or poorly lighted location is needed.

After this period of adjustment, sun or bright light is the preferred location, according to the kind of plant. Believe it or not, some cacti and many succulents can be sunburned if they stand too close to the glass of a sunny window. Elongated or abnormal growth is a sign that cacti and succulents aren't receiving enough sun or light, or are being watered too much.

The amount of water and the frequency of watering vary with the amount of light or sun. A potted plant dries out faster than those in a dish garden. Small cacti in individual pots need a little water every few days if soil has dried out. They can be watered with a syringe. Use the syringe sparingly for dish gardens that lack drainage holes.

Overwatering any month of the year is the surest way to kill cacti and succulents. Underwater rather than overwater, even during spring and summer, the active seasons of growth.

Fertilizing is not recommended for cacti and most

succulents. For the majority, there's nothing to be gained by trying to force them. They'll flower when they're mature. If they're fertilized or forced too much, they become subject to disease—and that's not typical behavior.

Fresh air, but not with an accompanying draft, helps to keep plants growing and healthy.

In spite of sun or bright light and fresh air, pests may appear. Pick off the white mealy bugs or darker scale insects with tweezers or a cotton-tipped toothpick dipped in denatured alcohol. For aphids, mites or red spiders, syringe the plants with water at room temperature or cautiously apply a diluted oil spray. Remove any infected plant to an isolated spot until it appears to be pest-free again, or so incurable that it had better be discarded.

Cacti

CEREUS is a common house plant, not attractive to look at in daylight but cherished for its flowers that open in the evening. Summer is the season of bloom. A bud starts to open early in the evening. For three hours or so, it's possible to watch the enormous flower open petal by petal. Then a sweet and rather heavy fragrance fills the air.

Cereus has a larger root system than do most cacti and so requires a large pot, and eventually a tub. As the plant grows, its stems will need support. Indoors in winter and outdoors in summer, scant watering in winter, regular watering in summer make up its schedule.

ECHINOCACTUS is familiarly known as barrel cactus. This group includes notocactus (ball) and gymnocalycium (chin cactus), recommended as house plants. The chaplet cactus with a garland of ivory-white blossoms is a choice gymnocalycium. Sand dollar (Astrophytum asterias) is a spineless, flattened echinocactus.

Barrel cacti, full grown, range from the size of marbles to plants eight feet tall and two feet in diameter in the Arizona desert. All are slow-growing. Plants mostly are ridged and thickly covered with spines. Flowers open wide to display several rows of satiny petals, which may be yellow, orange or some shade of red.

EPIPHYLLUM, or orchid cactus, comes not from the desert but from tropical forests and jungles. Anyone anywhere can grow an orchid cactus. In southern California, plants are grown in lath houses; small ones in hanging baskets; others, that reach three to eight feet tall, in pots or tubs with trellises to which plants are trained and tied. Elsewhere, grow epiphyllums on the sun porch, or in the basement, greenhouse or any room in the house where it won't be too prominent for about ten months of the year.

These are plain, practically ugly plants, except when the magnificent flowers open. Bloom starts in March, is heaviest in April and May, and peters out in June. The blossoms appear along the notched edges of the phylloclades or fronds which serve as stem and leaves and likely will branch. The center of the phylloclade is stiff, and the surrounding succulent portions store food. There are small-flowering varieties with blooms three inches in diameter. On larger varieties, a six-inch flower is ordinary, and some are twelve to fifteen inches in diameter. Colors are luscious pastels and brilliant salmon, orange, copper or red, from vermilion to maroon. Two or three shades may blend in one of the satiny, shining flowers. Incidentally, orchid cacti make good cut flowers.

Take care of an orchid cactus and it will grow and bloom resplendently. It needs a rich, humus soil and plenty of moisture. During the flowering season, water

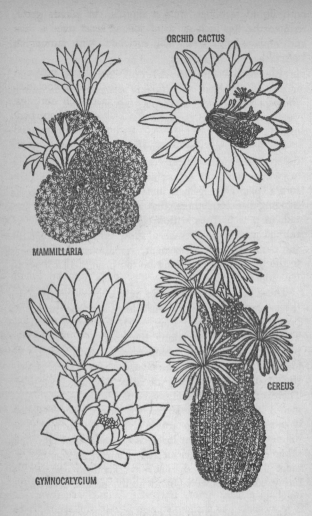

ORCHID CACTUS

MAMMILLARIA

GYMNOCALYCIUM

CEREUS

with liquid fertilizer once a month. As plants grow, remove the top inch or so of soil at least once a year and replace with fresh soil enriched with humus or leafmold.

Additional plants are easily grown from cuttings, which are six- to twelve-inch lengths of phylloclades. The first epiphyllums I grew were just such cuttings, wrapped in newspaper and carried about, undisturbed, in a suitcase for six weeks. By the time they had traveled from California to Connecticut a callus had formed over each cut, and the cuttings could be planted in pots of rich soil.

Full sun is not essential to bloom. Strong light or part sun is sufficient. Ventilate for fresh air.

MAMMILLARIAS are the pincushion cacti, which are easy to grow and include many not difficult to bring to flower. They have spines, and sometimes silky or silvery hair. Plants are round or columnar, and have a tendency to cluster together as they increase in number. Small smooth red fruits may form as the last of the flowers open. Powder Puff and Hummel's Powder Puff, an improved variety of M. bocasana, have white hair covering clustered globes. M. hahniana has violet-red flowers.

Closely related to the Mammillarias is a group called Coryphantha. They have larger flowers but more roots, and therefore need larger pots than do the little pincushions.

OPUNTIA, the prickly pear, isn't confined to deserts of the Southwest. It also grows in sandy stretches along the East Coast as far north as Long Island, and there are varieties hardy in Wisconsin, Wyoming and Canada.

Flat, thick, round or oval joints make up the stems, which frequently branch. Most varieties have spines on the flat surfaces. Some have hair. Plants are dwarf or tall, according to variety. Bunny Ears is the appropriate name of one variety, Angel Wings and Beaver Tail of others. I have never seen an opuntia flowering in the house. When they do bloom, flowers are lovely, and are followed by good-sized "prickly pear" fruits that turn red.

REBUTIA, the crown cactus, is one of the quickest and easiest to bring to flower in the house. On a mature plant, six or more blossoms may be open at one time. Shades of red, pink, orange and yellow offer a wide choice. Sun is necessary for this cactus.

RHIPSALIS is often called the mistletoe cactus because its small flowers are followed by white or colored berries. These are said to flower freely. Stems branch, and may be cylindrical, flat or angled, according to species. Since they droop, a hanging container is the best way to display them. Most of those in commerce lack spines.

CHRISTMAS CACTUS or crab's claw (Zygocactus) and EASTER CACTUS (Schlumbergera) are old favorites. They flower freely, the first in December or January, and the second in April. The latter should not be confused with Easter Lily cactus, small barrel-shaped plants with spines that open lilylike flowers in sun.

Tiny Christmas cactus plants with only half a dozen joints may be tipped with pendulous rosy-red blossoms if the right schedule is followed. New hybrids add new colors and earlier flowering. Thanksgiving cactus (Salmoneus) has scarlet or salmon-red flowers in November. Orange Glory, also early blooming, has large flowers of orange red. Amelia Manda has pale crimson blossoms; South Orange deeper crimson ones. There also are pink and violet-red varieties.

Christmas cactus trails as it becomes a large plant. Sometimes it is grafted to another upright stem so that there is a crown of blossoms. Easter cactus is a more upright and bushy plant. If possible, the large red or pink flowers are produced more freely than on Christmas cactus. There are several varieties of Easter cactus. Neither type has spines.

The trick in having Christmas cactus flower sometime

near the appropriate day is to enforce a dormant, dry period. Watering should be stopped in late September and not renewed until November, except for a light sprinkling about once every ten days to prevent roots from drying out. Resume watering little by little in November, and move the plant into more light or possibly into sun. Fertilizing is in order when new growth starts. Reduce watering gradually after flowers fade.

Succulents

So many succulents are easy to grow. An enormous number of plants are rightly called succulents, and sometimes it seems that the number of species and varieties that can be grown indoors is infinite. Many of these are ordinary, so an indoor gardener must become acquainted gradually with succulents in order to find out which ones will become favorites.

The differences are amazing. Consider crown of thorns (Euphorbia splendens) and poinsettia (Euphorbia pulcherrima). Color is the only thing the two plants have in common—red bracts on poinsettias and scarlet blossoms (true flowers) on crown of thorns. Euphorbia lactea, candelabra plant, doesn't even have the red flowers.

Crown of thorns is long-lived and undemanding. It flowers almost constantly, and the thorny stems are also dotted with small, soft green leaves. It grows slowly, but plants ten years or more old are often trained in circles or globes on coathangers or other wire supports. Euphorbia splendens bojeri, a dwarf variety, is often called "little crown of thorns." Euphorbia keysii is a new hybrid with bright coral-pink flowers in winter and spring—truly a lovely plant. Large red flower clusters and leaves are displayed by Hummel's Giant Christ Thorn.

The CRASSULA family offers even greater diversity.

Distinctly fun is bryophyllum, translated as "sprouting leaf." Bring home a leaf from Florida or break one from a plant indoors, fasten it to a window frame with a thumbtack and soon tiny plants are forming in the

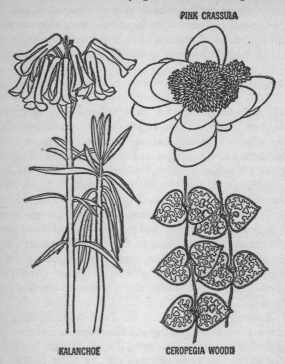

PINK CRASSULA

KALANCHOE   CEROPEGIA WOODII

scallops around the edges. When they are large enough to handle, they can be cut off and potted individually.

Other names for bryophyllum are air plant, life plant and floppers. Still another air plant is Kalanchoe tubiflora which grows quite tall, is topped with red blossoms and has spotted green leaves from whose tips plantlets sprout. Some other kalanchoes have the same habit.

The Christmas kalanchoes are hybrids of K. bloss-feldiana, prized for their clusters of small scarlet blossoms in winter. They are easy to bring into flower in succeeding winters, if a person remembers to feed in spring and enforce a dry, dormant period in fall.

Panda plant (K. tomentosa) has thick white wool covering its leaves, which are brown at the edges. Often listed as a kalanchoe is kitchingia, which comes from Madagascar. Kalanchoe beharensis, which also comes from Madagascar, is frequently labeled Kitchingia mandrakensis. This one has the largest leaves of all kalanchoes. They are usually rusty brown, and are thick and firm, with a plush texture. This plant, easy to grow to a height of eighteen inches or a little more in a pot, and to increase from leaf cuttings, is valued for flower arrangements.

If the only plant you've ever identified as a Crassula is the jade tree (C. argentea), with its crown of branches bearing small, glossy, succulent green leaves, there are many pleasant surprises in store for you. Among the Crassulas, one is called Hummel's Sunset, whose green leaves are edged with orange to red (rich coloring does not occur in full sun). Morgan's Pink crassula is a little plant with brushlike rose-pink blossoms topping the center; C. Schmidtii, another small plant, has rosy-red flowers.

Sedum, Sempervivum and Echeveria are other genera in the Crassula family. Echeverias form leaf rosettes with subtle tints and shades of color. Some leaves are further enhanced with a delicate silvery "bloom." Flowers are an added attraction.

The echeverias include a variety E. pulvinata, which is known as chenille plant (see page 80). Plushy leaves are edged with crimson, and the flower spikes display orange-red hues. Mexican snowball is the common name for E. elegans, whose rosettes of leaves are glaucous-blue to white. Blossoms are coral-rose. Mexican firecracker (E. setosa), naturally, has red and yellow flowers topping its rosettes of green leaves covered with silky hairs. A dozen or more echeverias are worth growing in the house and every one is a charmer.

Sedums and sempervivums have a good many varieties that are hardy outdoors in the northern states. By all means, select unusual non-hardy ones, such as Burro's Tail (Sedum morganianum) and Hummel's Golden (a variety of S. adolphi) for the house.

Succulents that belong to the Lily family include for the house stiff-leaved sansevieria, the aloes and haworthias with stiff basal rosettes of leaves, and the tongue-leaved gasterias. All four are noted for unusual mottling or marking of the leaves. Aloes in particular have worthwhile bloom. From the Milkweed family come the Starfish or Star Flowers (Stapelias), most curious plants, and Ceropegia, rosary vine, hearts-on-a-string, umbrella flower or sweetheart vine. The Amaryllis family contributes the Agaves with tough, odd leaves arranged symmetrically.

Sansevieria doesn't always have tall green leaves mottled cream or white and striped with darker green. Neither is it always called snake plant. Bow-string hemp, zebra plant, leopard lily, mother-in-law's tongue, lucky plant are other common names and if anyone isn't aware that it has earned the name cast-iron plant, let him buy one and find out for himself. S. hahnii is a variety that grows low enough to be included in dish gardens. S. goldeana has golden yellow bands along the margins of the leaves. S. Ehrenbergii is stunning, its steel-blue leaves edged with white and arranged somewhat like a fan.

Ceropegia woodii is the Rosary vine. Tiny heart-shaped leaves, green marked with silver, are spaced along trailing stems. Odd-shaped flowers in pink or light purple are so small they can go unnoticed. Several other ceropegias are available and all grow from tubers.

C. sandersonii is larger and has striking white and green flowers.

Named varieties of a few kinds of cacti and many of the succulents appear almost annually. These newer varieties may add a somewhat different colored flower, a change in marking or coloring of foliage, or an improvement in the habit of growth. They are the result of persistent selection on the part of patient hybridist-growers.

The confirmed collector of cacti and succulents not only buys plants from growers and hybridists but usually wants to try growing from seed. Some kinds of both cacti and succulents aren't difficult. Miscellaneous lots or mixtures of one type can be purchased. Rate for germination of seed and growth of seedlings varies. Some reach small specimen size in a year, others take much longer. Grafting is another interesting sideline for the serious amateur grower.

The finest collection of cacti and succulents, or arid plants, growing outdoors can be seen any month of the year, except October, at the Huntington Botanical Gardens, San Marino, Calif. Paths that wind through the twelve-acre planting permit close-up views of labeled plants. The best bloom on the South African species comes in November, December and January every year, and there is a fine display of color from mid-January to June. During summer most of the flowers open during the night and as William Hertrich, Curator Emeritus, said one August day, "I can never tell whether 200 to 300 or 4,000 to 5,000 flowers will open in a single night." Mr. Hertrich spent fifty years collecting, gathering, planning and supervising this magnificent garden of xerophytes.

An excellent indoor or under-glass collection of cacti and succulents, probably the best of its kind in the country, is to be seen at the Missouri Botanical Garden, St. Louis, Missouri.

CHAPTER XIV

INDOOR GARDENS

One house plant doesn't make an indoor garden, although it may be just what a room needs to look completely furnished and decorated. Any number of plants, from three up, are necessary for a contemporary or a traditional indoor garden.

Styles have changed as much as the selection of plants. Not too many years ago, an indoor garden was limited to a window or a dish, the latter planted with cacti or in pseudo-Japanese style. Recently, architects have been allowing space and places, specifically for plants, in house plans. Their ingenuity and skill have produced far more original ideas for incorporating plants than the glass wall with an indoor garden on one side, an outdoor garden on the other.

There are many practical ways to carry out the definition of a garden being a grouping of plants. As an outdoor garden starts at ground level, an indoor garden may begin at floor level, but doesn't always end there.

Five plants in containers on two levels make a dramatically simple garden that is the only important thing in the wide, almost square, entrance hall of one home. The plants are grouped to the left of the off-center door as a person enters the house. The largest plant is a four-foot-tall dracaena (a banana plant would also be good) in an octagonal cement container. At an angle, about eighteen inches away, is a dieffenbachia, and behind it a schefflera, both in simple brass containers. At an angle, but somewhat closer than the dieffenbachia, between the dominant dracaena and the outside wall, stands a bushy kumquat in a footed urn. On a simple polished wood shelf against the wall in a brass container is an aralia.

All of these plants look well for months in light only. Their care is limited to watering the soil and cleaning the foliage. Occasionally a yellowed leaf tip must be trimmed. If and when one plant looks sickly, it's easy enough to lift it out of its container and substitute another handsome foliage plant. The grouping can be changed quite often if desired, for there are so many foliage plants that are large and distinguished as well as sturdy.

In the living room of another house, the first thing that attracts a visitor's attention is a simple one- by four-foot garden one couple dreamed up, made and planted in front of a floor-to-ceiling window. For lack of a better name, I call it a tray garden. The tray, or form, is made of wood and lined with copper. The sides are two inches high and are framed with simple molding. An inch of large smooth white pebbles fills the tray, and four or five interesting plants are placed on the pebbles. Smooth black lava stones might have been used instead of white pebbles.

At Christmastime a tall, flowering poinsettia stands at one end of the tray. When its color goes, an evergreen bonsai takes its place. In summer, a caladium with richly marked leaves is a natural choice. No effort is made to cover the pebble surface of the tray with plants. One outsize plant close to one narrow end is balanced by three or four smaller but distinctive ones toward the opposite end.

The grouping of smaller plants at Christmastime includes kalanchoe to repeat the red and green of poinsettia. With the kalanchoe might be a peperomia and a philodendron.

Again, watering and snapping off dead flowers or yellowed leaves are about all the care that must be given. When a plant is past its prime, or one has become tired of it, it's a simple matter to take it into another room and substitute a fresh one.

Limited as these two gardens are in number of plants, they are in such important locations that, almost necessarily, the appearance must approach perfection at all times. This presupposes a collection of small to medium plants being grown more informally in some other room of the house. A reserve on which to draw is economically desirable, if only to save going out and purchasing new plants every so often.

Quite different is the floor-level garden along the glass wall of the living room of a modernized Victorian house. It's about three feet wide in the corner, tapers to about one foot at the other end. Length is six feet or a little more. In this garden, the plants grow in soil. Since the exposure is west, there is some color from flowers all winter. Impatiens with white and coral blossoms are pretty much in the foreground. Spathiphyllum, marica, umbrella plant, angel wing begonias build up in height toward the corner, where first a croton and, nearer the glass, a bougainvillea vine trained on a stout bamboo stake add bright foliage and flowers all winter.

The house site made it fairly simple to make this a garden in soil instead of pots, for the land slopes away from the house and the glass wall panels are an addition that rest on a foundation wall. Copper lines the sides of the small stretch of soil.

Picture window, glass wall or an interior wall of glass, brick or stone makes a background for indoor gardens, large or small. The garden area need not be rectangular. It can be as free-form as suits the location and blends with the rest of the room.

When the slope of the land and renovation of the house aren't accommodating enough in providing a garden site, there's real work attached. Sunken beds or boxes can be constructed so that the level of the garden parallels the floor. A project such as this is easier to accomplish when the house is being built. Raised beds can be equally effective, as well as far less trouble and expense to construct. Plan on a raised bed one to one and a half feet high, depending on the size of the plants that will be grown in it.

Whatever the basis of the garden, and whether the plants grow right in soil or stand in pots, the garden area must be lined with metal to prevent damage from water. Copper or aluminum liners are the best protection. Waterproofing must precede planting for a garden superimposed on wood flooring, arranged in beds or in a box sunk below floor level or above floor level, or in its own container such as the one-by-four-foot tray.

Instead of the wood frame so appropriate for the tray garden, the soil garden against the glass wall has a flagstone coping. Bricks also make a neat edging, as do marble splash rails from Victorian commodes. Raised beds require a simple, decorative facing. Popular for this purpose are bricks. Cinder blocks could be used in some rooms, as could tile, plastic and other surfacing materials.

The hint of a path can be achieved with marble or other stone chips, lava stones, tan bark, peat moss or similar materials. These materials sometimes are used for surfacing soil or concealing the peat moss or vermiculite packed around potted plants.

Plants can be selected to suggest a tropical jungle, a temperate forest, a desert scene or an old-fashioned garden with a few flowers and lots of green.

Sculpture or a lead figure is a distinctive accessory for indoor gardens. That is, if it is in scale with the area and the plants. Or, a garden could be planned to frame and set off a piece of sculpture.

The standard-size window with two panes of glass or small rectangular panes is transformed into a very different type of garden than would be planted at a picture window or glass wall. In a new or an old house, one standard window, two or three consecutive windows or a bay window require the same equipment for their metamorphosis.

The garden at any of these windows consists of potted plants, small, medium and large. Glass shelves across the windows are supported by metal brackets attached to the window frame in order to display the potted plants. Three glass shelves per window are about right—one across the center, and one midway across each pane of glass.

Shelves with a beveled edge can be purchased cut to the length of standard-size windows, with brackets to install them. Shelves in odd lengths or widths, or of thicker glass, will be cut to specification at a building-supply firm or glass shop. Narrow shelves can be cut to fit the long rectangular panel of translucent glass that is alongside many entrance doors. Each one may be long enough for only one plant, so choose an attractive one and use matching terra cotta or pottery saucers or coasters of appropriate material under each pot.

Brackets, such as the Victorian ones used for kerosene lamps, fastened to the window frame will hold larger potted plants like the plumbago or large-leaf begonia. Hanging containers of pottery, metal, reed or raffia will suspend plants from the window frame attractively, if desired.

Vines in pots at either end of the window sill can be trained along string or wire fastened to the window frame with thumbtacks. Vines grown in this manner are superfluous with curtains or draperies.

Although your plants will grow well at east, west and south windows, this type of garden can be enhanced with accessories. In fact, the use of accessories is one way to relieve the monotony of too much green in the cloudy winter months. Small figurines, paperweights, pressed glass, particularly in color, are possibilities. Don't use all of them at one time, and avoid overcrowding. Glass shelves will support just so many pots filled with soil and accessories without a crash.

If anything is not what it used to be, it is dish gardens. Shallow pottery dishes, rectangular or round, planted with cacti are still obtainable. They're more or less of a classic and, while they are an introduction to cacti, seldom satisfy the person who becomes fascinated with these plants.

Cacti, ivy and small philodendrons are no longer the main plants for dish gardens. Any small plant can be used and any sort of container. The important rules are to provide a bottom layer of stones or rough material for drainage, and to fill with a soil mixture good for the plants.

Oversize terra-cotta pots (a circular one eighteen inches wide can be found), modern designs in cement, interesting copper, brass and other metal containers including bread tins, pottery and porcelain all are used. The size of the container depends on where it will stand. The coffee table is an obvious place, but containers and plants can be obtained that are equally suitable and thrifty for mantels, end tables and dim places in living rooms, or for the sideboard or chest in a dining room. A huge shell might be planted for a terrace or recreation room. A china shell would be delightful on a dressing table.

Contemporary containers of terra cotta or cement probably need some good-sized plants such as spathiphyllum or dracaenas. Most containers, however, call for smaller plants such as Acorus, African violets, tiny Kurume azaleas, lacy selaginella, strawberry geraniums, miniature euonymus and dainty vines, including tradescantia and Cissus striata.

Dish gardens themselves are miniatures. They're also meant to be seen and enjoyed close at hand. A porcelain shell for a dressing table might display a wax begonia and helxine. For a large shell in a recreation room, good choices would be succulents such as kalanchoes, Hummel's Sunset crassula and aloes. A brass or copper pail is stunning with green foliage plants accented by one colored-leaved coleus. The choice of both plants and containers is endless.

The 1960's have brought out a container that is a cross between a full-scale garden and a miniature dish garden. A black iron frame or stand with three legs supports a white plastic tray (35 inches in diameter) that holds standard flower pots or pans concealed by quartz gravel. Its advantages include movability, size (big enough to be important) and simplicity. Although this is a heavy piece with half a dozen pots and gravel, it could be moved from one place to another or into brighter light periodically, if not daily, to benefit plants.

DISH GARDEN

Potted plants also can be switched in a moment for a party, a holiday or merely a change. The standing circular garden I saw displayed five plants—an evergreen bonsai in a twelve-inch pan close to the rim on one side and four other smaller plants—helxine, small-leaved ivy, aluminum plant and fatshedera—placed hit or miss in the remaining area.

Water gardens are a most successful idea, fully as successful as the two or three Chinese evergreens in a

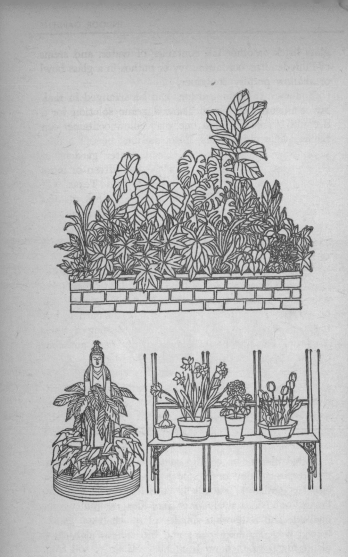

glass brick or other tall container of water, and stems of Philodendron cordatum, ivy or pothos in a glass bowl or shallow pottery container.

Honest-to-goodness gardens can be arranged in shallow containers of water. They're a fine solution for a decorating problem where only a shallow container can be used, as well as where light is poor.

Considerable experimenting with water gardens of all sizes has been carried on in the last fifteen or more years by plantsmen in New Jersey and Texas. Gil Whitten in Montclair, N.J., who probably has planted more water gardens than anyone else, is as enthusiastic as his clients, because plants grow so much more slowly in water than in soil that most gardens will not need replanting for more than a year.

Foliage plants are more satisfactory than flowering kinds for water gardens. Mr. Whitten has experimented with both. Some flowering plants such as begonias can be combined with foliage plants in a water garden, but they are not likely to look well for so long a time. African violets and plushy-leaved plants, cacti and succulents are not candidates for water gardens.

Philodendrons, large and small, are wonderful. Dracaena, dieffenbachia, pittosporum, podocarpus, nephthytis in variety, fatshedera are foolproof. Among trailing plants, pothos, cissus, grape ivy, creeping fig and tradescantia are fine, and some of them also offer contrasting foliage colors.

In addition to a shallow container of any material, various sizes of pinholders such as are used for flower arrangements, and floral clay to fasten the holders to the bottom of the container, are the equipment for planting a water garden. Plants should be taken gently from soil or sand so that roots will not be damaged. Shake first, and then wash off all particles of soil from the roots under running water and dip them in and out of water several times. Now the plants, roots and all, can be anchored on pinholders to stand where they are desired for an effective arrangement.

Add water until it's two inches deep or, if container permits, three inches deep. Three inches is maximum height, for the plants must neither drown nor suffocate. Pellets or pieces of charcoal dropped in the water will keep it sweet and prevent decay of roots and stems.

One of Mr. Whitten's water gardens was planted in a two-tiered brass container especially made for the corner of an apartment living room, to make use of a statue. Nephthytis plants were secured to pinholders in the lower tier. On the second tier a special metal base had a Chinese polychrome figure. Anchored in the water to soften the figure were two or three dieffenbachias with green and cream foliage. On special occasions the owner of this water garden adds gladiolus or other cut flowers, anchoring them on pinholders, too.

Replenishing water and keeping foliage clean by washing or spraying on an average of once every two weeks are the principal chores. Charcoal in the water means it doesn't have to be changed, merely added to as needed. In a few months, if plants such as nephthytis and some philodendron seem to be growing so tall that they might become leggy, pinch out the growing tips.

A water feature, of course, could be the focal point around which to plant a large, floor-level indoor garden. Small fountains and waterfalls can be purchased together with recirculating pumps so that the same water is used over and over again. Unlike a water garden, any water feature is likely to need constant maintenance. Take care not to let the waterfall or pool overwhelm the plants which, after all, are the real reason for indoor gardens.

CHAPTER XV

PLANTER BOXES AND ROOM DIVIDERS

Permanent structural planters in houses and apartments have made it possible for many more people to enjoy house plants. Room dividers, planter boxes, bins, planters are descriptive terms for this sort of indoor gardens. If the primary reason for installing any of these is its contribution to furnishings and decoration of the room, upkeep need be no more than that for a chair or table. On the other hand, a planter box built to house a collection of begonias or other favorites may call for all the indoor garden knowledge and skill a person has acquired.

Probably greater variations can be achieved in structural planters than in bona fide indoor gardens, which also are at floor level. The placement of these smaller containers, however purposeful, is less rigid than that of a full-fledged garden. Planter boxes and bins sometimes can be movable.

The fact that they can be moved doesn't reduce permanence. Since boxes and bins aren't an added extra but a considered part of architects' plans for many new homes, they are usually built-ins. When older houses are remodeled, built-in or movable planter boxes and room dividers provide an easy way to obtain a contemporary look.

Functions of planter boxes and bins—the latter are generally popular in Florida—are as many as their variations. At floor level, they can be placed to balance a furniture grouping, to indicate a glass wall, to carry the planting of a window equipped with glass shelves below the level of the sill, to furnish a foyer or entrance hall, however dim.

One of the most important roles is that of a divider between one room and another, or a divider that defines areas of space within one room. Planter boxes or dividers are particularly important between living and dining areas, in family rooms or kitchens, in entrance halls or in conjunction with the main door, to screen the immediate view into a home.

Against a glass wall or space divider, a planter box is essential. Without green plants at its base or the tracery of vines against the height of the glass, time and again someone unfamiliar with the house will walk into the glass panel. Planter boxes or raised beds are only two ways by which plants can complement a sheet of glass.

If the glass space divider consists of several panels held in place by means of wide frames, small plants can be displayed at various levels. A glass panel that abuts a wall of a room might have a free-form shelf of polished wood fitted into the corner and large enough to hold a plant chosen for its strong outline, as well as a telephone.

Planter boxes soften space dividers of other materials, such as plastic, filigree concrete, grille blocks of concrete, metal and mesh grating. A bamboo or slat blind gains importance as a space divider if it terminates at a planter box. By the same token, space dividers of any of these materials are excellent backgrounds for the plants.

The use of a three- or four-fold screen to display plants is less definite in a way, and is perhaps more of a party idea. A simple screen, with or without plants, is always a quick way to hide the children's play corner

or a sewing space when other activities take over in the evening. Painted shutters, bamboo or a burlap framed with bamboo make fine backgrounds against which potted plants can be hung by means of a special hook or a metal circle that slips under the rim of the pot and has a long hook attached. The screen is an excellent way for bringing orchid plants into living or dining room, or a small bromeliad with a striking flower spike arranged with other leafy plants.

It may not be fair at this date to say that the Pacific Coast leads in adapting planter boxes and room dividers to everyday living space, but certainly that region pioneered in their use. It still is an area where imagination is applied to ways of bringing plants into the home.

Neither shape nor height is a barrier to a planter box or room divider for a particular spot. The shapes and forms that have been built into floors, as well as at floor level (with sides), are as varied as imagination can work out.

Accepted as a natural and valuable part of the decorative scheme in the San Francisco area is the use of shallow planter boxes at floor-length windows to achieve continuity with garden beds on the other side. Variations in this sort of indoor planting are almost as many in number as the persons who own them.

Now and again, there's a location where the planter boxes cover such an extensive area that they are referred to as an indoor garden. A long corridor off which two or more rooms open becomes more than just a hallway if one side is lined with planter boxes. A glass wall, exterior or interior, may call for such an extensive use of planter boxes that they are the equivalent of an indoor garden.

Whether it's a planter box, room divider or bin, height is of utmost importance. It will have to be in good scale and proportion to the length of the container as well as to the particular location. But, height—or depth—also influences the welfare of the plants. Professionals who design and service these indoor plantings say that height of the box can be one of the chief causes of dissatisfaction.

Foliage plants, which are the basic material, are grown in pots from two and a half to twelve inches high, depending on the size of the plant and its root system. The planter box must be wide enough and deep enough to accommodate the tallest pot and some sort of packing around it, plus a minimum of one inch of drainage material underneath.

Of course, if you're having boxes, room dividers or bins built to display specific plants, the dimensions can be tailored to the pots in which they are growing. For existing boxes, plants must be chosen in sizes which allow the pots to fit comfortably. For shallow 4- to 6-inch planter boxes, plants in 3- to 4-inch pots are maximum. Don't cheat by trying to squeeze a plant into a smaller pot or by shifting it into a larger one, whichever would fit the structure. Some plants flower when they are potbound, but any plant has a lot of roots to grow underground when it's in too large a pot, before any luxuriant top growth and leaf production can begin.

The selection of individual planters is easier, for no one wants the rim of a clay flower pot resting on the edge of a decorative planter. Planters of all sorts are used. Contemporary in form and line are many made from concrete or cement, plastic, wood, wrought iron or a combination of bamboo and cane. Terra cotta is harder to find in many sections of the country, but large imported ones with simple lines, as well as Victorian or Florentine types can sometimes be found.

Antique or modern containers of brass, copper, porcelain or other ceramic are all acceptable. Personal preference and suitability for the room are the guiding rules.

More and more the clay pots in which plants grow are slipped into decorative container-coverings of straw, raffia or textured metal.

The brass-bound wooden tub is a standard planter, year in and year out. It may be modern or traditional, natural wood color or painted black, white or green. You may want to attach two good-looking, perhaps oversize, brass handles.

Large plants are the rule for planters which in some rooms measure twenty inches in diameter. Grape ivy trained on a seven-foot cone of wire mesh, an eight-foot tall podocarpus, a four- or five-foot dieffenbachia, a

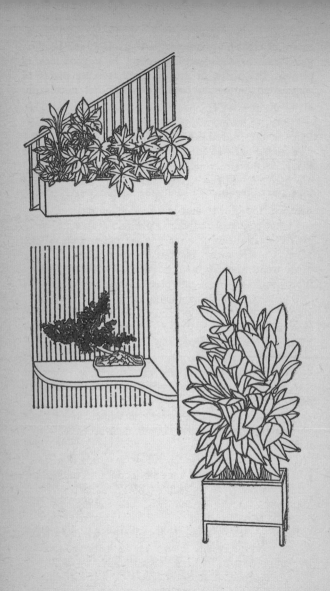

seven- or eight-foot fiddleleaf rubber plant, self-heading philodendrons—these are important in a good-looking planter. Use alone, or grouped with smaller plants of contrasting outline in harmonious but not necessarily identical containers.

For these large plants and sometimes enormous containers, a stand is often used to keep them off the floor and to add even more importance. Stands are sometimes made of matching materials. Again it may be a low wide tub or other container to match, overturned to support the planter. In some materials and styles, planters are footed.

All planter boxes and bins, room dividers and wooden containers should be waterproofed with a copper lining. Provision also must be made for drainage. Pebbles, stone chips or some kind of rubble is generally available and satisfactory. In a pinch, coarse builder's sand will do.

One to two inches of the drainage material should be packed over the bottom of the box or container. An inch is advisable even in the decorative container into which is slipped a plant in its clay pot of soil. This is insurance against the plant standing in a residue of water where its soil may become waterlogged and sour, a dangerous condition for the majority of plants.

There are two ways of planting. One, of course, is filling the box or bin with soil (this is not recommended for individual planters of any material or size). This can pose a problem of soil to suit two or three of the plants that require a rather special mixture or fertilizing. It also makes a planter, even a small box or room divider, heavy. It's messy to change the soil. Furthermore, city apartment dwellers aren't the only ones who have trouble finding enough soil to fill planter boxes and room dividers of any length.

The most practical way is to arrange the plants in their pots in the rectangular or free-form planter box or room divider—that is, after the layer of drainage material has been spread across the bottom. Peat moss or vermiculite are clean-looking, lightweight materials which are ideal to pack around the plants, between them, and between pots and the sides of the box and, finally, over the surface of the pots.

Probably other clean, light materials such as buckwheat hulls, which are used for mulching outdoor planting, also would be satisfactory. However, peat moss seems to remain the favorite because, when moist, it looks like rich brown earth. I like to use handfuls of peat moss that have been dropped in a pail of water and then wrung out.

Moisten packing material when the arrangement of plants is completed. At all times, keep it moist but not soggy, to add some of the humidity in which practically all plants, except cacti and succulents, thrive. Don't forget to water soil in the pots for the benefit of the roots.

Two other advantages accrue to this method of planting. One is that smaller plants in smaller pots can be placed on bricks or a cinder block so they'll stand at the same height as larger plants in bigger pots. The second is the ease with which the potted plants can be lifted out and others substituted. An ailing plant can be taken out without disturbing the roots of its neighbors. Best of all, a flowering plant or two can be set in place for a party, a special occasion or merely a change of scene. It's equally simple to set in place a different foliage plant or fruiting one to freshen up at any time.

The basic plants must be chosen from the lists of those that do well in the amount of light available and the prevailing temperature. Don't overcrowd. Not less than an inch should be left between pots of plants that are about the same size, so that damp peat moss can be packed between them. If plants are jammed together, it's an invitation to insects to travel from one to the other, and for decay to start from overlapping, damp leaves.

If high-branching, soft-foliage plants or treelike ones are used, by all means underplant. Many attractive creeping or trailing plants such as Ficus pumila, helxine, hemigraphis, pellionia, tradescantia or zebrina will be satisfactory ground cover under average growing conditions. Wax begonias, pinched back to keep them bushy and low, will flower in good light; small marantas and some small ferns and possibly even African violets are charming for underplanting.

Maintenance is no more difficult, and it may be less, in planter boxes and bins, room dividers and planters. It is kept to a minimum by selecting the right plants for the location.

CHAPTER XVI

OCCASIONAL USES THROUGHOUT THE HOUSE

A pottery horse carrying a cactus planted in its back is a gift that will amuse youngsters housebound with sniffles. This cute sort of planter, however, especially in multiple, can bore the adults of the family to the point of walking past it blindly for weeks before winter is over.

Not so the unusual small planter, carefully selected for the place it's to adorn. A deep saucer of old Flowing Blue, a maple salt box or a piece of driftwood hollowed out to hold tiny pots of cacti and succulents isn't likely ever to be unnoticed. Just as the wind-weathered driftwood is appropriate for cacti, so is the porcelain or china dish appropriate for a jewel-like arrangement of ferny selaginella, a seedling wax begonia in bud, a seedling impatiens in flower or other tiny living plants.

Ways and means for occasional display of plants are subject to changing—and sometimes fleeting—styles. One year, everyone has to have a small metal birdcage housing St. Louis ivy (Philodendron cordatum). Another year, every other person receives for Christmas a small rectangular shining brass planter stuffed with lily-of-the-valley pips.

In New England, wood containers, usually of maple, in such traditional forms as cradles, wall spoonholders, cranberry pickers and dry sinks are always popular (and sometimes in some rooms are just too obvious). On the West Coast, unusual hanging containers such as large wicker cagelike baskets from the Orient are used effectively. In the Southwest, terra cotta that isn't run-of-the-mill, and in the Southeast containers of woven straw, reed and similar materials may be used advantageously.

These as well as other means of display are more casual, but not less important, than window gardens, planter boxes and bins, and room dividers. Basically, there are three main types of such containers: the small or modest-size container, the hanging sort in a great variety of materials, and the stands and flower poles.

Special planters are sometimes coveted for a collection of special plants. Strawberry jars of terra cotta or glazed pottery start at a height of about six inches and range upward to approximately two feet, which is the size generally used outdoors. The pockets are perfect for herbs (one of a kind to a pocket), succulents that grow as rosettes, miniature roses, small African violets or their cousins, the trailing episcias. If a small strawberry jar, its pockets planted with lily-of-the-valley pips, is a Christmas gift, after bloom embed in each pocket a piece of helxine about the size of a twenty-five-cent piece. It soon will be a shower of green.

The soil mixture for the strawberry jar will depend upon the kind of plant selected for its pockets. Start by placing not less than an inch of drainage material across the bottom. Then ask someone to hold in the center a cylinder of newspaper into which sand is poured (leave the cylinder in place until planting is finished). Next, fill with the right kind of soil to the level of the first circle of pockets and set the plants in place, taking care to spread out their roots and water before covering with soil and then adding enough to reach to the next row of pockets.

The core of sand in the center provides an ideal way to water, for the water will drain through the sand to the lowest plants. The paper does not necessarily have to be pulled out, but daily watering will soon cause it to deteriorate.

Not everyone will want a strawberry jar for house plants, but rare is the home where a hanging container can't be placed effectively. Call them mobile planters, if you prefer. For some kinds of plants, such as the flowering browallia, lantanas, oxalis and many green or vari-colored vines and creepers, only a hanging container shows off their full beauty.

There was a time when the only hanging containers were the wire baskets sold by florists in early summer for porch decoration. These are still obtainable. As many if not more gardeners use redwood slat or solid hanging containers both indoors and outdoors. Wooden ones are rectangular, square or semi-circular. These "mobiles" come with three or four wires to attach to the sides and S hooks for hanging.

It is better to plant these hanging baskets than to set pots in them. The wire and slat-wood ones must be completely lined first. Florists use sheet moss, turning the mossy side outward. A flat green moss that can be cut and lifted in sizable pieces from the garden will be satisfactory. So will sphagnum moss. Overlap the moss, if necessary, to be sure no holes or breaks will spring open when the container is filled with soil.

This is one plant holder that needs no layer of drainage material. Fill half way or a little more with soil, and then take plants out of their pots and arrange them not far from the edge. Trailers around the outside and a moundlike plant in the center are ideal.

Incidentally, don't invest in the largest-size baskets for the house. Remember that plants in luxuriant leaf and flower add to the basket's breadth. Practically, a large wire or slat basket and a solid redwood one of any size is too heavy to lift from its bracket or hook.

And this has to be done at least once a week, so that the basket can be immersed in a pail of water for thorough soaking of the soil. Interim waterings must be done cautiously, so that water does not spill over onto floors, carpets or woodwork. To save time and cleaning up, keep an old tray handy to set on any surface under the hanging basket to catch drip.

Smaller and probably more practical, if not always capable of as lovely planting as the basket, is the old "gypsy kettle." Modern versions can be purchased in plastic, lightweight plated brass, and plain or embossed brass. Some follow the lines of a kettle, others are shaped and flared to hold a three-inch pot; still others are hanging planters that will hold trailers or a small bushy plant. Suitable brackets as well as chains are included with metal planters. Plastic ones are made in more than one style and size, with either rope or chain to suspend them. One style in plastic permits two or three different sizes to be hung one above the other.

Shallow saucerlike dishes of terra cotta or metal also can be suspended singly or in groups at different levels (not necessarily one above the other). These were first used along the West Coast and in the Southwest. The containers take small, dainty plants to grow in either water or soil—a small-leaved ivy, a delicate light green tradescantia, a small-leaved coleus in colors to highlight the terra cotta. The plants can be kept in place by small pinholders, such as are needed for water gardens.

Some persons are lucky enough to find nineteenth-century colored pressed glass shaped like a tumbler, with a rim under which are two holes through which cord can be knotted to suspend it. Modern pieces of glass, ceramic or metal may appeal sufficiently for the owner to find a way to hang them. When it comes to introducing plants into a home, don't be afraid to be original.

The plant stand, another tradition, is brought up to date every ten years or so. Tiered stands of metal are made in semi-circular and rectangular shapes, and with two or four shelves. Wrought-iron stands, shaped like espaliered trees, hold three to five or more potted plants on their branches.

The "flower pole" is an improvement on the stand, with arms to hold pots. This style is easy to turn so that plants on all sides receive maximum light. The pole consists of a cylinder of steel mesh that permits two adjustments of the metal saucers—at different heights on the cylinder and at distances between five and ten inches from it. The pole is strong enough to support nine four- or five-inch flower pots or pans, plus one eight-inch pot in the center of the base. If the plants would benefit, the mesh cylinder may be filled with damp moss to increase humidity.

Totem poles are something else. These are posts of sphagnum moss used to support vine-type philoden-

dron. They are anchored in the large pots required by these lush plants, and are often preferred to the lengths of cork or pieces of bark first used for supports. Totem poles, or moss sticks, as they are sometimes called, can be purchased ready-made. They are 2″ x 2″ rounded squares most often made eighteen inches long. If a taller one is needed, it wouldn't be difficult to make.

The sphagnum-moss totem poles also can be used as a base on which to train vine-type philodendrons with sizable leaves, or smaller-leaved grape ivy, cissus, neph- thytis, pothos, even flowering Glory Bower (Cleroden-

245

drum), passion flower or wax plant. These are large and important, and the flowering kinds are spectacular. All are for prominent places.

A really large plant in a good-looking container is as important in a room as furniture is and, according to some designers, can take the place of it. A happier solution is combining plants and furniture. Wrought-iron tables often provide holders for plants that can be seen through the glass top. They are made in dining-table and occasional-table sizes. Coffee and end tables of hardwood often are styled with a sunken, metal-lined planter.

Then there's the low table consisting of a cylinder of glass, covered with a wider circle of glass. The top is removable, so that the garden planted on the metal base of the cylinder can be watered and tended as needed.

The most recent trend, at present, is an area of plants on a bench, a long, low table or one long shelf against a wall. For this, a 2½-inch-deep metal tray is indispensable. Trays are made rectangular or square, but extra-long ones will have to be made to order. Fill the tray with two inches of pebbles, lava stones or marble chips and arrange potted plants to your taste. Keep water to the level of the pebbles.

On a wall bench or shelf, plants with a strong silhouette, such as Philodendrons Fosterianum, Florida, Imbe or Dubium, umbrella plant, some of the small palms, araucaria, are especially good. With one plant chosen for silhouette combine smaller ones with interesting foliage. A tray usually is placed toward one end of the long wood surface, and is balanced by a cushion or ornament somewhere on the remainder of its length.

Other easy-to-find planters for use on furniture or unadorned wood surfaces are low terra-cotta containers, a plain flower pan 12 inches in diameter, ordinary drainage tiles and cinder blocks (small potted plants in the holes). Probably more than one drainage tile and cinder block would be needed.

A rectangular tray of good length might be mounted on iron legs to hold it at the desired height from the floor in front of a window, to hide the yawning fireplace in summer or to take the place of a low table. If you're lucky enough to get hold of one of those giant clam shells, it could hold pots of jade tree (Crassula argentea), kalanchoes or other appropriate succulents or foliage plants and be placed on the concrete or flagstone hearth at one side of the fireplace.

In more formal rooms, lead planters in shell or other classic shapes are an excellent choice. In a sizable room, a small piece of statuary might be combined successfully with a minimum of well-chosen plants.

Lead planters, shells, simple urns or painted clay pots, each holding one plant, contribute a sense of freshness and aliveness when placed on a console or ornamental bracket or a column. The support with its plant, singly, in pairs or grouped, becomes an architectural feature to reckon with. One or two planters of this sort, each holding an elegant plant (for example, an Indica azalea or Christmas kalanchoe) are equally effective on a sideboard, commode or chest.

On sideboards, chests and end tables, as well as on window sills, cache pots also are used in pairs. These ornamental pots are most commonly found in beautiful porcelain, simpler pottery and muted tole. The range of sizes is limited. Cache pots are strictly ornamental, but are never so lavishly decorated as to compete with the plants whose pots they conceal. A pair makes a nice accessory for a room.

Cache pots certainly are more usable than the jardiniere, that large receptacle for plants, usually made of ceramic and often so ornamented as to be almost ugly. The jardiniere of 1900 to 1910 that held the palm in the parlor and, a few years later, the Boston fern, probably will return in another few years as a prized "antique" container for an eight-foot podocarpus or ten-foot Monstera deliciosa. If it does, be sure to put in the bottom of the jardiniere a two-inch layer of drainage material. One fault with jardinieres was the water that always collected around the base of the flower pot (a jardiniere was heavy to lift).

Perhaps the jardiniere won't make a comeback, for the trend continues toward simpler and more functional ways of living with plants. Don't select too many kinds of planters for any one room, whether it does or doesn't have an indoor garden, planter box or room divider. Don't concentrate all of the occasional planters, large and small, in the living and dining rooms. The bathroom is a perfect place for plants that must have humidity, so try one or two on lamp brackets, or a small planter on a corner shelf. The kitchen is a convenient place for watching plants that grow fast. Living with plants can apply to hallways as well as foyers, to bedrooms as well as recreation rooms.

CHAPTER XVII

ARTIFICIAL LIGHT

The table lamp that gave enough light for reading after dark and had a base commodious enough for a philodendron or pothos vine to be planted in soil made its appearance during the 1940's. It was novel, and women everywhere bought it. The base, by the way, was usually copper or brass.

The pothos or philodendron had to be replaced sooner or later, pretty much as it always had to be when it stood in pots on a mantel or window sill without benefit of artificial light during evenings and cloudy days. To the person who didn't go in for house plants, or had never thought they could be grown under electricity, that simple lamp seemed quite wonderful.

Experiments with growing plants under artificial light had been going on almost continuously for many years. In 1893 at Cornell University, Liberty Hyde Bailey was trying out arc lamps in the greenhouses. The Plant Industry Station of the United States Department of Agriculture at Beltsville, Md., in 1918 started tests with artificial light for growing chrysanthemums under glass. At the Boyce Thompson Institute in Yonkers, N.Y., studies began in 1924 and have continued ever since.

Only two or three styles of lamps can be purchased twenty years after that first table model appeared in the 1940's. A table lamp tall enough to support brackets for flower pots under its beneficial light can be found if one hunts for it. However, it's not a lamp that most people would buy for their living room. Every so often, a standing lamp designed to display plants, in addition to giving satisfactory light, appears in the general furniture market.

Pole lamps, or a tree of lights, with three or more fixtures, also support potted plants in some instances. Still another use of a tree of lights is to serve as the core of a round table with a planter encircling the pole at table level.

A table with a lighted glass-enclosed compartment is currently on the market. Stands equipped with lights are not decorative enough for anyone except a confirmed grower of certain kinds of plants.

Artificial light serves two divergent functions for plants. It can be rigged up purely and simply to stimulate growth and flowering and perhaps to speed propagation. Or, it can be used to dramatize an indoor planting, spotlight an important specimen or generally enhance any display or decorative use of plants after dark.

Dramatic lighting is much more subtle than the people who bought those first planter lamps ever dreamed it could be. On the other hand, it can be achieved in the simplest way. One white 60-watt light bulb is the only investment one couple makes for a stunning effect. A large-leaved philodendron growing on bark is the only ornament on a commode against a wall. The raw white globe concealed below is pointed so that its white light forms a halo on the wall behind the plant.

Colored bulbs, spotlights and floodlights all can be tried to bring out fresh values in plantings, if they're placed at safe distances. Before cornice and cove lighting became accepted practices in living rooms, no one probably would have thought of moving the sofa and its companion end tables far enough away from the wall so that palms and philodendrons more than twice as high could be grouped behind one end of the sofa. Dramatic is the right word when the four warm white 40-watt rapid-start fluorescent lamps behind the cornice over the sofa are turned on.

Beyond a doubt, modern lighting makes it possible for plants to grow healthily in locations where twenty years ago they would have shriveled or faded to pale ghosts of themselves. That is, modern lighting to live by, not special lighting for plant culture. For example, a spacious built-in desk along a windowless wall is adequately illuminated in three ways: fluorescent lamp under the lowest overhead shelf, soffit illumination and a recessed ceiling light over each corner of the desk. Each ceiling light is one 150-watt spot incandescent lamp which shines directly down on a rich green foliage plant. Pull-down lamps over end tables flanking a sofa keep the planters on the end tables growing, green and occasionally flowering.

The artificial light so badly needed if plants are to live in a room divider or on a shelf which is never touched by daylight, let alone by sun, can be effective after dark without being an eyesore in daytime. Indoors, fixtures and bulbs should be concealed, as they are for decorative lighting of an outdoor garden after dark.

Select fixtures that won't permit lights to shine into the eyes of the people who share the room with plants. Arrange bulbs or tubes so that circles of light from each one do not overlap and create too much heat for the plants. Above all, before starting to light plants, make sure that fuses are adequate for the additional load.

Mazda or fluorescent lights, alone or in combination, are recommended for the average home. Fluorescent light alone seems to be becoming general among indoor gardeners intent on growing a collection of plants that need pampering and on carrying on all operations with special plants such as African violets and other members of the Gesneria family.

Mazda light, which projects itself farther, must be placed at a greater distance from the plants than are fluorescent tubes. If the mazda is the floodlight type of bulb with a built-in silver reflector, it could be suspended from the ceiling or other high point and focused to shine down on the plants. But a floodlight whose purpose is to silhouette leaves and stems of a vine against a glass wall will have to be placed some distance away, at floor level and focused at an angle. One floodlight may suffice for a glass panel, three or more may be needed for a glass wall.

Interesting illumination, but not silhouetting, of a planter box against a glass wall can be obtained with ceiling spots. Flood or spot incandescent lamps, each perhaps 100 watts, can be used in the circular recessed overhead fixtures. Such lighting undoubtedly is beneficial to the plants, but it is not the sort that dedicated growers use.

Fluorescent lights should be no more than twelve inches away from the plants. The white tubes simulate sunlight and are said to deliver more energy than colored tubes. If fluorescent tubes are suspended from chains, they can be raised or lowered according to the amount of light needed by the plants.

Growers and collectors of African violets, episcias and other gesnerias, and orchids are more interested in the beneficial aspects of artificial lighting than in the decorative ones. Supplementary light is an aid to bringing difficult plants, such as crossandra, into bloom and speeding flower development on others, such as anthuriums, that will live but may only produce foliage in reduced light.

Growers of such specialized plants find lighting equipment is neither elaborate nor prohibitively expensive. Probably the highest-priced item is the two- or three-tiered stand on wheels equipped with fluorescent lights. These are widely used for collections of African violets.

Not every African violet fancier grows his plants in tiered carts. Some are equally successful in such unlikely places as basements and other dark rooms where the plants stand on tables or benches above which are installed fluorescent light tubes on chains. Almost any kind of plant can be grown successfully in such a setup. Here, after one has learned how much light is needed, African violets can be kept in constant bloom and additional plants propagated without difficulty.

Rectangular fluorescent lamps on legs and with reflector tops are available to place over plants on a table or shelf. I suspect these are used mostly by collectors when they display a few of their plants in living or other rooms. They could be placed over a few plants in dingy places to keep them growing steadily and looking healthy. However, simple installations of one or more bulbs or lamps are adequate—and relatively inconspicuous.

One method that has worked wonders is a combination of 100 watts of mazda light and 100 watts of fluorescent. Remember that the mazda light bulb must be farther away from the plants than the fluorescent. One 100-watt mazda bulb may be sufficient for some groups of plants.

For a smaller planter, a 275-watt sun lamp will be beneficial if turned on for an hour at a time. The sun lamp must be far enough distant not to scorch or burn foliage.

Fluorescent tubes, which are so generally used by amateur growers at the present time, are of several kinds. Daylight tubes, warm-white and cool-white types, are most popular, alone or in combination. It is generally recommended that the tubes have reflectors.

When one learns how to regulate the lighting, plants will grow for an indefinite period. How long and how frequently illumination is given depends on many factors. Lights aren't necessarily turned on every day, or on any one day for longer than a couple of hours. One woman who grows African violets in the basement of her house in New Jersey burns two fluorescent tubes of 40 watts each about twelve hours a day in midwinter.

Even if she could grow her African violets in rooms with spacious windows, she still probably would depend to some extent on artificial light. It is the only way to counteract the short and cloudy days that prevail during winter in New Jersey and many other northern states.

Without adequate light, even foliage plants make spindling or leggy growth in winter. Light is one of the factors that are absolutely essential for even, steady growth. Commercial growers have developed great skill in the use of artificial light to stimulate bloom for a specific time on cut flowers and potted plants.

The current trend toward fluorescent light may be reversed in another one to five years. Research and experiment by scientists and by professional and amateur growers are in continual progress.

For up-to-date information, the best source is the Extension Service of your state agricultural college. The local lighting or utilities company is certain to have information available and to be willing to discuss and advise on your problems.

CHAPTER XVIII

EQUIPMENT FOR PLANTING
AND MAINTENANCE

To keep one or one hundred house plants handsome and healthy, fall, winter and spring, the essential tools can be kept conveniently on a small shelf or stored in little space in a cupboard. There's no need to build bins for soil, or even to keep soil on hand. Day-to-day care and any emergency can be managed without difficulty, thanks to the modern packaging of planter mixes, fertilizers and sprays that are sold in neighborhood stores.

The first piece of equipment everyone needs is a watering can, unless you're willing to use a teakettle or a pitcher with a good spout for pouring. Watering cans of copper, brass or pottery are decorative, and the plastic ones come in cheerful colors. Plastic is, of course, the lightest to carry.

Professional watering cans are less glamorous in appearance but no more efficient than the decorative ones, for all of them have a long spout to be poked in between the foliage and pour water on the soil. All the materials are fashioned into cans of different capacities. A one-quart can supplies water for a good collection of house plants without having to be refilled.

When shopping for a watering can, you should also get a syringe or spray bottle for squirting a mist of water over foliage. As essential as watering the soil is the mist which not only keeps foliage clean, but also supplies humidity, so essential to many plants, to the atmosphere. Rubber bulbs or glass bottles with pumps are generally available.

On the shelf near the syringe, keep a small soft brush for dusting off hairy- and plushy-leaved plants and a sponge for wiping off large and harder leaves with water. Another item to be included in such equipment might be either an aerosol spray or a bottle accompanied by applicator to coat the foliage of philodendron, ivy and other hard-surfaced leaves. These liquids make foliage lustrous and can be washed off with cold water if you decide clean leaves with their natural luster or mat finish are more to your liking. These sprays are harmless; their use is a matter of preference.

Miniature tools are sold separately or in sets. The most useful one has a small rake at one end, a forked blade or shovel at the other. With it, surface soil can be cultivated or loosened. If no one has given you a shiny brass one, an apple corer or discarded table fork will be almost as efficient. A small trowel comes in handy for filling pots with soil; a sharp knife for taking cuttings.

Those who do a great deal of transplanting may crave a potting stick made of aluminum. A twelve-inch wood label also does the job of working soil or other growing medium down into a pot. A professional gardener wouldn't be without one.

A bundle of labels, or some kind of marker on which names can be written, is kept on hand by many indoor gardeners. Often needed are twistems in short lengths, or special clips, to fasten a vine-type philodendron to its totem pole or to train another vine in the way it should go.

Gadgets are endless, and often ingenious. Some of them are fun, but few are absolutely essential to maintaining an average house plant. Any one of several gadgets can be inserted in soil at the side of the pot to indicate by color or some other means when it's time to water. Humidifiers range from gadgets to automatic electric ones. The latter are needed chiefly for African violets and other plants that must have high humidity.

Specialized plants such as any of the gesnerias and orchids are almost certain to need some special equip-equipment items. Awareness of these comes from catalogues and from talking with other growers.

Trellises to fit any pot up to five inches in diameter, totem poles and bark supports are possibilities. These usually are purchased as needed, as are brackets, hangers, hanging baskets and the like.

The medicine end of the shelf needs only three items for all ailments. An aerosol spray bomb contains an all-purpose mixture to subdue aphids, white flies, mites and, so the claim runs on some brands, mealy bugs. Nevertheless, keep a box of cotton-tipped picks and a small bottle of alcohol beside the bomb. Dip a pick in alcohol to remove mealy bugs and scale insects that cling to stems and in axils of leaves.

This arsenal is sufficient for homeowners whose interest in plants is for decoration and for indoor gardeners with a collection of average plants. Hundreds of plants, especially firm-leaved foliage ones, never attract insects or break out in spots. Specialists in cacti, orchids and some of the flowering plants may need a small sprayer and a more diversified kit of chemicals to be prepared with water.

Soil and Fertilizer

A suburban or country garden is no longer the chief source of soil for potted plants; and nothing could take up less space on a shelf than modern fertilizers.

Fertilizers come as a liquid in a bottle, as powder in an envelope no larger than a seed packet, as capsules and pellets. Some are food for a wide range of foliage plants, others are special formulas for azaleas, African violets and plants that need specific nutrients. Directions and timing on the bottle, packet or tube should be followed exactly.

A small cache of charcoal is advisable. Charcoal is used widely as a purifying agent in refrigerators and air conditioners because it has the ability to absorb gaseous impurities. Small pieces of charcoal from a wood fire or pellets of charcoal dropped in a water garden keep the water sweet. Finely ground charcoal is included in some planter or soil mixtures.

Soil from the outdoor garden, particularly if it's a good, brown, loosely textured loam, can be the basic growing medium for a vast majority of plants. With it are mixed peat moss, humus, leafmold, sharp sand, volcanic rock and fertilizer—two or more in varying amounts according to the plants that are to grow in it. Piles of these various materials need no longer be kept on hand. Nor does one—whether one lives on Long Island or in Minnesota—have to go outdoors on a dreary winter day and try to fill a pail with soil because a pot was knocked over and broken and the contents scattered. Soil, humus, peat, leafmold and other ingredients now are packaged in bags of various sizes to hold amounts from twenty-four ounces to ten pounds. Better yet, soil formulas are packaged.

One more hurrah—these packaged formulas and mixes usually are stamped "Sterilized." Thus, there is no need for baking soil in the oven, soaking with fumigant or applying something to prevent damping-off, a serious threat to seedlings.

Formulas are carefully worked out for packaging so that they are suitable for African violets, bromeliads, orchids, foliage plants, or azaleas that have a preference for acid soil. One mix is especially for starting seedlings and rooting cuttings.

Planter mixes, consisting of various materials but with not a particle of soil, first came to indoor gardeners' attention about 1950. A planter mix is a growing medium formulated especially for the culture of indoor plants. Anyone who questions the value of a planter mix need only grow two of the same kind of plant side by side for six months—one in a pot of soil, the other in a pot of planter mix—to be convinced.

Planter mixes never form a surface crust, as soil mixtures do. Such a crust prevents thorough watering and inhibits aeration, among other handicaps. On the contrary, a good planter mix is porous for both water and air; it supplies nutrients and remains fresh and sweet even when impurities such as alkali are a residue from watering.

A planter mix may consist of as many as eight elements, but so thorough is the job that it's difficult to recognize any of them. Peat moss, peat humus, one of several types of leafmold, charcoal, perlite, humisite, volcanic rock and pea pebbles are widely used materials. Redwood and oak leafmolds are both good, but they supply quite different nutrients.

While it may not be necessary to keep planter mixes and special formulas on hand, because they're so easy to purchase, it may be advisable to keep other potting supplies. Pebbles, bulb fiber and vermiculite for bulb forcing come in small packages. Lava stones, marble chips or your favorite surfacing for gardens are good things to have on hand for emergency replacements.

If a flower pot breaks, never toss it in a garbage can

or trash basket. Break it up in smaller pieces and store in a bag or extra flower pot. Pieces of flower pot are called crock, and are essential for drainage. Select a piece of the right size to put over a drainage hole, so that soil or planter mix won't be washed out but drainage of water will not be impeded.

Pots

Pots are standard containers for growing plants. The standard pot and classic shape is the one made of clay, usually quite distinctly reddish in color, but often more yellowish, depending on the place where the clay came from. Glass, metal, ceramics and plastic have been used to fashion pots similar to the clay ones. In spite of the use of these materials and the styling innovations, clay pots reign almost unchallenged.

The round clay pot is usually called a flower pot, although it houses more foliage plants than flower plants. Size is according to measurement and refers not only to pots, but in catalogues often indicates size of plants.

The standard pot, in which the inside depth equals the inside top diameter, comes in sizes from 2½ or 3 inches to 15 or more inches. Smallest of all is the thimble or thumb pot, used for shamrocks. The 3-, 4- and 5-inch pots are in greatest demand; few persons except those who grow cacti use many 2½-inch pots.

The azalea pot, with an inside depth about three-fourths of its inside top diameter, accommodates not only azaleas, with their thick, shallow ball of roots, but also other plants with similar root systems. Bulb pans or half pots are, roughly, half the depth of standard pots, regardless of diameter. Rather squatty clay pots are made especially for African violets.

Clay pots and pans are more porous than others, which is fine in greenhouses and planter boxes, but less than ideal in rooms with high temperatures and dry air. Many plants from the florist now come in pots that have been painted white on the outside. Paint seals the porous exterior and thus prevents too rapid loss of moisture from the soil. However, don't paint pots while plants are growing in them.

One of the greatest advantages of a clay pot is the round hole in the center of the bottom. Its purpose is to assure drainage. This it does perfectly. Simple saucers are made to go under the pots and are in matching sizes.

Clay pots in 3- and 4-inch sizes, plus a few larger ones, are convenient to have on hand. Bulb pans, for example, are good for sowing seeds and rooting cuttings. A small supply takes little space, for pots of the same size and shape can be stacked one inside the other.

Many fancier pottery pots and more colorful plastic ones should be ignored. Their lack of porosity is more than offset by the faults of attached saucers and no drainage holes. In some cases, pots have two tiny holes just above the attached saucer but these are not as efficient as the drainage holes in clay pots. Few plants thrive in pots with attached saucers and no provision for drainage, even though the pots are of glazed pottery.

There are some plastic pots of good quality being manufactured. These have holes in the bottom of the pots, and matching saucers. Both round and square ones are made in a range of sizes.

Wick-fed pots are made in glass, pottery and plastic. They copy the lines of the clay pots. The pot fits snugly into a stand of the same material which is a reservoir for water. A woven-glass wick leads from the drainage hole into the reservoir and carries water to the soil, by means of capillary action. Wick-fed pots are a safeguard for watering soft-leaved plants. It is said that the reservoir needs to be refilled on an average of once every ten days for an African violet.

Woven-glass wicks can be purchased in lengths cut for

clay, glass or plastic pots in widely used sizes. The wicks also can be purchased in rolls, priced by the foot. Thus it is possible to convert any clay pot into a wick-fed one. Wicks must be set in place before pots are planted. Pull about an inch of the wick through the hole into the pot and unravel it so it spreads out over the bottom like petals of a flower. Proceed to fill and plant pot as usual.

Occasionally, pots of other materials are introduced. Pressed vermiculite and ceramic variations are most usual. Before investing, be sure the new kind has all the advantages of a clay pot.

Indoor gardening doesn't require a collection of tools such as accumulate for outdoor gardening. Minimum but adequate equipment includes the following:

1. Watering can
2. Rubber syringe
3. Small cultivator
4. Small soft brush and a sponge
5. Charcoal
6. Fertilizer—liquid, powder or pellet

For emergency action against insects, add:

7. Aerosol bomb of all-purpose spray
8. Cotton-tipped picks and alcohol

CHAPTER XIX

PLANTING AND TRANSPLANTING

A family, as it grows larger, looks for a larger home. And plants require new pots from time to time, depending on how fast they grow.

Jerusalem cherries are planted and transplanted three times between February, when seed is sown, and December, when the fruiting plants are offered for sale in stores. Seedlings are transplanted in rows into flats, then by May into individual small pots, and in September shifted into larger ones.

Unless the pot is broken accidentally, no house plant needs repotting oftener than once a year. Many slow-growing ones can go for two or three years without being repotted. Mature or full grown plants never have to be transplanted, unless you want to.

Years ago, every house plant was repotted annually in order to provide it with fresh soil in which to grow. This was done whether the plant went back into the same size pot, or had grown enough to warrant one a size larger. Modern cultural methods based on planter mixes and entirely different types of fertilizers have done away with the need to change the soil periodically.

One plant per pot is the rule. The choice of clay, glazed pottery or other ceramic, plastic, glass or metal is according to the owner's preference (professional growers for many reasons always use clay). For satisfactory growth, a pot must meet certain specifications. These are as follows:

DRAINAGE . . . . At least one hole in the bottom.

SIZE . . . . Big enough to hold the roots in normal position, but not much roomier.

TRANSPLANTING . . . Only one size larger than the present pot.

CONDITION . . . . Clean inside and outside.

The cutting, as soon as it has developed roots, should be planted in a 2½-inch pot filled with a suitable soil mixture or planter mix. By the time the cutting is large enough to be regarded as a plant and to flower (if the reason you have it is for its flower), it probably needs a 3-inch pot. The wax begonia that has flowered all winter in a 3-inch pot should by spring have a large enough root system to fill a 4-inch pot.

Whenever roots have worked their way through the drainage hole of a pot, the plant is potbound. A potful of roots is a sign that it's time to shift the plant to a larger pot. But if it's flowering or making obvious top growth, postpone the transplanting until activity wanes.

When several plants are to go in one pot or in a decorative container, choose a container large enough to accommodate the root systems of all. Plants also must have room for top growth to develop naturally.

Crowding six plants in a pot only large enough for three leads to one-sided plants or tall, straggling ones.

If house plants are moved in their pots into the garden for summer, transplant those that need it either before this move, or shortly before they are brought back indoors in early fall. Some people prefer spring, some fall for this transplanting. There's no decision to make for plants such as geraniums, begonias, coleus and iresine that are taken out of their pots and planted right in the ground. However, I prefer to leave in their pots those azaleas that will be brought back indoors, poinsettias and specimen plants.

If there's no garden into which plants can be moved, time essential repotting or transplanting at the end of the dormant season, or season of inactive growth. Thus, early February is an ideal time for cacti, late winter for ferns.

Some house-plant owners and decorators say they prefer standard clay pots when a mossy green coating collects on the outside. This may be aesthetic, but for planting and transplanting all pots should be spick and span. The green coating clogs the pores of the clay, so soil moisture is retained. However, it may harbor disease. It won't take many months to decide which state is preferable.

Pots can be used over and over again, so long as they are scrubbed each time. Let pots soak for a few hours, or overnight, in a tub or pan of water. This will loosen much of the earth and any growth or roots clinging to the sides. Most pots can be cleaned down to their surface by rubbing them with newspaper. For stubborn areas, a stiff brush may be needed.

Unless all materials are thoroughly clean, disease spores or insects may be transferred to the new plant. Soil diseases are particularly difficult to combat.

All clay pots should be soaked in water before planting. Then the porous surfaces will be full of water and will not draw moisture from the soil or planter mix with which it's filled.

Before transplanting, plants must be removed intact from the pots in which they have been growing. There's a right way and wrong way of doing this, just as there is for lifting kittens and puppies. Don't take hold of the top or even the main stem of the plant and try to pull it out. Instead, take hold of the pot so that the stem of plant is between first and second fingers and the tips of the fingers rest on the far edge of the pot. Then turn pot and plant upside down and rap the edge sharply against the edge of a counter or table. The plant will slide out with roots and soil intact. Turn right side up and set in the new pot that's all ready for it.

Before any plant is taken from its pot, have right at hand a selection of clean pots in various sizes, some crock, pebbles or other rough material for drainage and the right soil or planter mixes.

Place a piece of crock over the drainage hole, spread an inch or more of drainage material, and cover this with the soil or mix until the pot is about half full. Now press the soil down firmly. Then look over the plant to judge how high soil must be to hold it at the right level. This should be the same height as in the old pot, so follow soil line on stem. When finished, soil level should be about an inch below the rim of the pot.

After the plant has been knocked from its original pot, set it in the new one that has been prepared and hold it upright in the center. With the other hand, fill in around the plant with soil, pressing it in, around and over the roots. This is the moment when a potting stick or 12-inch label comes in handy. Work it up and down in the soil around the sides of the pot to help settle it and to prevent pockets where water can collect. Finally, firm soil with the fingers, tap the pot to settle its contents and water thoroughly.

Newly potted plants should be kept out of sun, regardless of how much sun they need to grow. Keep them shaded lightly and watered as necessary until, after a few days, they look perky and fresh enough to stand being moved to their permanent location.

There's no trick really to planting in pots or containers. The method is substantially the same for first planting and later transplanting. The various steps and motions become automatic after a little practice in potting. Even if every single plant has to be shifted into a larger pot once a year—though this never happens—it can be done efficiently and quickly by having all materials spread out within reach of a cleared working space.

For seedlings and rooted cuttings, small pots are filled in the usual way and the growing medium firmed in place. Transplant and space out seedlings in a flat of rich soil after they show their second pair of leaves. When they have developed into young plants, each one can be potted individually. Both times, place deep enough so that its first pair of leaves rest on the soil. Use a pencil to open a hole in the center of the soil in the pot, and push soil firmly but gently around the seedling to hold it in place.

When cuttings can't be pulled out of the sand with a slight tug, roots have formed. They should be transplanted fairly promptly into a richer growing mixture, since the sand in which roots formed offers little or no nutrients. As on seedlings, root systems are so small that an opening in the 2¾-inch pot of soil can be made with a pencil.

Don't transplant seedlings, rooted cuttings, bromeliads, begonias or any other house plant just for the sake of repotting. This is not a cure-all. Neither growth nor bloom will be stimulated by repotting in the middle of a plant's dormant season; nor will it be if the plant isn't receiving enough light or sun in dark winter weather or any other time of year, or if temperatures are too high, or frost has touched the leaves.

It might be worth repotting if water stands on the soil surface or collects in the bottom of the pot or saucer. In such a case, repot to correct the poor drainage. Only aquatic plants thrive in water.

Simple repotting can be done, if necessary, while plants are flowering or growing actively. Transplanting and shifting into a larger pot delays bloom and new growth. Not until roots have grown to fill the new container will new growth be noticeable above soil.

A specimen plant—such as oleander, banana, podocarpus or sweet olive—so large that it is growing in a pot or tub 12 inches or more in diameter, is rarely taken out and transplanted. Instead of changing the soil completely, the top one or two inches are carefully removed once a year. A fresh soil or planter mix, enriched according to the needs of the plant, replaces the old. Take care not to disturb roots, particularly the fine feeding roots, in making this substitution. In the case of some plants, two inches of the old soil can be removed safely; of others, only one inch.

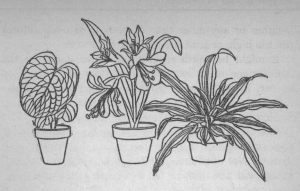

CHAPTER XX

UPKEEP—BY WEEK AND SEASON

This much can be said for indoor gardening: weeds are not the plague that they are outdoors. Neither are insects. I've never heard of or owned a house plant that had to be sprayed every ten days, as do a good many out of doors, at certain seasons.

These two pleasant facts reduce house-plant and indoor gardening care to a routine. Instruction tags on plants sum up the best conditions for their survival and continued growth. To be sure whether the plant has been settled in the most favorable location, look at it carefully every day for a couple of weeks.

One or two green leaves are almost certain to turn yellow and fall off and, if there are flower buds or fruits, a few of these may drop. Such losses aren't indicative of a trend, but are a natural aftermath of the move from a greenhouse or florist shop to an apartment or house. If such behavior continues after two weeks, look for a more suitable place for the plant—and a more suitable plant for that particular place.

Daily inspection of a new plant or a new planting is the only way to become acquainted with its needs. Generally speaking, African violets and the majority of foliage plants need to have their soil watered every day. In your house or apartment, certain factors may make watering essential twice a day, or perhaps only three times a week. This the owner must find out.

Five important points to remember in growing foliage plants have been summed up by one of the largest growers and distributors of these plants in the United States. Because they're worth knowing, we list them here:

1. Soil mixture should be heavily organic. For instance, one part garden soil, one part sand and two parts peat moss make a good soil mixture.
2. Regular feeding is important, to keep plants growing and in good leaf color.
3. Temperature should be a minimum of 65 to 70 degrees, and higher than this for certain varieties.
4. High relative humidity is important.
5. Shade is needed all year—light shade during the northern winter months and heavy shade during summer.

Flowering plants demand more care to keep them growing satisfactorily and blooming on schedule. Least care of all are fruiting plants, cacti and succulents. However undemanding, no indoor plant can be neglected indefinitely.

Fifteen minutes a day should be ample time to tend about one hundred plants in the house. Once every two weeks, an extra hour or so will be desirable. Important seasonal chores take longer, just how much longer depends on the number and the kinds of plants. To sum up the attentions that consume the quarter-hours and hours:

DAILY:

Water, if needed.

Pinch off dead blossoms and yellowed leaves.

Tuck in or bend a vine tendril in the way it should go.

Isolate any plants on which insects or abnormal growth such as leaf distortion is noted.

WEEKLY (or every two weeks):

Wash, hose or dust off foliage of all plants.

Give deep soaking by immersing in a tub, sink or pail of water to those plants that require it.

Spray or otherwise treat for insects and disease.

Fertilize plants that need it.

Pinch back any plants whose growth would benefit thereby. That is, when vines are producing smaller leaves spaced farther apart, pinch off as far back as normal growth (stick these ends in water to root). Also pinch out the growing tip on each stem of a wax begonia or plant of similar habit that should be bushy.

Turn all plants a quarter-turn to assure even growth.

SEASONAL:

• *Fall*—Move plants indoors from garden, terrace or porch.

Prune or trim plants for shapeliness (azaleas, hibiscus, etc.)

Cut back stems of old begonias and geraniums to 2-inch stubs.

Divide overgrown plants and replant separately.

Replant dish and water gardens, also indoor gardens and planter boxes, as needed.

Induce rest periods on cacti and others that are inactive.

Plant bulbs to force.

271

• *Winter*—Feed as necessary, particularly to speed bloom on poinsettias and the like.

Start spring-flowering indoor bulbs.

Continue to water bulbs after bloom.

• *Spring*—Increase shade where needed.

Move plants outdoors to garden, terrace or porch after all danger of frost is past.

First, renew or replace soil, and fertilize those that need it.

Transplant as needed.

• *Summer*—Induce rest period for amaryllis and related bulbs.

Inspect plants outdoors for adequate moisture and possible insects.

Take cuttings of geraniums, begonias, coleus and many other soft-stemmed plants in August.

Selecting plants for their lasting qualities as well as their attractive appearance is sensible. But the amount of attention they need will be determined by the conditions under which they must grow at home.

Factors for Growth

LIGHT needed for growth is the basis for selection. The majority of flowering plants must have sun. The amount varies from wax begonias, that bloom in next to none, to geraniums, that need all possible sun to produce a flower. Colored-leaved plants are more richly hued if they receive some sun part of every day that it shines.

Green-foliage plants and a handful of flowering plants and bulbs need only light to look their best. Again, the amount varies with the plant. For example, in too bright light the healthiest-looking ivy breaks out with red spider, which turns leaves yellow or gray.

Too bright light and too intense sun can have an adverse effect even on plants that need light and sun. For example, many begonias flourish in a sunny location in winter, but must be shaded or moved to another location in spring as sunlight becomes more intense. This is true also of African violets and some other plants.

Picture windows can pose a problem. Those that face east or west are favorable locations for many house plants in fall and winter. A northern exposure, if not shaded by evergreens, is safest at all seasons for the greatest number of plants. South, the desirable exposure for flowering plants in standard-sized windows, can be devastating to them in a picture window. Even in winter, when bright sun pours through the expanse of glass with or without being reflected from snow, plants literally cook near picture windows facing south.

If sun is desirable but should be filtered or diffused, this can be accomplished with sheer curtains, bamboo or slat blinds or possibly with Venetian blinds. Adjustable ones will be most convenient. For some foliage plants, bright light must be filtered. As light and sun increase in intensity in spring, they can be reduced by the same means.

The plant that needs more light than is available anywhere in your home probably can be grown successfully if you will use artificial light judiciously (see page 253).

TEMPERATURE is second in importance only to light when plants are being selected. Professional growers stipulate three ranges.

Cool or cold means 40 to 45 degrees minimum at night, and 10 to 15 degrees higher (55 to 60) during the daytime.

Moderate temperature is interpreted as 55 degrees minimum at night; 65 degrees, or two or three degrees higher, during the day. This range in a greenhouse classes it as a cool greenhouse.

Warm conditions (the old-fashioned phrase was "stove conditions") are based on 62 to 65 degrees at night, over 70 degrees during the day. Keep daytime temperatures between 70 and 77 degrees if possible. Few plants can survive temperatures of 80 degrees or higher.

Generally speaking, house plants grow most satisfactorily in the cool end of their temperature range. Many more kinds of plants, particularly flowering ones, can be grown successfully in daytime temperatures averaging 65 degrees than can be grown in higher temperatures. When prevailing temperatures are 70 degrees or higher, tropical foliage plants are the safer choice.

Fluctuations in temperature are hard on plants. House plants just don't grow if they are kept for any length of time in lower temperature than that most favorable for their growth. A considerable and almost uncontrollable difference between day and nighttime temperatures indoors can occur in regions where winters are severe. The drop will be even greater close to windows.

When forecasts predict a bitterly cold night, it isn't necessary to move all plants near a window to a warmer area. Far less work is involved in slipping sections of newspaper between the plants and the windowpane. They'll be untouched by frost, because newspaper provides such good insulation.

In greenhouses, plants are grown at lower temperatures than are maintained in homes, but in greenhouses humidity is much higher.

HUMIDITY is essential to the satisfactory growth of all house plants except cacti and succulents. Bromeliads have built-in humidifiers. For other plants, some means must be devised for adding humidity to the air.

Humidity and temperature are closely related. It's humidity rather than temperature that creates the tropical atmosphere of a greenhouse. The higher the temperature in a house, the greater the humidity must be for plants.

Low humidity is most keenly felt by plants in fall

274

and winter when windows are closed and the heat for the house is turned on.

The simplest and least objectionable means of supplying humidity is to grow plants on watertight trays or saucers which hold an inch of pebbles or stone chips and are kept filled with water just to the level of the pebbles. The water evaporates in the heat of the room and adds moisture to the air around the plants. Water must be replenished as often as needed. Watering the soil or other medium in which the plants grow is a separate chore.

The planter box or room divider that houses potted plants surrounded with peat moss presents no problem of humidity. Moisture is supplied to the air by keeping the peat moss damp. Shallow water gardens, if they're wide enough and not overplanted, will add moisture to the surrounding air through evaporation and thus benefit specimen plants near by.

Various other means are used to increase humidity. Hanging tins that will hold water behind radiators is one. Setting decorative pots or pans filled with water among groupings of plants is another.

The rubber syringe, spray bottle or fog sprayer which emits a fine mist of water provides temporary relief from dry air. If it's beneficial to some plants, and if you have the time, this mist could be sprayed daily on foliage or into the air around plants.

Finally, special small humidifiers, operated by electricity and plugged into a wall socket, can be purchased. A humidifier could well be a good investment for orchids, African violets and other special plants. It shouldn't be necessary for the vast list of run-of-the-mill foliage and flowering plants.

Air conditioning of the house or apartment or of one room in which plants may be growing has so far brought to light differing opinions. In some sections of the country, growers report that air conditioning maintained in a house or room is as satisfactory for plants as for humans. Others say that it seems to be all right in hot weather. One or two growers say that practically all plants, except the xerophytic ones, grow well in air conditioning. (Since the xerophytic ones have adapted to dry soil and air, it seems to me they're the ones that should do best in air-conditioned rooms.)

On the other hand, from Florida come complaints that air conditioning makes the atmosphere too dry for plants. This also was my experience with plants in air-conditioned offices in New York City. Tropical foliage plants certainly would not react well to air-conditioned rooms, and probably some others couldn't stand air-conditioning.

Therefore, be careful in your choice of plants for rooms that are air-conditioned for the family's comfort, and use judgment in deciding which ones will thrive best in such circumstances.

FRESH AIR at regular intervals is essential to many plants. Just how plants, for which air and ventilation have always been considered vital in heated rooms during winter, react in air-conditioned rooms where windows cannot be opened is another unanswered question.

When plants are first moved back into the house, or indoor gardens are planted in fall, the need for air is probably greater than at any other time. Some means will have to be found for admitting air and letting it circulate without creating a draft. A cold draft can cause a cherry or pepper to drop its fruit overnight. Many tropical foliage plants such as crotons and soft-leaved plants such as all the gesnerias are especially sensitive to drafts.

Daily ventilation, therefore, must be accomplished in cold weather by lowering a window from the top for a period each day. Shield the plants, if necessary, from a draft. Weatherstripping on windows eliminates one means of entry for cool air in winter.

Plants are much more sensitive to gas than people are. The slightest trace escaping from a kitchen range or furnace will ravage plants. Yet many persons whose homes have central gas heating grow an assortment of plants with great success. If there's any doubt, choose only the hardiest sorts with leathery or waxy leaves for kitchens with gas ranges—and place them near windows rather than near the stove.

WATERING is the most puzzling of all chores, as well as the one needed most often. Some plants normally require a little water every day. Soil around a few, such as the umbrella plant, should never be allowed to dry out. At the other end of the scale are geraniums and any number of others whose soil should be almost dry to the touch before it is watered again.

The natural inclinations of plants for water can be turned topsy-turvy by conditions of light, temperature or humidity under which they are growing. Sunny days and general outdoor-weather conditions are other influences. No one can tell another person how often or how much to water plants. Each person must learn for himself.

Plants that thrive in wick-fed pots present no problem. The old and often repeated question of whether it's best to water the soil at the top of the pot or water in the saucer beneath is unanswerable. The method isn't as important as supplying the soil or other growing medium with water. The only reservation on watering from the top of the pot is the warning to take care not to splash water or leave drops on leaves that are soft, hairy, woolly or plushy. Actually, this is true in regard to any kind of leaves: a drop on the glossy leaf of a begonia in sun can cause brown spots.

Water at room temperature is essential for African violets and tropicals. It is desirable for all plants.

Overwatering is general. It's safer to underwater, for plants sooner or later indicate their need by starting to droop or wilt. Certainly avoid overwatering until you learn how much your plants can take.

Dormant or rest periods are naturally dry ones. Water only often enough—perhaps once a month—to keep roots from drying out. Cacti and bulbs need a rest period as dry as this for months every year. Foliage and flowering plants need a little more watering in their dormant period, for it is one of inactive growth rather than complete rest.

FOOD is as essential to plants as it is for people and animals. Fertilizing at regular and timely intervals maintains vigorous growth as well as production of healthy foliage and flowers.

Fertilizer should never be given on a hit-or-miss schedule. Nor will an application compensate for prevailingly cloudy weather or lack of light during winter months in northern areas.

Plants need fertilizer as well as water to spur growth when their dormant period ends. They also need regular feeding, once every week or two, to force them into bloom at certain times of year.

More flowering plants than foliage ones need special planter mixes and regular fertilizing to maintain a good appearance. Foliage plants should not need fertilizing for the first six months after they're brought into the home from a greenhouse or florist.

Liquid or dry fertilizer is simple to supply. Feed only when soil or other growing medium is moist, never when it is dry.

Overfertilizing can cause abnormal growth or excess production of leaves. Overwatering may be the cause of leaf fall. Insufficient light, coupled with high temperature and low humidity, may be the reason for a halt in growth or the production of leaves that are smaller than normal.

Taking care of any of these elements will not counteract absence of another one. If a plant isn't behaving as it should, check light, temperature, humidity, fresh air or drafts, watering and fertilizing. If each one is being supplied as it should be, shop for another plant to grow in that location.

Insects and Diseases

Cleanliness is the most effective deterrent to insects. Sterilized soil is probably most important to prevent disease.

Keeping leaves clean and free of dust, soot and oil is as important as watering the roots. Spray vigorously with cool water or wipe clean the leaves of all foliage plants at least once every two weeks. Using a small soft brush, clean the leaves of African violets, peppermint geraniums and others that are hairy or plushy.

Almost as important to the plant as cleanliness for freedom from insects and disease is favorable location, temperature and watering. Too much sun can make a plant look almost as sickly as aphids can. Aphids and mealy bugs are the two most common pests. Shrubby, woody-stemmed plants may be susceptible to scale.

Daily or even weekly inspection of every plant in the house should bring to notice any that shows a sign of an insect or a disease. Remove it at once so that it won't infect its neighbors, and don't return it until you're positive it's clean and healthy.

Aphids, red spiders, mealy bug, white fly and scale are sucking insects that penetrate into leaf or stem. Nicotine sulfate always has been the standard remedy. Special formulas to be diluted according to directions on the bottle are available. Still other formulas of modern chemicals are prepared for other insects.

Nowadays, however, all-purpose sprays consisting of several chemicals and effective against more than one pest are more general. House-plant insecticides are packaged in aerosol, push-button bombs, as are those for gardens. No mixing and a fine enveloping spray make bombs the easiest method of control.

Old-fashioned methods work well for some insects. A good method—tedious but certain—is to remove mealy bugs and scale with a cotton-tipped toothpick dipped in alcohol. If it won't harm the plant—it would an African violet—spray leaves and stems vigorously with water after insects have been cleaned off. Mealy bugs are said to breed in dust and heat.

Red spiders are too small to be visible, but their presence can be known by a rough or cobwebby feeling to the undersides of leaves (ivy is this insect's preference). Red spider is much easier to prevent than to eradicate. Vigorous spraying of upper and under sides of leaves with cool water every week, without fail, is the best preventive. "Give them pneumonia to get rid of them" commented one professional grower. Foliage plants suspectible to red spider should be located where sun or light and heat aren't too much for them.

Thrips and other mites also are too small to see but their presence can be recognized by distorted leaves and flowers, stunted growth and discoloration. Miticide sprays in aerosol bombs should control thrips and mites, especially on African violets and cyclamen.

Diseases are usually recognized by spotting or imperfections on foliage or rotting of the stems. These seem to me too difficult for amateur gardeners to fight in the house.

Mold or mildew which coats leaves and possibly stems with gray or white can be traced to overcrowding of plants, poor ventilation or insufficient light. Correcting the condition will prevent future outbreaks. Since molds spread, isolate plants and dust them with sulfur.

For every plant that may be attacked by an insect or a disease, there are fifty others that never are. When trouble appears, try to keep it from spreading to other plants. Often it's more sensible to discard an infected or diseased plant than to attempt a cure and risk returning it to its place.

Vacation Time

When tulips, lilacs and roses are flowering outdoors, house plants aren't as important as they have been during the preceding eight months. As many of the house plants as can be spared from their accustomed places need a vacation.

Vines and many of the foliage plants can be used in wrought-iron or wire stands to decorate the porch or terrace for the summer. Oleanders, hibiscus, sweet olive, podocarpus and other plants in tubs or large pots also should be moved outdoors. Possibly they, too, can stand on porch or terrace, near the main entrance, or in a group somewhere in the garden.

Smaller plants in 3- to 5-inch pots are best retired somewhere in the garden to rest. Few house plants except beloperone (shrimp plant) and geraniums need a fully sunny spot in the garden. Foliage plants and ferns require a location in full shade. At least part shade is desirable for all indoor plants, for whether they flower, fruit or produce handsome leaves indoors, summer is their time of inactive growth.

African violets, gloxinias and all other gesnerias, as well as any other plants with hairy, plushy or brittle leaves, need go no farther than a sheltered corner of the porch. In fact, since this sort of plant cannot stand exposure to rain, wind or summer sun, they can stay right in the house.

Potted plants do best and are easier to lift in the fall if they are sunk in the ground up to the rims of their pots. To prevent roots from growing into the earth and anchoring the pots, scatter an inch of cinders under each one. If there are a good number, it will save time to dig out an area and spread the cinders before arranging the plants.

Before they're placed in the ground, look over each plant. If it has insects or disease, discard, because the condition will worsen by September. Trim straggly ends from vines and cut back tall, drooping or sprawling growth on geraniums, alternanthera and similar upright plants. These tip ends can be cuttings to root in sand (see page 290).

Don't forget all about these house plants on vacation. Take time about once a month to look at them. If rainfall has been sparse, they'll need watering. If insects have found them, spray without delay. If, suddenly, some plants are growing very fast, by all means prune or trim.

Cacti and succulents may remain indoors or be moved outdoors. This is determined partly by their size, partly by where and how they're growing.

Flowers in vases may replace small dish gardens about the house in summer. Cut flowers can be added regularly to water gardens to keep them seasonal. Planter boxes, room dividers and indoor gardens can be pretty well stripped of plants, but don't let them look utterly vacated.

Cut branches of rhododendron or other evergreens last well in water and are a simple way to fill planter boxes and room dividers. Or, you may wish to leave key plants in place in gardens and planters and fill in with a minimum of cool-looking plants such as caladiums.

If there's no garden to which the winter stand-bys can be moved, switch them around in order to find room for at least a couple of caladiums and gloxinias.

When you go away for vacation, it is no longer necessary to hire someone to come in and water or to decide whether it's the lesser of two evils to worry about the house plants dying or the failure of a makeshift self-watering system.

Tests at the Agricultural Extension Service at Rutgers University in New Jersey have provided a simple solution. Seal each plant in a polyethylene plastic bag and forget about it.

Don't water plants before they're sealed, for then there would be the danger of leaving them too wet. Use one bag for each plant, seal tightly, and leave in the usual location. They should survive for several weeks without watering.

Various self-watering gadgets have been marketed over the years. One of the best which might be used for plants too large or awkward to seal in polyethylene is a small but deep plastic funnel with an extremely narrow neck. There's a tiny opening in the end of the neck, through which water drips slowly into the soil. Stick the funnel, at an angle, neck down into the soil. Just before you leave on vacation, fill the funnel with water.

CHAPTER XXI

SEEDS AND CUTTINGS

In the case of many kinds of house plants, growing your own from seeds or cuttings is more than a possibility. Neither method brings results of a size for decoration within any three-month season. There's a certain pride, however, in pointing out a plant loaded with flowers or displaying unusual leaves and saying, "I grew that one myself—started it on the kitchen window sill."

When seeds are sown, it takes from six months to seven years to obtain mature plants that are ready to flower or show full beauty of foliage. For example, seeds of coleus sown in February will grow to bright-leaved plants by summer, but the orchid hybridist who crosses two plants must wait five to seven years after the resulting seed is sown to see whether the flowers are worth while.

Cuttings root and form plants in less time than it takes to grow them from seed. Stem cuttings are the most dependable kind, although many people are successful with leaf cuttings of certain house plants.

However long or short a time it takes for plants to develop, seedlings and cuttings require daily attention in the beginning, and several transplantings plus regular attention for a year or more. Don't expect every seed to sprout and every seedling to grow into a flowering plant, or every cutting to form roots.

A great many foliage house plants for retail sale are produced by professional growers from cuttings. If they are sold as small plants that have been shifted only once or twice in pots, the price is much less than for a three-foot philodendron or podocarpus, however promptly its cutting rooted and however rapidly the plant grows. Many flowering plants, whether grown from seed or cuttings, are exacting in their demands until they reach bud or bloom and can be sent to market.

The list of house plants worth growing from seed in the average home is fairly short. Those whose interest in African violets or any other plant branches off toward hybridizing will set up special facilities to grow the seeds from which brand-new varieties must come.

It's interesting to sow a packet of geranium or coleus seeds to see how many different kinds of flowers and leaves will appear. From one package of geranium seed I have obtained some plants with single flowers, others with double ones, and in all shades of red, pink and white, plus some with a center eye in a contrasting color. Admittedly, a few plants were "blind" and never flowered, and the rest took months to reach the flowering stage.

Another reason for growing house plants from seed is to obtain, inexpensively, a quantity of plants such as Christmas cherries or peppers to give as gifts. Then, too, it's so difficult to buy any primroses except the large-flowered rose-colored ones that it may seem necessary to start Fairy or Chinese primroses from seed.

Just for fun one winter, I let the spike of rose blossoms on veltheimia form seed pods. After they were thoroughly dry, they were sown in a pot and germinated well. The first year they grew into little shining green plants in a small flat. By the end of the season each plant had formed a tiny bulb, so the next year, after a rest period, the bulbs were planted individually in small pots. It took five years and at least two more shiftings into larger pots before the veltheimia bulbs reached flowering size. Even then, both the foliage rosette and the flower spike were smaller than those from a mature bulb that had been purchased. But it was a great satisfaction to grow our own.

Generally speaking, I would recommend that no house plants be grown from seed that can be grown from bulbs or propagated from cuttings. Wax begonias, for example, are far simpler to increase from cuttings, if only because their seeds are so extremely fine that they need special handling. Annual vines that do well indoors, such as black-eyed Susan or clock vine (Thunbergia alata), cathedral bells (Cobaea scandens) and passion flower, aren't difficult. Neither are herbs such as basil.

If you want to try growing your own primroses, coleus and geraniums, buy seedsmen's packets that will contain a selected strain. Don't expect remarkable plants from seed of any old blossom on your own geranium, coleus or primrose. In catalogues, seeds are usually found under the heading "House Plants" or "Greenhouse and Conservatory Plants." Try to resist buying seeds of plants you know grow best in a greenhouse.

Seeds may be sown any time from late January to July or August. During the rest of the year, germination will be slow or poor simply because it just isn't a good season for seeds to sprout. Coleus, impatiens, browallia and others that double as bedding plants outdoors and house plants in winter should be sown between February and April, transplanted into the garden when all danger of frost is past, and cuttings taken in August and rooted to obtain new plants to bloom indoors during winter.

Choose a bulb pan or pot or a clean coffee can in which to sow seeds. Fill it to within an inch of the top with a sterile seed-starter mix, vermiculite or peat moss. I've had good luck with vermiculite, which is always sterile.

Small seeds should be pressed lightly into the growing medium, larger ones covered one and one-half times their size. Water lightly and cover with a small pane of glass. In addition, place newspaper over the glass at first. Seeds should germinate within two to three weeks if they are in a warm, light place and the growing medium is kept moist but not soggy.

As soon as any seeds sprout, remove the newspaper and glass and place the container where it will receive plenty of light. The greatest hazard for tiny seedlings is a disease called "damping off" which causes them to keel over. The disease is most likely to break out during a spell of dark, damp, cool days. It is prevented, for the most part, by sowing in sterilized soil or other sterile medium.

As soon as the second pair of leaves appears, the seedlings should be pricked out. A mixture of one-third compost, one-third sand and one-third peat moss or humus is good. Fill a small flat or cigar box and prick out the seedlings in rows, spacing them one to two inches apart. Never let the seedlings dry out, but don't permit the soil to become soggy. Seedlings can use all the sun available during late winter and early spring, as well as a little fresh air every day.

By April, May or early June, depending on when seeds were sown and seedlings spaced out in flats, the young plants can be transplanted into individual pots. The soil mixture prepared for the flat is equally good for pots. Each one can go into a two- or three-inch pot, depending on how much growth it made in the flat.

Of course, bedding plants can be transplanted right into the garden. Other young house plants can be kept in their small pots in a coldframe or sheltered place outdoors all summer. By fall, they'll undoubtedly be ready for a larger pot unless they already are in 3-inch pots which are so well filled with roots that the plants should start to flower.

Seedlings and young plants can't grow steadily if they're neglected even for a day or two. They must never lack water. As they progress from seedlings to

full-fledged plants, pinch off growing tips of stems to make them bushy and to prevent legginess. Seed-grown geraniums tend to become leggier than commercially grown ones.

Cuttings are a shorter and more carefree route to plants than are seeds. "Slip" is the everyday word for a cutting. Countless persons, from Colonial days to the present, have shared an admired coleus or begonia with a friend or neighbor by giving them a slip. Often, cuttings are rooted in water without thinking. For example, when ivy is cut to bring indoors and placed in a bowl of water, the stems invariably form roots.

Stem, leaf, rhizome and root are types of cuttings, all of which must be placed in some medium that will encourage the development of roots. This may take two weeks or two months.

June to August is the important time each year for taking cuttings. These usually are soft-stemmed ones of new growth that form roots speedily. By September, coleus, wax begonias, impatiens, scented geraniums and many other house plants that have spent the summer outdoors are much too large to take back into the house. The solution is starting new plants from cuttings during summer.

Stem cuttings from some plants root so easily that they need only be placed in small glasses of water. Impatiens, coleus and wax begonias are typical. Geraniums sometimes root in water, but it is safer to place them in sand. In either case, geranium cuttings take longer than the three others mentioned. The average soft-stemmed cutting roots within two to three weeks. Cuttings of plants with harder stems, such as podocarpus, may take closer to two months.

In the case of a host of plants, take stem cuttings by using a sharp knife to remove three- to four-inch lengths from the tips of stems. Strong, healthy plants are the source of promising cuttings. Weak or spindling growth yields poor cuttings and poor new plants. Take cuttings from the most vigorous growth, which may be at the base of old plants, rather than the tips of top growth.

When you have a handful, look over each one and make a clean, sharp cut just below a node (nodes are the places where leaves appear along the stems). At least two nodes should go below the water or sand in which cuttings are placed to root, so trim off the leaves in these places.

Unless you are certain that a cutting will root in water, fill a bulb pan or other container with sand—clean, coarse, sharp builder's sand. Sand is good, because water drains through it and won't collect to start rot of stems.

Cuttings need bottom heat and moisture in order to form roots. One of the best ways to keep the sand moist is to insert, in the center of a 6- or 8-inch bulb pan, a thumb pot with its drainage hole plugged with paraffin, putty or a cork. If the little pot is filled constantly with water, this will seep out through the porous sides to keep the sand moist.

Before stem cuttings are inserted in sand, dip the cut end of each one in a rooting hormone, either liquid or powder. This is sold in small bottles under various trade names. It is also beneficial for large-leaved stem cuttings to reduce the size by folding each leaf in a triangle and trimming off the edge with the sharp knife. Always pinch off flower buds. Press sand very firmly around each cutting.

The pan or container of cuttings should not stand in sun. Even in a light place, shade them for a couple of days with a tent of newspaper. This should prevent wilting of leaves.

After a couple of weeks, root development can be tested by tugging the cuttings slightly. The sand does not contain any nutrients for the new plant, but leave the cuttings until you're sure that enough roots have formed.

Stem cuttings need only develop roots to become a complete plant. Any other sort of cutting must progress through more stages, since leaves and stems as well as roots must form.

African violets and some of the begonias are most commonly rooted from leaves. A firm mature leaf with its stem, cut from an African violet, will require about ten months to produce a new small plant of flowering size.

African violet leaves will root in soil or water. Many people swear by the water method. The stems are thrust through wax paper, fastened to cover the glass, so that they touch the water but the soft blades do not. Or the leaves can be placed at an angle in a pot of damp sand so that stems are out of sight.

When leaves are rooted, plant them in small pots filled with soil rich in leafmold. Eventually, when clusters of young plants have sprouted, cut off the parent leaf. When these little plants are big enough to handle, separate them carefully and plant each one in a 2-inch pot. As soon as they become potbound, shift to 3-inch pots, in which they should flower.

The large leaves of Rex begonias are used for either of two kinds of cuttings. Leaf sections are perhaps easier to root. Cut the large leaf into triangular sections so that the base is at a junction of veins. Then thrust these pieces point down in a pot of damp sand and cover with a pane of glass. The other method relies on the whole leaf, which is cut on the underside in several places at the junction of the veins. Fasten this with hairpins or something similar so that it rests right on sand. Roots will form at the cuts and, given time, small plants will appear on the upper side. In contrast to African violets, these begonia leaf cuttings take months.

Results are much more successful under greenhouse conditions than under those of the average home.

Since even heat and constant moisture are essential for seeds to sprout and cuttings to root, many ingenious types of equipment have been made to provide these conditions in a house. Miniature greenhouses, less than a foot long and a foot high are made with a traylike base and a plastic top shaped like a greenhouse. A rectangular aquarium, cleaned and sterilized, with a glass top and sand covering its base, can be most satisfactory.

Covering any small container with plastic may do away with the need for special equipment. A bag used for packaging fruits and vegetables or for packing sandwiches will do. Since plastics vary in thickness, and different plants need different amounts of moisture, watch closely to determine how tight to close the bag or seal the pot.

Few house plants are multiplied by root cuttings, but the rhizomatous begonias can be increased in number by making cuttings of the rhizome or fleshy rootstalk. Cut off two-inch pieces of the rhizome, lay on sand and cover lightly with sand.

Air layering is a tried-and-true method of bringing down to pot level rubber plants and dracaenas that grow taller and taller but lose all leaves except a cluster at the top of the stem. This feather-duster growth is not as likely to occur with Ficus decora and F. pandurata as it was with the older, less handsome F. elastica. Air layering, however, is a good way to propagate tall-growing types of begonias which are difficult to root from cuttings. It's also a practical way to obtain new plants of oleander, croton and pandanus, which are hard to root and may become leggy.

Nothing is removed from the plant. Cut a notch in a side branch or on the stem just under the topmost cluster of leaves. Or girdle the branch (remove the bark) where it is desired that roots should form. On begonias which are softer-stemmed than oleanders and crotons, cut halfway through a branch at a joint and insert a label or splinter to keep the cut open. Then wrap the cut area with damp sphagnum moss and bind it to the stem with raffia. The covering in greenhouses used to be a flower pot, split lengthwise, but this has been superseded by an outer wrapping of plastic.

The inner wrapping must be kept constantly moist to stimulate rooting. Roots eventually will show outside of the wrapping. When there are sufficient roots, cut off the new plant and pot in a proper planter mix.

Summer is not the only time to increase plants by cuttings. From most of the begonias, except the little wax one (B. semperflorens), it is better to take the cuttings in late winter or early spring when new growth starts.

The best time and the special techniques for cacti, orchids and other house plants in which one may specialize can be learned from others who grow and increase such plants successfully. Bulletins and other publications issued by national societies dedicated to the plant also are helpful.

The growing of orchids from seed is a highly technical process, as is the division of large, old orchid plants. The orchid cactus (epiphyllum) is often grafted to force earlier maturity and flowers.

Some plants, of course, reproduce without recourse to seeds or cuttings. Bryophyllum, kalanchoes and some other succulents develop tiny plantlets along the edges of their leaves. Strawberry geraniums (Saxifraga sarmentosa) and spider plant (anthericum) send out long runners with small plants at the tips. Don't be too hasty about snipping off these new plants and potting them. Wait until you can see that they are complete plants with roots and leaves, and until they are sizable enough to handle easily.

By all means try air layering and, if there's a reasonably suitable place, try stem cuttings of common plants. As for seeds, experiment with ones that are easy to grow before investing in special equipment for the demanding kinds. Fresh seeds usually germinate, but the many months of care to bring plants to maturity may be the stumbling block to success.

HOUSE PLANTS FROM SEED

EASY TO GROW

JANUARY TO MARCH	GERMINATION IN WEEKS
Abutilon (flowering maple)	2 to 3
Asparagus Fern (A. sprengeri)	4 to 6
Begonias, wax—various strains	2 to 3
Browallia speciosa major	2 to 3
Cathedral Bells (Cobaea scandens)	2 to 3
Clock Vine (Thunbergia alata)	2 to 3
Christmas Cherry (Solanum)	3 to 4
Coleus	2 to 3
Cuphea (firecracker plant)	2 to 3
Fuchsia	4 to 6
Impatiens	3 to 4
Kalanchoe	1 to 2
Morning Glory	1 to 2
Passion Flower (Passiflora coerulea)	2 to 4
Primula obconica	3 to 4
Primula Chinensis	3 to 4
Sensitive Plant (Mimosa pudica)	3 to 4

APRIL TO JULY	
Christmas Pepper	3 to 4
Primula malacoides (fairy primrose)	3 to 4

JULY TO AUGUST	
Cathedral Bells (Cobaea scandens)	2 to 3
Clock Vine (Thunbergia alata)	2 to 3
Geraniums	4 to 6
Grevillea robusta (Australian silk oak)	2 to 3

NOT SO EASY TO GROW

JANUARY TO MARCH	
Calceolaria	2 to 3
Cineraria	2 to 3
Crossandra	7 to 12
Cyclamen	3 to 4
Dracaena	5 to 7
Naegelia (temple bells)	2 to 3
Shamrocks	1 to 2
Streptocarpus	2 to 3

CHAPTER XXII

FUN FOR CHILDREN

Three or four flower pots and some seeds to plant in them keep little children busy and happy on a rainy afternoon. In another few days they'll probably dig up the seeds to see if they're growing. And when they find no sprouts or flowers, that ends that project.

There are some good tricks, however, old as the hills but bound to fascinate a youngster the first time he's given the materials to try them. Think back to the time when your mother or a teacher gave you some lentils and an old saucer. They were dried lentils from a package on the kitchen shelf.

Spread a layer of lentils on a saucer and add just enough water to moisten them (do not fill the saucer with water). Set on a window sill, and in less than a week stout little green shoots will appear.

Patterned on this idea is the combination of two packages usually to be found in stores in midwinter. The little packet has seeds of a land cress (not water cress), which sprouts quickly. The large bag contains a light, porous material resembling vermiculite, if it isn't that. Instructions say to fill a soup or cereal dish with the contents of the larger bag, moisten and press the seeds into it. Before many days, you can almost hear the sprouts popping from the seeds.

If any seed packets have been left over from last spring's outdoor planting, let the children have them. Bean seeds spaced out on a damp blotter sprout in a few days. They don't grow to crop size indoors, but they're big enough for youngsters to note that the seed coat breaks to let the plant emerge and that the two sides of the bean seeds shrivel as the sprout grows. Fill the holes in damp sponges with leftover radish, lettuce, alyssum and dwarf marigold seeds for quick greenery if not flowers.

As old as the lentil trick is starting carrot, beet and white turnip tops. These root vegetables are sold most of the year, shorn of their tops and packaged in plastic bags. The whole root vegetable needn't be sacrificed to juvenile horticulture.

Slice off the top of any of these, plus an inch or so of the vegetable itself. Then arrange in saucers or coasters holding about a half-inch of water. In less than a week, ferny green leaves are shooting up from carrots, tiny green and red ones from beets, and coarser bright green ones from turnips.

The kitchen is the source of other seeds for planting. Let the youngsters collect seeds from oranges, lemons, grapefruits and dates. Suggest that they soak them overnight in a glass of water and then plant them in a pot, covering them with about a half-inch of soil. Keep them shaded, and water daily until sprouts appear. About a month later, suggest fertilizing by means of a plant tablet. They'll be nice little green plants that no amount of neglect can kill, although any dreams of gathering oranges or dates should be quashed gently.

Avocado or alligator pear seeds are fun to make grow.

Turn the large pits over to the children and show them how to put three toothpicks into each one to suspend it over water in a saucer or a glass. The water should just touch the tip of the pit. In about three weeks roots emerge and top growth starts. After the top growth has lived on water for two months, let the children start to add soil gradually to the water. When the plant seems strong enough, move it into a pot of soil.

CARROT

For a sweet-potato vine, select a plump, firm sweet potato, which actually is a tuber, and stick toothpicks into its sides so it can be suspended over a Mason jar with one tip in the water. Persuade the youngsters to leave this in a dark place for ten days so roots will grow. Then they can bring it out and place it on a light or sunny window sill to watch its green stems and leaves grow. Some sweet potatoes make bushy green plants, but most of them produce vines that will need training on strings, unless they're set on the crossbar of the window so the vines can hang down.

Lentils, bean seeds on blotters, carrots and beets are long-lived enough for little children. Sustained interest and sustained day-to-day care can't be expected until children are close to ten years old. Then the demand may be for a "plant of my very own."

Seeds to sow may satisfy the request after January,

and in the fall they can have bulbs to plant. Give them half a dozen bulbs of Bermuda buttercup (Oxalis cernua), and two or three lachenalia or lily-of-the-valley pips, none of which have to be placed in the dark after they've been planted. All of them bloom promptly and without fail.

Sea onions (see page 178) aren't very easy to buy, but if you find one, children will be fascinated. It's more

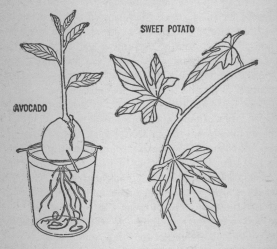

SWEET POTATO

AVOCADO

common in Europe, where the juice from its leaves is used to cure cuts, bruises and other ailments. The green bulb grows to enormous size and will flower without being planted. However, potted half in and half out of soil, it will grow, flower and produce new little bulbs. When the skin of the bulb turns from green to brown, peel it off. Eventually from the side of the bulb, new little bulbs can be seen. They'll fall off, and when they're as big as grapes they can be planted separately in pots.

Children of any age prefer to do their own seed

planting. A supply of paper cups and a bag of planter mix is recommended by the garden-minded parents of two youngsters. The paper cups fit on a narrow window sill and minimize the problem of drip. Fill the cups to about three-fourths of their height, then plant seeds and cover lightly. Three large seeds such as nasturtiums and beans are enough per cup, or five or six smaller seeds such as radish seeds.

Morning glories and moonflower vines are good choices because, once they sprout, they grow fast. Morning glories will bloom in about ten weeks. Nasturtiums, zinnias, gourds, decorative and edible peas and beans are other annuals whose seeds are large.

An early-flowering dwarf marigold such as a Petite mixture, alyssum, Sensation cosmos, balsam and impatiens have smaller seeds, but they sprout quickly and dependably. Again, only three seeds to a cup. Most of these annuals will bloom around Eastertime if they have enough room to develop into proper small plants.

Ask a friend who's going to Florida to bring back a couple of leaves of bryophyllum, and explain that they need only be wrapped in paper and stuck in a pocket of a suitcase. When you receive them intact, give them to the youngsters to fasten to the window sill with thumbtacks and suggest that they watch what happens. (New little plants will appear along the edges.)

A strawberry geranium with runners and a rosary vine are other curious plants that children may enjoy. If you see a strawberry geranium with runners it is worth buying, for soon tiny and perfect plants appear at the tips. The rosary vine has heart-shaped leaves with silvery markings hanging from delicate stems. It's always interesting, not only for its leaves but also because it has odd little flowers and, sooner or later, bulbils in the axils of the leaves. The bulbils look like beads and are responsible for its name. They can be planted to obtain more vines. Some people call this plant hearts-on-a-string because of the shape of its leaves.

The reason for a plant's name is likely to be of interest to children. To show them how seeds sprout, plant some against the side of a glass which has been filled with sand and watered. The seeds won't grow in sand but they sprout as they do when wholly covered with soil. Action—in this case the beginning of growth—holds the attention of youngsters.

CHAPTER XXIII

ODDS AND ENDS

Adults who are looking for action find it in resurrection plant and in redwood burls. It's hard to believe that either of these tan to brown lumps could become green and ferny-looking so quickly after it's placed in a bowl of water.

Resurrection plant (Selaginella lepidophylla) grows wild in Texas and Mexico. During months of arid weather, it dries up into a ball of dead-looking fronds. In water, these become soft, green and fernlike.

When you get tired of looking at a resurrection plant, withhold water and let it dry up again. It will keep for years and still be capable of revival in water. This is a low plant, so don't select too deep a bowl for it.

Redwood burls come from the big trees (Sequoia sempervirens) that grow only along the Pacific Coast from the vicinity of San Francisco northward. The burls are abnormal growths that appear along the trunks of these magnificent trees. They vary greatly in size. Place a burl in a container of water and soon graceful, fine, green sprouts appear, with soft bright green needles clustered along the stems. They will grow in water to four, possibly six inches. They bring a touch of the woods indoors and require no care except water to keep them green.

Neither resurrection plant nor redwood burls need sun to keep them green. Nor do they need much water—about an inch at all times should be enough. Charcoal pellets in the water will help to keep it sweet.

Insect-eating Plants

Perhaps the most curious plants in the world are those that eat insects. No fertilizer is needed by these plants that are equipped to lure, trap and then absorb flies, beetles and other juicy bugs.

Easiest to obtain, and probably longest-lived in the house, is Venus flytrap (Dionaea muscipula). Charles Darwin, the English scientist and author, wrote that Venus flytrap "is the most wonderful plant in the world." It is native only to a small swampy area near Wilmington, North Carolina. The plant is a rosette of stems and leaves. Each leaf consists of two lobes edged with "teeth."

When an insect alights on the leaf, sensitive hairs cause the lobes to close up and the teeth cage the insect within. Small insects may be released, but flies or beetles cause the lobes to close more tightly and secrete a fluid which "digests" the meal. In about ten days the trap resets itself. From time to time, a leaf will wither and turn brown. Snip it off.

Because Venus flytrap grows in a bog, it must have moisture and humidity to live indoors. The pamphlet that comes with the plant suggests three inches of peat moss, sphagnum moss, vermiculite or similar material as a growing medium. Keep this constantly moist. To guarantee humidity, a container such as a fish bowl or brandy glass can be used and covered with clear plastic between feedings. Leave the plant uncovered when it's moved outdoors in its container for the summer. Sun and warmth are needed for growth.

When the Venus flytrap is indoors where there are no insects for it to catch, give it occasionally a tiny piece of meat, preferably something soft like chopped beef. Too large a piece may cause the leaf to turn

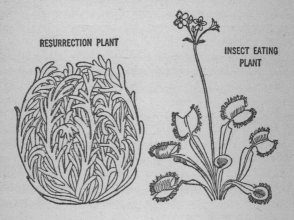

RESURRECTION PLANT

INSECT EATING PLANT

brown, in which case it must be snipped off. If the Venus flytrap is fooled into closing by touching its lobes with a pencil, they will reopen in a few hours. At no time should plant fertilizer be added to the medium in which this insect-eating plant is growing.

Sundew (Drosera rotundifolia) and pitcher plant (Sarracenia purpurea), two other insect-eaters, also grow in bogs but are more widely distributed over the country than is Venus flytrap. Glands in sundew's flat little leaves exude drops of sticky fluid that glisten like dewdrops and attract insects to become tangled in the bristles.

Pitcher plants have tall leaves formed like pitchers,

that are usually filled with water and drowned insects. They're green to purple in color. Nectar on the outside of the leaves attracts bees, ants, spiders, wasps, moths and flies to the lip of the pitcher. Once over the edge, downward sloping hairs lining the pitcher prevent insects from escaping.

Mix peat moss and humus or leafmold as a growing medium. Shallow dishes or bowls are best. Spread a layer of sand for drainage, with charcoal on top, then the peat mixture in which the plants are to grow. Often these plants are grown in covered bowls or terrariums to maintain humidity.

By all means, move any of these three insect-eating plants outdoors for the summer. In midwinter they are dormant, or inactive in producing new leaves.

Terrariums

The best-known terrarium is the small-size round fish bowl filled with partridge berries, the cover tied on with a red ribbon, which is a standard Christmas item in florist shops. Generally speaking, a terrarium holds more than one plant, and is known as a miniature garden under glass.

That plants would grow in bottles, fish bowls and aquariums was learned accidentally by a London physician, Dr. Nathaniel Ward, early in the nineteenth century. Large rectangular cases with metal or wood bases, glass sides and glass covers flat or pitched like the roof of a greenhouse are called Wardian cases. Before people learned to grow African violets, they were often displayed in Wardian cases.

Now terrariums, smaller and more decoratively shaped than a Wardian case, are preferred. Round or rectangular aquariums will accommodate a number of plants and permit them to be arranged as a scene.

Glass jugs, brandy snifters and large wineglasses also are planted with scenes in miniature.

A piece of glass cut to the right size to cover the opening is as essential as the glass container. The glass cover fosters humidity and thus makes it possible to enjoy many plants that otherwise would not grow in a living room.

A woodland scene, a bit of the tropics, a small flower garden are possibilities for a terrarium. The only rule is to select plants that grow in the same kind of soil and at about the same rate, and need more humidity than is in the air of the room.

Woodland plants brought back from vacation or dug up during a walk on a November afternoon are one possibility. Look for partridge berry, small violet plants, bunchberry, wintergreen, rattlesnake plantain and pipsissewa. Small ferns such as spleenwort and polypody are real finds. Ground or princess pine (lycopodium) in either trailing or upright form will look like miniature shrubs and trees in a terrarium. Carefully lift some sections of moss, too, and lichens if you see any.

In garden, greenhouse or florist shop, look for wax begonias, Johnny-jump-up seedlings, a strawberry geranium or small-leaved ivy. Small pteris or table ferns won't shrivel up in a terrarium as they do in pots in a warm room. Any of the selaginellas or helxine make nice ground cover.

Wherever plants come from, a terrarium should provide loamy soil and perfect drainage. To insure drainage, cover the bottom of the glass with a thin layer of charcoal and over this place an inch of peat moss mixed with coarse sand.

A mixture of two parts garden soil, one part peat moss and one part humus or compost makes a good soil. Spread it at least two inches deep everywhere and in some places higher, in order to create a scenic effect.

Cover the roots and firm the soil over them. Give

each plant enough room. If they're crowded together, foliage may be damaged.

Here and there, a stone may imitate a cliff, or the soil may be built up to indicate a hillside. Pine needles mark a path among woodland plants, stone chips through the cultivated ones.

When planting is finished, water and set the glass cover in place. The terrarium should stand where it will receive plenty of light. However, sunshine will shorten its life. Watering should be needed not oftener than once every two weeks, and perhaps less than that. When drops of water collect on the cover, move the glass to one side for a brief time. Water evaporates from the soil and transpires from the leaves to condense on the glass and drop down to moisten the soil again.

Aquarium Plants

Many plants will grow in a water garden (see page 229). However, only a few plants can live submerged in water or floating on its surface. These are commonly planted in aquariums.

Aquatic plants should have their roots anchored in the sand which covers the bottom of the aquarium. It's easier to set them in place and pour a little sand over the roots before the aquarium is filled with water. If there's water already in it, use long-handled kitchen tongs to get the plant down in the sand and then push some sand over its roots.

Long, pale green, translucent leaves are characteristic of eel grass (Vallisneria). Several small arrowheads (Sagittaria) as well as anacharis (Elodea canadensis), with short leaves on long, trailing stems, are good. Perhaps the prettiest is Cabomba, with finely divided leaves.

Plants to float on the surface include Salvinia, with tiny heart-shaped, bright green leaves, the mossy azolla, and water lettuce (Pistia), with a small rosette of velvety, light green leaves.

If the aquarium is large enough, water snowflake with little white blossoms and water poppy with little yellow flowers could be planted in small pots of soil to stand on the sand bottom. Leaves and flowers of these two plants will float on the surface of the water.

An umbrella plant, in its pot of soil, shouldn't be submerged. It can be effective in the corner of an aquarium if it stands on an overturned pot or upright brick. The rim of the umbrella plant's pot should be at the surface of the water, so the base of the plant isn't submerged.

Bonsai

Appreciation of bonsai, the potted dwarf tree of Japan, has been increasing steadily in this country. This is no ordinary potted plant. It is a tree, a shrub or a group of trees that, by artificial dwarfing grows in a small shallow container and creates an artistic and scenic effect.

Bonsai are not house plants. During the hundreds of years that bonsai has been cultivated as an art in Japan, the living materials have been only outdoor plants. Furthermore, bonsai in their containers are kept outdoors most of the time. They are brought indoors, briefly, to be displayed effectively on special occasions.

Authentic Japanese bonsai live for a great span of years and their size is amazing in comparison to their age. A cut-leaf maple, twenty-five inches high with a trunk two and a half inches in diameter is over eighty years old. It grows in a round pottery bowl not more than ten inches in diameter. A group of pines, nine trunks growing from one stump and the tallest one eighteen inches high, is more than 125 years old. A juniper thirty-one inches high with a trunk six and one-half inches in diameter is more than 300 years old.

Flowering plants such as cherry, peach, crabapple, quince, camellia, wistaria and pomegranate also are trained as bonsai. Too large flowers are considered out of place, so bonsai cultivators in Japan have evolved a camellia with blossoms no larger than fingertips. In or out of flower, a bonsai must be shapely.

Pots are chosen with as much care as the plants to be trained. As one Japanese explained it, the pot should set off a bonsai much as a frame is selected to complement a picture.

The art of bonsai is one that has been developed in Japan since the twelfth century or earlier. It is all too easy to attempt a bonsai and end up having only a dwarf shrub growing in a pot or a mass of twigs laden with flowers. To the student of bonsai, the trunk of the tree, the spread of the roots, the distribution of branches, all of which may be trained to give an aged appearance, are important.

According to the Japanese way of thinking, bonsai gratify a person's love of nature. They are important plants and are displayed carefully, indoors and outdoors, so that they will be uncluttered by other plants or accessories.

Some of the Japanese teachers of bonsai who have lectured in the United States in recent years have expressed tolerance of the American tendency to display a bonsai indoors most of the year. It is easier to obtain a true bonsai, even on the East Coast, than it was a decade ago. Anyone who is fortunate enough to own one is quite likely to enjoy it indoors for the greater part of the year, even if it is a hardy, woody plant.

Exposure to the elements is recommended by the Japanese for these sturdy bonsai. Certainly one that is displayed in the house for enjoyment during winter or for four to six months of every year should be moved outdoors in early spring. Don't wait until all of the house plants are moved outdoors and leave the bonsai to rusticate with them. A bonsai deserves a location outdoors where it can be seen to advantage without being smothered by other plants or accessories.

Indoors and outdoors, a bonsai will have to be watered. Sprinkling is the easiest way to avoid run-off, but enough water should be given to soak the soil deeply. Frequent light watering is not good. Whether a bonsai will need watering daily, twice daily, every other day or once a week depends on the kind of plant and the conditions under which it is being displayed.

These long-lived plants should be fertilized once a year, not oftener, with an organic fertilizer. Sprinkle or wipe off foliage to keep it clean, just as you do ordinary house plants. Occasionally, trimming to retain shapeliness may seem desirable. You may want to do this yourself or prefer to consult the person who trained the bonsai.

Lectures and demonstrations have been given in many places in the United States in recent years. On the East Coast, the Brooklyn Botanic Garden has done a great deal to bring bonsai to the attention of the public. A sizable collection of bonsai is maintained at the Brooklyn Botanic Garden. On the West Coast, a California Bonsai Society has been established with headquarters at the California Museum of Science and Industry in Los Angeles.

If it can be summed up in one phrase, bonsai is a more disciplined way of growing plants than Westerners have ever practiced. Contemporary architecture has made it possible for more Westerners to live with plants and, although the arrangement of them is often casual in comparison with bonsai, recognition of the individual beauty of plants has grown. In many homes, there is a place for a bonsai as well as typically western groupings of plants.

APPENDICES

A SELECTION OF HOUSE PLANTS FOR PREVAILING DAYTIME TEMPERATURES

70 DEGREES OR HIGHER

FOLIAGE

Bromeliads
Cacti and Succulents
Columnea
Croton
Dieffenbachia
  (Dumbcane)
Dracaena
Ficus decora and
  F. pandurata
Grevillea
  (silk oak)
Maranta
  (prayer plant)
Palms
Pandanus
  (screw pine)
Peperomia
Philodendrons
Pilea
  (aluminum plant)
Pittosporum
Schefflera
Schismatoglottis
Syngonium
Ti Plant

FLOWER

Acalypha hispida
  (chenille plant)
Anthurium
  (flamingo flower)
Ardisia (fruit)
Episcia
Gloxinia
Kohleria
Ruellia
  (velvet plant)
Spathiphyllum

VINE

Hemigraphis
Passiflora
  (passion flower)

65 TO 70 DEGREES

FOLIAGE

Acorus
Araucaria (Norfolk
  Island pine)
Podocarpus
Rhoeo discolor
  (Moses on a raft)
Saxifraga (straw-
  berry geranium)
Tolmiea
  (piggy-back plant)

FLOWER

Azaleas
Carissa
  (Natal plum)
Gardenia
Malpighia
  (miniature holly)
Osmanthus
  (sweet olive)
Plumbago
  (leadwort)
Trachelospermum
  jasminoides (Con-
  federate jasmine)
Wax begonias

VINE

Cissus
Hoya
  (wax plant)
Jasminum
  grandiflorum
Pothos
Tradescantia

UNDER 65 DEGREES

(Cool room, exterior glass wall, unheated enclosed porch or sunroom)

Fatshedera

Citrus trees
Geraniums
Miniature roses

Ivy

A SELECTION OF HOUSE PLANTS FOR PREVAILING SUN AND LIGHT

FULL SUN

FOLIAGE	FLOWER	VINE
Cacti	Abutilon (flowering maple)	Jasminum grandiflorum
	Acalypha hispida (chenille plant)	
	Beloperone (shrimp plant)	
	Cuphea (firecracker plant)	
	Euphorbia splendens (crown of thorns)	
	Geraniums—all kinds	
	Hibiscus	
	Marica (apostle plant)	
	Miniature roses	
	Oxalis	
	Plumbago (leadwort)	
	Trachelospermum jasminoides (Confederate jasmine)	

SUN FOUR HOURS A DAY
(East or West Window)

Alternanthera	Ardisia (fruit)	Hemigraphis
Anthericum (spider plant)	Azaleas	Hoya (wax plant)
Coleus	Carissa (Natal plum)	Passion Flower
Croton	Cestrum (jessamine)	
Grevillea (silk oak)	Citrus fruits	
Iresine	Clivia (Kafir lily)	
Rhoeo discolor (Moses on a raft)	Gardenia	
Ruellia (velvet plant)	Gloxinia	
Saxifraga sarmentosa (strawberry geranium)	Impatiens (patience plant)	
Tolmiea (piggy-back plant)	Kalanchoe	
	Osmanthus (sweet olive)	
	Saintpaulia (African violet)	

314

DIRECT LIGHT
(No Sun)

FOLIAGE

Cordyline terminalis
(ti plant)
Ficus decora and
F. pandurata
Helxine
(baby's tears)
Pandanus
(screw pine)
Peperomia
Philodendrons
Pittosporum
Podocarpus
Schismatoglottis
Syngonium
(or Nephthytis)

FLOWER

Begonias
Episcia
Malpighia
(miniature holly)
Spathiphyllum

VINE

Pothos
Tradescantia

MINIMUM LIGHT

Aglaonema (Chinese
evergreen)
Aloe
Araucaria (Norfolk
Island pine)
Aspidistra
(saloon plant)
Bromeliads
Crassula
(jade plant)
Dieffenbachia
(Dumbcane)
Dracaena
Fatshedera
Ferns
Maranta
(prayer plant)
Palms
Most philodendrons
Pilea
(aluminum plant)
Schefflera (Australian
umbrella tree)

Anthurium
(flamingo flower)

Cissus
(kangaroo vine
and grape ivy)
Hedera (ivy)

VINES AND THEIR USES

Vines are plants with slender stems incapable of supporting themselves. They climb by tendrils or other means, trail, creep, clamber or twine. The following lists are made up from plants discussed in several chapters.

FOLIAGE

NAME	EXPOSURE	MEDIUM
Cissus		
antarctica	Light	Soil
discolor	Light	Soil
rhombifolia	Light	Soil
striata	Light	Soil
Ficus (fig)		
pumila	Filtered light	Soil
radicans	Filtered light	Soil
Hemigraphis (red ivy)	Light	Soil
Ivy	Indirect light	Soil or water
Pellionia	Filtered sun	Soil
Philodendron	Light	Soil or water
Pothos	Indirect light	Soil or water
Tradescantia	Bright light	Soil or water
Zebrina	Bright light	Soil or water

FLOWERS

NAME	EXPOSURE	COLOR
Allamanda	Full sun	Yellow
Bougainvillea	Full sun	Pinks and reds
Clerodendrum	Full sun	White and red
Hoya carnosa	Part sun	Pink
Jasmine		
J. grandiflorum	Part sun	White
Lantana		
sellowiana	Sun	Lavender
Passiflora		
P. coerulea	Sun	White, blue and rose
P. coccinea	Sun	Scarlet
P. racemosa	Sun	Red
Petrea		
P. volubilis	Sun	Lavender purple
Ruellia		
R. amoena	Part sun	Red
R. makoyana	Part sun	Rose
Schizocentron		
S. elegans	Sun	Rosy purple, spring and summer
Thunbergia	Sun	Apricot
T. alata		

TOTEM POLES OR BARK
(Vines that can be trained upward against a support)

Cissus antarctica—Kangaroo vine
Cissus discolor—Begonia cissus
Cissus rhombifolia—Grape ivy
Clerodendrum thomsonae—Glory bower
Ficus pumila—Creeping fig
Hedera—Ivy

Hemigraphis colorata—Red ivy
Hoya carnosa—Wax plant
Nephthytis—Arrowhead
Pellionia
Philodendron—all climbing or trailing kinds
Pothos—Devil's ivy
Rhaphidophora—Shingle plant

TRAILING OR CREEPING VINES
(Fine ground covers for indoor gardens and planter boxes)

Ficus pumila—Creeping fig
Ficus radicans—Climbing fig
Hedera—small-leaved varieties such as Hahn's Star

Helzine soleiroi—Baby's tears
Hemigraphis colorata—Red ivy
Pellionia
Selaginella

HANGING PLANTS

Some plants aren't strictly vines, either climbing or trailing, but have long arching or drooping stems that show off to best advantage if they are kept in hanging containers, on shelves or brackets. These "hanging" plants include:

Anthericum—Spider plant
Asparagus sprengeri—Emerald Feather, Asparagus fern
Begonia weltoniensis
Begonia foliosa
Browallia speciosa major—Sapphire flower
Campanula isophylla—Star of Bethlehem
Ceropegia—Rosary vine
Ivy geranium—(summer flowering)

Nierembergia gracilis—Cup flower
Oxalis cernua—Bermuda buttercup
Rhipsalis—Mistletoe cactus
Saxifraga sarmentosa—Strawberry begonia
Sedum morganianum—Burro's Tail
Streptosolen jamesonii—Orange browallia
Verbena—Peruvian flame

SEASONAL TIMETABLE

WINTER
(December, January, February)

BLOOM ....Holiday gift plants and bulbs planted in fall and winter for forcing are the chief sources. On the majority of house plants, flowers are scarce until mid-February.

SEEDS ....Start in late January or early February and continue until July (see page 286).

BULBS ....Plant amaryllis in December. Continue to plant lily of the valley and paperwhite narcissus every two weeks into February. Start gloxinia, achimenes, caladium and other spring and summer-flowering bulbs between Feb. 22 and March 15.

DORMANT ....Cacti, ferns. Cacti start new growth and bloom in March.

SPRING
(March, April, May)

BLOOM ....Lengthening days and stronger sun bring ordinary plants such as begonias and geraniums, exotics such as anthurium and camellias into bloom. Every week sees more kinds of begonias flowering. Late-planted bulbs and other seasonal plants flower too.

SEEDS ....Continue sowing. Transplant seedlings started earlier.

CUTTINGS ....To have zonal geraniums flowering by early winter, take cuttings in late May or early June.

VACATION .... When all danger of frost is past, move as many house plants as possible outdoors to garden, porch or terrace. Transplant as needed.

SUMMER
(June, July, August)

BLOOM .... This is the season of minimum bloom, since the majority of plants are in a state of inactive growth. Most of the begonias are resting, but hollyhock begonia flowers in summer and now, if ever, the calla begonia should bloom. Specialties of the season are cereus, oleanders, bulbs planted in late winter and several relatives of the winter-flowering amaryllis (see page 160). Hibiscus blooms steadily outdoors.

SEEDS .... Pot individually early-sown seedlings, transplant late-sown ones.

CUTTINGS .... June through August are the important months for taking cuttings of soft-stemmed plants (page 289).

FALL
(September, October, November)

BLOOM .... African violets head the list of flowering plants indoors. Oxalis, nerines and other bulbs add their blossoms to those of such seasonal plants as plumbago, wax begonias and shrimp plant. Fruits are turning color on ardisia, citrus and similar plants. Geraniums that have flowered outdoors all summer will not continue to do so indoors.

BULBS .... Start easy-to-force kinds in soil or water.

CUTTINGS .... Continue to take from soft-stemmed plants. As soon as cuttings taken earlier have formed roots, plant in small pots.

INDOORS . . . . Bring back into the house in early September, before frost, all plants that have summered outdoors. In November, start fertilizing poinsettias to stimulate bloom.

DORMANT . . . . Reduce watering of Christmas cactus to force bloom. Reduce watering of other kinds of cacti to induce their annual rest period.

PLANT SOCIETIES

Many plant societies have been formed because of widespread interest in growing a particular kind of house plant. Most of these societies are national organizations, but some of them also have regional and local groups.

Annual membership fees, usually modest, are charged. The benefits from membership are many, and the knowledge to be gained thereby comes from several sources. Some organizations publish bulletins at stated intervals. Yearbooks, newsletters, handbooks for judging, annual meetings, flower shows, library and information services are among the various advantages offered by national plant societies. Most of them emphasize two or more of these means of communication between members.

Some national plant societies, such as the American Camellia Society and the American Poinsettia Society, were formed primarily by outdoor growers of the respective plants. However, such organizations also include in bulletins or other publications data of interest to those who can only grow the plants indoors.

National societies of possible interest to house plant growers with the name and address from which information may be obtained are as follows:

AFRICAN VIOLET SOCIETY OF AMERICA, *Inc.*

Membership Secretary: Mrs. Robert Wright
P.O. Box 1326
Knoxville, Tenn.

AMERICAN AMARYLLIS SOCIETY

Executive Secretary: Dr. Thomas W. Whitaker
Box 150
La Jolla, Calif.

AMERICAN BEGONIA SOCIETY

Membership Secretary: Mrs. Dorotha Waddington
1135 No. Kenter Ave.
Los Angeles 49, Calif.

AMERICAN CAMELLIA SOCIETY

Executive Secretary: Joseph H. Pyron
Box 465
Tifton, Ga.

AMERICAN FUCHSIA SOCIETY

(Members primarily grow fuchsias outdoors in mild climate)

Secretary: C. T. LeHew
1633 Moreland Dr.
Alameda, Calif.

AMERICAN GESNERIA SOCIETY

Membership Secretary: Mrs. Betty K. Buchanan
712 Ebenway Dr.
Nashville, Tenn.

AMERICAN GLOXINIA SOCIETY, INC.

Membership Secretary: Mrs. Norman J. Cherry
P.O. Box 608
Merrick, N.Y.

AMERICAN HIBISCUS SOCIETY

Executive Secretary: James E. Monroe
Box 144
Eagle Lake, Fla.

AMERICAN ORCHID SOCIETY, INC.

Executive Secretary: Gordon W. Dillon
Botanical Museum of
Harvard University
Cambridge 38, Mass.

AMERICAN POINSETTIA SOCIETY

Executive Secretary: Mrs. R. E. Gaunt
Box 94
Mission, Texas

BROMELIAD SOCIETY, INC.

Membership Secretary: Mrs. Jeanne Woodbury
1811 Edgecliff Drive
Los Angeles 26, Calif.

CACTUS AND SUCCULENT SOCIETY OF AMERICA, INC.

Editor: Scott E. Haselton
132 West Union Ave.
Pasadena, Calif.

CYMBIDIUM SOCIETY OF AMERICA, INC.

P.O. Box 1670
Pasadena, Calif.

EPIPHYLLUM SOCIETY OF AMERICA

Secretary: Mrs. Gene Luckenbacher
4400 Portola Ave.
Los Angeles 32, Calif.

INTERNATIONAL GERANIUM SOCIETY

Secretary: Mrs. Vernon Ireland
1413 Bluff Drive
Santa Barbara, Calif.

OREGON ORCHID SOCIETY, INC.

(Out-of-state members welcomed)
Secretary: Dorothy Sibert
4670 N. E. Holman
Portland 18, Oregon

DO'S AND DON'T'S

To be certain of having house plants that are healthy, handsome and vigorous calls for good judgment in their selection and care.

DO'S

1. Do buy as many plants as possible locally. Many of them cannot be shipped with complete safety in winter, and some are hard to pack so that they will arrive undamaged at any time of year. Larger sizes can be purchased locally, too.
2. Do be guided in selecting house plants by the amount of sun or light available, and by prevailing temperatures.
3. Do hunt for house plants and bulbs that flower in direct or reduced light instead of in sun.
4. Do keep foliage clean.
5. Do learn the names of your plants, preferably their botanical names. Common names vary from place to place, and several plants may share the same name.

DON'T'S

1. Don't overwater at any time of year.
2. Don't fertilize during cloudy, dark winter weather. Food cannot compensate for lack of sun, or stimulate growth when other factors are unfavorable.
3. Don't repot in winter unless the container or pot breaks.
4. Don't move plants away from windowpanes or glass walls on cold winter nights. Slip sections of newspaper between glass and plants for insulation.
5. Don't hesitate to discard exhausted, disease-ridden or insect-infested plants.

Axil—The upper angle formed by the stem of a leaf and the stem of the plant from which it grows.

Bract—A modified leaf, often reduced in size and sometimes colored. Examples: red bracts that form poinsettia "flowers," and the "petals" of shrimp plant.

Bulb—A thickened bud, usually underground, capable of producing a new plant. Also a fleshy tuber or corm that resembles a bulb.

Bulbil—A small bulblike bud, usually produced in the axil of a leaf and capable of producing a new plant.

Calyx—The outer circle of a flower, usually green or leafy-looking; occasionally prominent.

Cool Room—A room with temperature minimum 40 to 45 degrees at night, 55 to 60 degrees daytime.

Crock—Broken pieces of clay flower pots used when planting to improve drainage.

Cutting—A portion of a plant cut off and treated so as to produce a new, small plant.

Dormant—Resting or inactive in growth.

Flower—A blossom, usually colorful. A flower consists of the following parts:

> *Calyx*—the outer circle of sepals, usually green.
> *Corolla*—the ring of petals, usually colorful.
> *Stamens*—slender filaments tipped with anthers bearing the pollen.
> *Pistil*—the ovule-bearing and seed-bearing organ, often hidden in the center.

Force—To bring into flower in advance of the normal blooming time.

Frond—The leaf of a fern or a palm.

Fruit—The part of the plant that holds the seed. It may be a small, inconspicuous seedpod, or may be large and colorful as an orange.

GENUS—A subdivision of a plant family. The first word in a botanical name is the genus, as in Euphorbia pulcherrima (poinsettia), or Euphorbia splendens (crown of thorns).

GLAUCOUS—Covered with a "bloom" or white substance that rubs off.

HERB—Specifically, a plant used for its scent, flavor or medicinal value. Botanically, a plant lacking woody stem structure.

HUMIDITY—The amount of water vapor in the air.

HYBRID—A plant resulting from the crossing of two different plants of the same species, and differing markedly from either of its parents.

INFLORESCENCE—The manner of bearing flowers; usually used to describe flowers that lack soft petals.

LEAF—The expanded organ, usually green, growing laterally from a stem. The parts of a leaf are:
> *Blade*—the broad expanded portion.
> *Petiole*—the stem by which the blade is attached to the main stem or branch of the plant.
> *Stipule*—a basal appendage, of which there are usually two, looking like small leaves, below the leafstalk.

LOAM—An easily handled, fertile soil, either black or brown, coarser grained than clay, finer than sand and containing organic matter.

MEDIUM—A nutritive mixture or substance in which plants grow, such as soil, peat moss, vermiculite, etc.

NATURALIZE—To grow or to become established as if native.

NODE—The joint along a stem from which a bud or leaf grows.

OFFSET—A small plant that develops at the base of a mature one and in replica of it.

PINCH—To shorten stems by pinching out the bud or tip.

PIP—A fleshy rootstalk, as of lily of the valley.

POTBOUND—The state of a plant when the roots cram the pot and work through drainage hole in the bottom.

PRICK OUT—To transplant tiny seedlings from pots, in which seeds were sown, to flats.

PROPAGATE—To increase in number.

RHIZOME—An underground or rootlike stem, usually thicker than above-ground stems.

SERRATE—Saw-toothed.

SHRUBBY—Growing like a shrub, with many low, woody stems.

SLIP—A cutting.

Species—A group of plants that possess in common one or more distinctive characteristics.

Specimen—A plant grown by itself for effective display.

Sucker—A stem or shoot of underground origin characterized by rapid vertical growth.

Totem Pole—A cylinder of sphagnum moss to insert in a pot for the purpose of training and supporting a plant such as philodendron.

Tuber—A short, fleshy, usually underground stem or shoot bearing minute scale leaves with buds in their axils. A tuber produces a new plant.

Variety—A plant within a species, but having some identifying characteristic of its own that separates it from others of the species.

Vein—A sap-carrying vessel that forms the framework for the tissue of a leaf.